FROM WISE
TO WISE MEN

FROM WISEGUYS TO WISE MEN

The Gangster and Italian American Masculinities

Fred L. Gardaphé

Routledge
Taylor & Francis Group
New York London

Published in 2006 by
Routledge
Taylor & Francis Group
270 Madison Avenue
New York, NY 10016

Published in Great Britain by
Routledge
Taylor & Francis Group
2 Park Square
Milton Park, Abingdon
Oxon OX14 4RN

Printed in the United States of America on acid-free paper
10 9 8 7 6 5 4 3 2 1

International Standard Book Number-10: 0-415-94648-4 (Softcover)
International Standard Book Number-13: 978-0-415-94648-3 (Softcover)

Library of Congress Cataloging-in-Publication Data

Catalog record is available from the Library of Congress

Taylor & Francis Group
is the Academic Division of Informa plc.

Visit the Taylor & Francis Web site at
http://www.taylorandfrancis.com

and the Routledge Web site at
http://www.routledge-ny.com

DEDICATION

This book is dedicated to my godfathers:
Uncle Louie, 1934–1959, who died a wiseguy;
Uncle Pat, 1925–2005, who died a wise man.

ACKNOWLEDGMENTS

This book was conceived and written during one of the most demanding periods of my life. That it got done when it did is due to the strength of friends and family who supported me through it all.

Rachel, Mary Jo Bona, my sister, Kathy, and my brothers, Paul and Michael, were all voices that called me home from the wilderness. Chickie taught me how to listen to the secrets of the desert, and how the sun and Italian soul food could help heal deep wounds and strengthen one's spirit. Ana taught me how to stop running away from the self that this book kept uncovering. Norma provided me with a port in a storm where I could regroup and get back on track with the book's thinking and writing.

Jo Hendin never gave up faith that what I was doing was necessary. Lucienne Kroha's invitations to McGill University were the first public testing grounds for some of the ideas here. Other speaking opportunities came through the generosity of Dennis Mooney of the University of Pittsburgh, Djelil Kadir of Penn State University, Alan Perry of Gettysburg College, and many organizations through the New York State Humanities Council Speakers Bureau; these invitations were all testing grounds as well. Thanks to Anthony Julian Tamburri, Anna Camaiti Hostert, Bret Carroll, and Regina Barreca, whose interest and invitations to contribute to their book projects helped me to get earlier versions of some of this thinking out to readers. Stan Pugliese heard an early paper at the 2001 American Italian Historical Association Conference and introduced me to Routledge.

Thanks to Jeanette Vuocolo, I became aware of and in touch with Maria Manhattan and Antonio Petracca, the artists whose work appears in Chapter 10. Sandra Mortola Gilbert, Felix Stefanile, and Robert Viscusi, and Antonio D'Alfonso of Guernica Editions all generously allowed me to reprint their poems *in toto*.

Mille grazie to the great folks at Routledge who helped me rewrite and ready this book for public consumption:

Karen Wolny, my first editor, who signed me to a contract; Bill Germano, who picked up the project along the way; Richard Tressider, my Project Editor; Jane McGary, my kind and demanding copy editor who cleaned up quite a mess; and Kimberly Guinta, editor extraordinaire who helped me to re-envision early drafts and to rewrite this book.

Finally, a great big *grazie* to Zara, my muse in many ways.

TABLE OF CONTENTS

ix

INTRODUCTION

Italian gangsters,
all my life Italian gangsters;
you too, Leonardo, and Galileo,
and you too Pop.[1]

—Felix Stefanile

This book is the result of a good thirty years of my own fascination with the gangster figure, both in real life and in fiction. It comes a long time after my first writing on the subject back in high school, when I did a senior paper on the Mafia in the United States in response to my schoolmates' taunts that I came from Mafia land and didn't even know what the Mafia was. Years later I wrote a chapter, "Godfathers as Heroes," in *Italian Signs, American Streets; The Evolution of Italian American Narrative* that became the basis of a college humanities course on the gangster in Italian American literature which I have taught a number of times at Stony Brook University; much of this book's content has come out of lectures and discussions in that course.

I have been interested in what it means to be an Italian-American man since I first realized I was a man and an Italian American. It started at a pretty early age. When I was ten, my father was murdered, and I was told over and over that I was now the man of the family. Having no idea what that meant, I learned it the way I had learned almost everything else up to that point—I simply began imitating the men in my life. I have been especially interested in the effects that macho behavior has had on the meaning of being an Italian-American man because it is the only way most of us know how to be men.

Although the book's origins are complex, I have tried to keep its premise simple. I wanted to investigate the figure of the gangster in Italian-American literature and film to understand how the use of this stereotypical figure by Italian-American artists shows the interactions of Italian and American cultures. I began to see the portrayal of various gangsters in literature and film as sites for studying Italian, American, and Italian-American cultures during the periods when these figures were constructed. What I found was that the figure either attracted or repelled people, sometimes for the same reasons.

Since the gangster's earliest appearances in American cinema, there has been regular association between the gangster figure and the Italian-American male. In Felix Stefanile's poem, "A Review of the Film *Godfather VII*," quoted in the epigraph of this chapter, the gangsters created by Hollywood eventually come to represent all Italian and Italian-American men past, present, and future. But what does it mean when a culture's masculinity has been co-opted by a stereotype?

Perhaps no cinematic figure has had such a profound effect on the development of an ethnic stereotype than has the American gangster. Formal protest of the image of Italians as gangsters dates back at least to a letter New York City mayor Fiorello La Guardia wrote to protest the very first gangster film, *Little Caesar* (1930): "Mr. Hays would not dare to produce such a picture with a Jew as that character—he would lose his job if he did."[2] There was, however, little organized outcry by Italian-American organizations over portrayals of Italians in the media before the appearance of Mario Puzo's novel *The Godfather* (1969) and later the films based on the book. Since then, for more than half a century, local and national Italian-American organizations have expended a great deal of energy and money to fight the seemingly incessant portrayal of Italian Americans as gangsters. They have claimed a few victories, such as getting an Al Capone museum in Chicago to shut down and a restaurant chain to change its advertising pitch, but the image of the Italian as a gangster is as strong as ever in

American culture. The gangster, especially the Italian gangster, has captured an important place in society by his proven ability to help exploiters of the image separate people from their money. What the gangster means in American culture, how that is expressed in literature and cinema, and how Italian-American artists use the figure differently from artists of other ethnic groups are among the questions that led to the writing of this book.

The image of the gangster has been very frustrating to some Italian Americans, a frustration that surfaces in such publications as *Finalmente! The Truth about Organized Crime*, by Richard A. Capozzola. A retired New York state educator and administrator who also served as police commissioner for Westchester County of New York from 1974 to 1978, Capozzola argues that the defamation and denigration of Italian Americans through the news media and Hollywood should be "equated to ethnic genocide." He finds the origins of the Mafia mania in the Kefauver Senate Crime Committee hearings of 1950–1951. Based on the information provided by John Scarne, "the world's foremost authority on gambling" and author of *The Mafia Conspiracy*, Capozzola proposes that the Mafia is a government fabrication designed to keep the eyes of the authorities on Italians, all the while overlooking the real sources of crime in the United States. Capozzola's point is that anti-Italian sentiment born out of the Mafia myth has kept the best of Italian-American culture out of sight and the worst of it in everyone's face.

Capozzola's self-illustrated history covers a twenty-year period, stopping at the murder of Joseph Colombo, but not short of suggesting that the shooting of Colombo was orchestrated by a government agency interested in eliminating the Italian American Civil Rights League. Capozzola's evidence comes from his own feelings and from a conversation Scarne had with gangster Frank Costello, who told him "no mob guy did the job." Capozzola wants readers to see what he calls "the real Italian Americans," and to understand that the gangsters on the screen have been used to keep Italians down.

As far-fetched as his claims may seem, Capozolla does have a point. From its first appearance in the film *Little Caesar*, the gangster stereotype has been associated with Italian culture. A study conducted by William DalCerro notes that there were one hundred "mob movies" made before Coppola's *The Godfather* (1972), and more than three hundred after it.[3] While other American ethnic groups—notably Jewish, Irish, African, and Asian—also have been cast as gangsters, most often the immediate ethnic association of the gangster is with Italian Americans and the mythic antecedents of U.S. organized crime: the Mafia of Sicily, the Camorra of Naples, and the 'Ndrangheta of Calabria. There are many reasons for these associations.

First, there actually were Italian gangsters; second, they appeared in the United States at a time when fear of immigrants, especially those from southern Europe, was common and strong enough to warrant public outcries that readily blamed any unsolved crime on an Italian immigrant. Third, Italians were not quick to (re)present their own culture to the public; this is explained by what David Richards refers to as "the privatization of culture," the idea of being Italian in the home and American outside the home, which enabled others publicly to present Italians any way they pleased.[4] The result was that the people of the United States first learned about Italian immigrant culture through media portrayals of those accused of being involved in organized crime. Italian immigrants were seen as people who clung to their foreign tongue and their dark foreign ways. Their inability to organize effective campaigns to counter the negative media portrayals left unchallenged the articles in national papers, a flood of Hollywood gangster films, and later, live televised hearings of congressional investigations into organized crime. And so these portrayals became, for most people, introductions to Italian-American culture. Italian Americans are still trying to find a way to keep the media from using their culture to fulfill America's addiction to the gangster figure, as evidenced by the swarm of protests surrounding the HBO television series *The Sopranos*.[5]

Although Italian Americans can probably find enough evidence to suggest an Anglo conspiracy to use their culture for profit, they would have to account for the powerful representations of Italian Americans as gangsters created by members of their own culture—those whom activists sometimes call "Uncle Doms" because they seem to be giving Americans the Italians that everyone expects.[6] However, besides protesting what they can see, Italian Americans need to learn how to see beyond the surface of most representations of the gangster, especially in the works of their own writers, filmmakers, and artists.

Many of the earliest depictions of the Italian male in American cinema were problematic: the stock characters of the stupid immigrant and the exploited worker or the exotic foreign lover à la Rudolph Valentino, but early Italian-American writers and directors were often involved in such creations, hesitant to portray the Italian except as a marginal workingman, as Frank Capra did with Mr. Martini in *It's A Wonderful Life* (1946). Beginning with Mario Puzo's *The Godfather* (1969) and continuing in the novels of Don DeLillo, the gangster in literature, theater, and film has more often than not been the product of Italian America's own sons and daughters. It is not that there have been no gangsters from other ethnic groups: from F. Scott Fitzgerald's *The Great Gatsby* to William Kennedy's *Legs*, the gangster figure looms large in the American imaginary. However, little has been done to explain just how this characterization has fashioned notions of masculinity in Italian and American cultures.

From Wiseguys to Wise Men examines the impact the gangster figure has had on the construction of the Italian-American man. Recently, the largest bomb in the history of the world was termed "the mother of all bombs." When I heard this I thought, "Only in the United States could they create a mother that gives birth to destruction." A bomb is a nongendered object, so why call it "mother?" Could it be that it is typical of traditional American masculinity to blame any kind of damage on the mother? This would never happen in Italy, where the mother–child relationship and the public image of the mother figure are quite different. This could be the key to seeing a fundamental difference between Italian and American versions of masculinity: the relation of the male to the mother is not the same. The gangster offers a site for investigating different notions of the role mothers play in the creation of masculinities. This book looks at performances of masculinities, especially at its origins in the male's relationship to the female, and in his separation from his mother.

Beyond his impact on gender definitions and family relationships in the United States, the gangster also figures as a means of transgressing the social boundaries set up by definitions of class. Frederic Jameson writes: "If we want to go on believing in categories like social class, then we are going to have to dig for them in the insubstantial bottomless realm of cultural and collective fantasy."[7] Jameson leads the way through his view of the gangster as a key player in Mafia movies that "project a 'solution' to social contradictions—incorruptibility, honesty, crime fighting, and finally law-and-order itself—which is evidently a very different proposition from the diagnosis of the American misery whose prescription would be social revolution."[8] While Mafia movies may keep us from thinking about revolution, they also focus our attention in other directions.

During the 1960s, when slogans like "Power to the People" surfaced to shake the complacency of the U.S. working class, Italian Americans gained their share of power in a society that only a generation earlier had exploited them as workers. The gangster became the symbol of the transformation of the Italian-American male from worker to power broker. He took power and became a social parasite — a stable partner to the economic system that had kept him trapped until he took his future into his own hands, along with his gun.[9] This was not a revolutionary but a *reactionary* act. As Michael Klein observes:

> Hollywood films seldom foreground their ideology — more often it is encoded within the conventions of a popular genre: science-fiction, westerns, thrillers, gangster films.... These films are often fantasies, in some cases fantasies of a special kind in that in restructuring the past, heightening/stylizing the present, or projecting a future, they may defamiliarize and thus clarify aspects of their audience's present situation, or provide a forum for the expression of contradictions, concerns and feelings that the dominant culture represses.[10]

The gangster has become a necessary figure in U.S. culture and some Americans are obsessed with gangsters. In this book, I explore the gangster as a figure who embodies traits that the dominant culture represses. I use the figure to gain some insight into the past, present, and future of U.S. culture. I see the gangster as a mode of being a man, a road map for the directions taken by variants of masculinity in America, and as a model for moving from poverty or the working class to the middle or upper class, and, therefore, as a trope for signifying the gain of cultural power that comes through class mobility.

I want to make it clear at the outset that I am speaking of the gangster as an artistic device rather than as an actual thug belonging to a group of organized criminals. Although I have investigated the histories of actual gangsters, the real ones interest me less than the imagined ones, and so I have focused on representations of the gangster. The gangster that most interests me, then, is the figurative one with the capital "G," who has likely influenced more imitators than any real criminals met in histories and biographies. Robert Warshow, in an essay often (perhaps too often) quoted, points out that while there are real gangsters, the "Gangster" is "primarily a creation of the imagination. The real city, one might say, produces only criminals; the imaginary city produces the gangster; he is what we want to be and what we are afraid we may become."[11] Around this fictional gangster, others form a feudal fraternity. Within this system, the gangster is the leader who receives the efforts of everyone's work, and who then doles out a share he deems appropriate for each member. In return, the gangster provides direction and protection. The gangster is the man of action who knows how to get things done and who has a strong sense of two worlds: the one inside the gang and the other outside.

The truth is that the fiction of the gangster is stronger than the facts, and the facts of American history will never be as attractive as the fictional myths that have been created around the gangster. Prior to Puzo's *The Godfather*, the gangster was usually a singular individual whose gang dissolved when he was jailed, killed, or reformed. Through the films of Francis Ford Coppola, Martin Scorsese, and Brian DePalma and the books of Mario Puzo, Gay Talese, Frank Lentricchia, Don DeLillo, and Anthony Valerio, most Americans have come to know the gangster as a more thoughtful, well-rounded figure; a man who thinks before he acts, who rarely pulls the trigger of a gun. From *The Godfather* to *The Music of the Inferno*, a novel by Frank Lentricchia, Italian-American culture has grasped the figure of the gangster and elevated it from the status of a common criminal to a trope that can explain much about Italian culture and American society. It is my contention that the gangster, in the hands of the Italian-American artist, becomes a telling figure in the tale of American race, gender, and ethnicity, a figure that reflects the autobiography of an immigrant group just as it reflects the fantasy of a native population.

This study examines those representations in three sections. Part I, "Romancing the Gangster," shows how fiction took the flimsy reality of the gangster's life and made it legend. Chapter 1, "Origins of an Archetype," sets up a framework to show the historical and social contexts of the creation and use of the gangster figure. I search for this gangster's archetypal roots through the mythic figure of Hermes and explore the character as a storytelling device. From there I move into contemporary representations of the gangster. Chapter 2, "The Gangster as Culture Hero," identifies a new function for the gangster as presented in Mario Puzo's novels, *The Fortunate Pilgrim* (1964) and *The Godfather* (1969), and in Francis Ford Coppola's films.

Part II, "Realizing the Gangster," looks at attempts by writers and filmmakers to present the gangster life through a realistic lens. In chapter 3, "The Truth about Gangsters," I use Gay Talese's *Honor Thy Father* and *Unto the Sons* to demonstrate the great attraction the gangster has to the typical Italian-American man as a model for manhood, as well as Ben Morreale's novels, *A Few Virtuous Men* (1973) and *Monday, Tuesday ... never come Sunday* (1977). Chapter 4, "Rough Boys: The Gangsters of Martin Scorsese and Michael Cimino," analyzes the figure of the gangster in their films, constructed in imitation of a mainstream American model of manhood at the cost of repressing and misrepresenting an Italian model of masculinity.

Part III, "Reinventing the Gangster," explores attempts to use the gangster figure to create new ways of reading Italian-American culture. In chapter 5, "Queering the Gangster," I look at how Giose Rimanelli's *Benedetta in Guysterland* and Frank Lentricchia's *The Music of the Inferno* and *Lucchesi and the Whale* explore the deviant sexualities of their gangster characters to debunk traditional notions of Italian and American masculinity, and to show how the development of a tradition of humor and parody helps readers grow beyond the confines of the romanticized and realized gangster figures. Chapter 6, "Female Masculinity and the Gangster," shows how Louisa Ermelino creates new notions of masculinity, first in a male character in her novel *Joey Dee Gets Wise*, and then through the female characters of *The Sisters Mallone*. Chapter 7, "The Gangster as Public Intellectual," uses Don DeLillo's novels, *Americana* and *Underworld,* and Anthony Valerio's novel, *Lefty and the Button Men,* to explore what I call the creation of the "gangster of the intellect." Chapter 8, "Fresh Garbage: The Gangster as Today's Trickster," explores David Chase's television series, *The Sopranos* and Tony Ardizzone's novel, *In the Garden of Papa Santuzzu.*

In part IV, "Looking for a Few New Men," the book turns toward an examination of new models for American manhood and suggests that the wiseguy can indeed become a wise man. This section examines writers whose fictions imagine a place beyond history, outside of history, where new ideas of manhood can be proposed, explored, and realized. Chapter 9, "New Directions in Italian-American Manhood," suggests that repetition of history is stagnation. Here I use the poetry of Felix Stefanile, Sandra Gilbert, and Robert Viscusi; Robert DeNiro's film, *A Bronx Tale,* based on an original one-man show by Chazz Palminteri; and the plays of Richard Vetere to demonstrate the possibilities of a post-gangster American manhood. The book concludes with chapter 10, "From Macho to Zero: Redesigning Italian-American Masculinities," which meditates on the future of the gangster figure. I look at Robert Viscusi's novel, *Astoria*, the one-man show, *Blood Type: Ragu*, by Frank Ingrasciotta, and novels by Jim Provenzano and Anthony Giardina to suggest what the future may hold for the gangster figure and ultimately for Italian-American men.

I

Romancing the Gangster

1

ORIGINS OF AN ARCHETYPE

The gangster as the public knows him today is a strange mixture of fact and fiction. The figure that first appeared in newspapers and newsreels of the 1920s has grown to heroic proportions. Disseminated through powerful mass media exposure, the gangster provides subliminal guidelines for manhood and serves as a cultural icon, reflecting changing notions of masculinity in the United States. The gangster emerged in response to the evolution of corporate capitalism in the early twentieth century. Although criminal gangs had long occupied American cities, the Prohibition Act of 1920 and the desperate poverty brought on by the Great Depression in the 1930s provided opportunities for individual crime leaders to emerge and thrive.

During the late 1920s and early 1930s, the exploits of gangsters such as Al Capone, John Dillinger, "Baby Face" Nelson, and "Pretty Boy" Floyd became national news, fueled fictional accounts, and captured the popular imagination. These real-life gangsters rose above ordinary criminals by committing their crimes with bravado; they were all blatant transgressors of the boundaries between good and evil, right and wrong, and rich and poor. As corporate capitalism promoted consumerism and widened the gap between rich and poor, Americans became infatuated with the gangster, a man of humble origins who affected stylish dress and fancy cars, defying the boundaries separating social classes.

These increasingly fascinating characters began to appear in American films during the late 1920s and early 1930s. Early films often portrayed gangsters as degenerate and overly feminized men losing their independence in the new capitalist society, but later films recast them as men who wielded power through sexuality and guns. Films such as *Little Caesar* (1930) and *Scarface* (1932) established a lasting association in popular culture between the gangster and particular ethnic groups: Jewish, Irish American, African American, Asian, and—especially—Italian American. The cinematic images of masculinity associated with these ethnicities stereotyped and marginalized these groups. This marginalization was amplified in the 1960s and 1970s when, amid growing feminist criticism of conventional understandings of manhood, the ethnic gangster embodied the masculine qualities under attack. Al Capone's rise to iconic status came during America's "Roaring Twenties," a time of excess and changing morality stimulated by a booming economy. At the same time, reactionary religious and social activist forces then exerted enough pressure to lead Congress to pass the Volstead Act, legally prohibiting the production and sale of alcoholic beverages. This created a ripe opportunity for smart street thugs to thrive in the resulting black market. A legend in his own time, Capone became a symbol of contemporary power; right or wrong, Capone's actions told Americans that crime didn't just pay—it paid handsomely. His legend became the basis for the many gangster films of the 1930s. Later, as the New York police detective Remo Franceschini witnessed during his surveillance of John Gotti, the real gangsters started imitating the characters in the *Godfather* films. After a generation, one could hardly tell the difference between the real and artificial gangster.[1] This transference of fact into fiction, and the subsequent influence of fiction on fact, is the subject of this book.

Through books such as Mario Puzo's *The Godfather* (1969), Gay Talese's *Honor Thy Father* (1971), and William Kennedy's *Legs* (1975), and especially through the films of Francis Ford Coppola, Martin Scorsese, and Brian DePalma, the American ethnic gangster of fiction eventually became more rounded, more thoughtful, and less inclined to act violently. These more recent depictions represent the efforts of ethnic groups to take control of their own stories, and they also reflect advances in cultural analysis made by feminist critiques of masculinity.

As African Americans began breaking down the social and economic barriers of earlier times, filmmakers began to exploit the black man in gangster films such as *Shaft* (1971) and *Black Caesar* (1973). The black gangster then became a kind of revolutionary figure as African Americans began making their own films and music. Rap groups like Public Enemy, Niggas with Attitude, and Capone-N-Noreaga adopted the powerful gangster pose to depict ghetto life in the 1980s and 1990s. Their "gangsta rap" was featured in gangster films such as *Colors* (1988), *New Jack City* (1991), *Boyz N the Hood* (1991), and *Menace II Society* (1993).

The gangsters' actions also reflected changing notions of manhood. Historians such as David Ruth have suggested that the gangster figure helped shift ideal masculinity away from traditional qualities such as honor to traits like violence, independence, and the ability to exploit the social system.[2] These aspects of the gangster have captured the public imagination from the 1930s to today. Whether a distilled version of the Italian stereotype, an imitative performer of gangsta rap, or a newly sensitized Mafia man, à la Tony Soprano, the gangster continues to reflect cultural perceptions of true manhood. More than an urban evolution of the western outlaw, the gangster came into American culture at a time when great change was occurring in American society and he has remained there in one form or another ever since.

The goal of this first chapter is to explain why America keeps creating this figure and exporting it throughout the world. What is it about the gangster figure that keeps people returning to the theaters for more, and why are the gangsters usually Americans of Italian descent?

HERMES AND THE EMERGENCE OF GREEK DEMOCRACY

The importance of retrieving ancient archetypes—character and event types that recur widely in world mythologies—and using them to help understand contemporary human behavior has been well established by psychologists such as Carl Jung. The Greek god Hermes came to represent popular appropriation of the trappings of aristocratic culture, and he can be seen as an archetype for performing masculinity. There must be something archetypal in the gangster figure, I thought, for it to wield power over artists and audiences. As I searched throughout the cultural warehouse of Western civilization, I found my way back to Greek mythology and came across two aspects of Hermes that suggested him as a possible pathway to understanding the behavior of the American gangster and its representation in American culture.

Hermes, son of Zeus and the nymph Maia, served many functions in the Greek pantheon, and these roles changed over time. Norman O. Brown writes in *Hermes the Thief*, "The story of the infant Hermes' theft of the cattle of his elder half-brother, Apollo, represents the original core of the mythology of Hermes and reflects the primitive mores of Greek pastoral tribes."[3] Hermes wants to be considered an equal to Apollo, so he steals the cattle. To the ancient Greeks, equality was a reasonable rationale for thievery. Hermes tells his mother that "her scruples about his activities are childish; that he intends to put his own interests first and follow the career with the most profit in it; that a life of affluence and luxury would be better than living in a dreary cave; that he is determined to get equality with Apollo—by illegal means [thievery] if he cannot get it by legal means (that is, by gift of Zeus)."[4] As Brown points out, Hermes' intention to profit from his work connects him to the negative qualities of the newly developing commercial culture. Thus, Hermes becomes a figure associated with both the idea of clever thievery and the idea of profit. Brown also identifies Hermes as a trickster, whose "trickery is never represented as a rational device, but as a manifestation of magical power."[5] Hermes, like any gangster kingpin, is the wiseguy, the man with the plan.

Beyond Hermes' relevance as a model for the gangster figure in society is his development as a god during a period of transition in Greek history. The societies of the Hellenic states changed radically from 1500 to 500 BC, as the decline of the self-sufficient family and tribe and the rise of monarchy forced a new organization onto the family. Over this time, class divisions were created and the landowning aristocracy gained control over some states. Popular resistance to aristocratic repression led in some states, notably Athens, to nascent forms of constitutional democracy. Brown writes: "In this vortex of social change were crystallized other phenomena which are themselves potent catalytic agents—the development of slavery, the codification of law, the invention of money."[6] He notes a corresponding shift occurring in the Olympian pantheon. "The component gods were given ranks and positions analogous to the component orders in society. Hermes, previously an independent and autonomous trickster, becomes the subordinate of Zeus the King, his messenger and servant-in-chief."[7] Hermes becomes the patron of "a class of 'professional boundary-crossers'—skilled and unskilled workmen" subordinate to the king, representing "service obtained beyond the boundary, from outside the family."[8] In essence, he becomes what today we might call a "godfather" figure, one who connects the family to the world outside its boundaries and oversees the interactive mechanism between those inside and outside the family.

But as Brown points out, Hermes' image eventually became tarnished. In the time of Hesiod, around 700 BC, the figure of Hermes became associated with the sinister through his giving to Pandora, a woman whom Zeus created to answer to Prometheus' theft of fire, the box of woes that triggers her "mind of a cur and a stealthy disposition[9]". Through this act, Hermes plays a role similar to that of Eden's serpent in Christian myth. He begins to represent a power against familial collectivism and for acquisitive individualism. Hesiod interprets Hermes' trickery as a design to gain profit. Wealth, up until this point, came the old-fashioned way, through the gods, and this was the ideal of success. But the new way to succeed was through individualism. Hermes became the model for the self-made man who gains power through profit, the antithesis of the behavior championed by Hesiod, Solon, and Plato who, in Brown's words, "begin to use 'theft' and 'robbery' as interchangeable metaphors in their denunciations of acquisitive individualism, thus ignoring the earlier distinction between forcible and fraudulent appropriation."[10]

Enacted here is the traditional battle between the powerful and the helpless. "The theme of strife between Hermes and Apollo," writes Brown, "translates into mythical language the insurgence of the Greek lower classes and their demands for equality with the aristocracy."[11] Hermes goes on to become god of the lottery, the means by which Athenians (after 487 BC) elected public officials. The lottery, Aristotle wrote in *Politics and Rhetoric*, reflects "the democratic principle of the absolute equality of all citizens."[12] In the *Hymn to Hermes*, the aspirations of the industrial and commercial classes are projected onto the figure of Hermes; their conflict with the aristocracy is projected into the conflict with Hermes and Apollo. On a final note, Brown tells us that "Hermes' intrusion into the musical sphere [through his invention of the lyre, which he gave to Apollo to make amends for his cattle thievery] paralleled the initiation of the lower classes into the cultured pursuits previously monopolized by the aristocracy."[13]

In sum, Hermes becomes a champion for equality through the acquisition of what the ruling class has. He is, thus, an archetype of the gangster, especially the fictional gangster seen as a trickster figure used to represent deviant forms of behavior against which a society can form its ideas of proper behavior, and to create a sense of shared cultural identity.

THE GANGSTER AS TRICKSTER

The trickster archetype is one that provides for chaos and change. He takes people to places outside the boundaries of traditional and normal society; he reminds them that culture is human-made; and he shows them that those who reach for too much will eventually lose everything. Thus, the gangster can be seen as a natural trickster figure. Stanley Diamond, in his introduction to Paul Radin's *The Trickster*, writes that civilization changes the primitive trickster into "a segregated and vicarious aspect of human experience" by suppressing the concrete image of the trickster and changing it into "the problem of injustice."[14] The "dual images of the deity as expressed in the trickster" that "are fused in the network of actions that define primitive society"; they become separated into the two distinct, abstract notions of good and evil. And this, says Diamond, is what enables the development of "moral fanaticism, based as it is on abstract notions of pure good, pure evil, and the exclusive moral possibility or fate of any particular individual—what may be called moral exceptionalism."[15]

In the moral fanaticism of Anglo-American–based culture, good and evil were separated, and as Americans strove toward the notion of pure good, they had to be able to measure their progress by personifying evil in others. As Paul Radin remarks, "Our problem is thus basically a psychological one. In fact, only if we view it as primarily such, as an attempt by man to solve his problems inward and outward, does the figure of the Trickster become intelligible and meaningful."[16] The only way to understand the trickster, then, is to "study these myths in their specific cultural environments and their historical settings."[17]

The mythographer Karl Kerényi sees the trickster figure as the one who brings disorder to a system: "Disorder belongs to the totality of life, and the spirit of this disorder is the trickster. His function in an archaic society, or rather the function of his mythology, of the tales told about him, is to add disorder to order and so make a whole, to render possible within the fixed bounds of what is permitted, an experience of what is not permitted."[18]

The trickster also works to help us organize our sense of community. Carl Jung sees the trickster as "[a] collective personification ... the product of a totality of individuals ... welcomed by the individual as something known to him, which would not be the case if it were just an individual outgrowth."[19] The trickster, Jung writes, serves as a reminder of our shadow selves:

> The so-called civilized man has forgotten the trickster. He remembers him only figuratively and metaphorically, when irritated by his own ineptitude, he speaks of fate playing tricks on him or of things being bewitched. He never suspects that his own hidden and apparently harmless shadow has qualities whose dangerousness exceeds his wildest dreams. As soon as people get together in masses and submerge the individual, the shadow is mobilized, and, as history shows, may even be personified and incarnated.[20]

Jung sees trickster stories as having therapeutic value: "It holds the earlier low intellectual and moral level before the eyes of the more highly developed individual, so that he shall not forget how things looked yesterday."[21]

Seeing the figure of the gangster as a trickster helps to explain America's fascination with this character. Society needs a figure that can represent fringe behavior against which the mainstream can formulate its values and identity. The Mafia myth has thus served an important function in American society in defining both what is and is not American and what is and is not acceptable behavior in American society.

THE GANGSTER IN AMERICAN CULTURE

In *The New Science*, the eighteenth-century Italian philosopher Giambattista Vico identified what he called the mythic stage of history, which developed after families and social institutions were established. During this mythic stage, an aristocracy formed against which the common people revolted as they attempted to gain greater control of their lives. Out of this struggle rose heroic figures to replace the divinities of the previous age, what Vico calls the poetic age, as models for human behavior. Vico claims that this shift occurred when people moved away from an agrarian environment and into an urban one, and from a theology based on fear of the gods to one in which man would begin to struggle with the gods. Vico theorized that men rewrote the stories of gods in myths that gave the gods human qualities. The result was that people could then "sin with authority"; after all, if a god could sin, then humans couldn't be expected to behave much better.[22]

The key to understanding this mythic mode lies in Vico's suggestion that "poets do not make ethnic myths; they simply record in allegorical poetic form, the histories of their people."[23] Myths are histories that over the years become stories that change as the need for different lessons arises in each generation. Thus, it is possible to look at the stories created around Italian Americans to determine how what once was history has now become myth.

What kinds of gangster myths have been created from yesterday's recording of reality? The gangster in literature, theater, and film, more often than not, has been the product of Italian America's own sons. Mario Puzo, Francis Ford Coppola, Don DeLillo, Martin Scorsese, Brian De Palma, Gay Talese, Frank Lentricchia, and Anthony Valerio are just a few of the artists who have been drawn to the figure of the gangster. In their hands, the gangster has become a cultural figure of mythic proportions.

The critic Richard Gambino noted in 1975 that "the mafioso rivals the cowboy as the chief figure in American folklore, and the Mafia rivals the old American frontier as a resource for popular entertainment."[24] Robert Warshow also saw this connection, but in a more fragile vein:

> The Western film, though it seems never to diminish in popularity, is for the most of us no more than the folklore of the past, familiar and understandable only because it has been repeated so often. The gangster film comes much closer. In ways that we do not easily or willingly define, the gangster speaks for us, expressing that part of the American psyche which rejects the qualities and the demands of modern life, which rejects "Americanism" itself.[25]

Warshow goes on to say, "What matters is that the experience of the gangsters as an experience of art is universal to Americans."[26]

Gambino does not see this role of the gangster, nor does he see the gangster as a universal figure. Instead, he argues that the gangster, when presented as Italian American, has created a great obstacle for Italian Americans in their attempts to become accepted as good American people. Beyond identifying the obvious problem of discrimination, Americans, especially Italian Americans, must understand why contemporary America needs the gangster, and why this mythic figure needs to be an Italian American.

Just as European colonists needed the American Indian as a primitive "other" against whom they would fashion their social mores and cultural identity, contemporary Americans need an "other" with whom to contrast their culture, especially since communism stopped being perceived as an internal threat to U.S. democratic structure and socioeconomic order. The Anglo-American Protestant Christian culture of the nation's founders looked for a separation of good and evil; this created a worldview that posits Christians as good, and non-Christians, if not evil incarnate, then at least prime suspects for evil's presence. The fundamental structure of the United States requires, in spite of the professed separation of church and state, an embodiment of that evil.

Once the Native Americans had been dispossessed and reduced to a remnant, the United States had to find and maintain another "other" against which the nation could build its social and cultural identity. Key candidates were those self-sustaining groups or tribal cultures that were able to survive within their own cultural and often geographic boundaries inside the United States. The Italian-American gangster makes a perfect "other" by virtue of his connection with a tribal culture that does not play the game of capitalism according to the rule of law or the Protestant work ethic; gangsters have not resigned themselves to working hard so that others can get rich. The Italian gangster often rises out of poverty or from America's working class through a world that depends not on his individuality but on his ability to contribute to the betterment of the entire community of criminals. When he fails, the gangster is usually killed or turned over to the authorities for imprisonment, and inevitably another leader arises, promising to improve on his predecessor. His reward is power inside and outside his ethnic community.

There have been three stages of development of the gangster figure within American popular culture, and each stage reflects a different function for the gangster. The first is the early use of the gangster as minstrelsy, as a way of performing Italian culture in an effort to control the perceived threat to mainstream American culture posed by the difference introduced by a wave of Italian immigration. This stage began with the rise of Al Capone and faded with the Vietnam War, but it revives whenever a non-Italian puts on the mafioso mask to perform the gangster. A second stage began when Italian Americans started to use the figure of the gangster as a vehicle for telling their own stories of being Italians in the United States. The third stage started when Italian Americans began to parody, and, in doing so, renounce, the gangster figure as representative of their culture, as a means of gaining control of the story.

During the first stage of representation, the gangster figure emerged when the nation was shifting from an agrarian to an industrially based economy; this was also a time when immigration to the United States was at its highest and xenophobia was rampant. Italian immigrants encountered a great deal of discrimination from established Americans, leading to the development of negative stereotypes. In *Wop! A Documentary History of Anti-Italian Discrimination* (1999), Salvatore LaGumina presents a great deal of evidence of these negative portrayals as they appeared in the mainstream U.S. media of the late nineteenth and early twentieth centuries. At this time, people also felt the loss of old-fashioned American individualism as the country's economy became more corporate. David Ruth, in *Inventing the Public Enemy: The Gangster in American Culture, 1918–1934*, argues that as America's urban centers grew, as the U. S. economy was becoming more corporate, and as the government became more bureaucratized, the American was losing the traditional sense of individuality. Amid this social upheaval, the gangster became "a central cultural figure because he helped Americans master this changing social world."[27] Just as the gangster came to represent America's struggle with the advent of image-driven consumption, Ruth sees the gangster as moving ideal masculinity away from its traditional basis in "male honor" to a basis in violent, aggressive behavior that reflected a man's ability to control his world. Nowhere was this more obvious, writes Ruth, than in the representation of the gangsters' treatment of women. A defender of "conservative gender values" on the one hand, the gangster also enacted an "openly expressive sexuality" that was becoming more acceptable in urban life.

Before the invention of the gangster, Ruth writes, crime was (re)presented in films through a deranged individual who performed his deeds singlehandedly in urban slums. Based on the realities of 1920s and 1930s, crime scenes in films such as *Scarface* (1932), *Little Caesar* (1930), and *The Public Enemy* (1931) moved from ethnic ghettos to downtown commercial centers. This enabled the criminal to resemble more closely those in the rising business class rather than the dark, ethnic foreigners of earlier depictions. Thus, the criminal rose in class and assimilated to mainstream culture just as American urban white ghetto ethnics were trying to do the same. Easier access to stylish consumption through fancy dress and cars blurred the earlier lines that separated the social classes. As street criminals began associating with the upper echelons of society, it became harder to tell the gangster from the corporate elite. The central ethnic figure in this first stage of representation, in spite of the fact that other ethnic groups were involved in organized crime, is the Italian—but not just any Italian.

The prototype for this gangster is Al Capone, whom Ruth calls an "attractive and repulsive" figure that "illuminated the lives of urban Americans."[28] Capone's story, as a microcosm of how the individual could "escape from obscurity to wealth, power, and fame," also epitomized the gangster's adoption of corporate strategies through the need to "organize or perish." *Little Caesar*, based on Capone's life, catapulted the gangster figure into American consciousness and opened the way for the creation of a new genre of film. The great social impact of *Little Caesar* has been attributed to its being one of the earliest "talkies," but the film did more than let audiences hear the gangster's voice and violence. The film scholar Jonathan Munby says:

> The gangster film is a genre like pornography and the horror film, held in contempt socially and intellectually not because it may corrupt and not because it is artistically inferior to other kinds of film but because it realizes our dreams, exposes our deepest psychic urges ... The genre speaks to not merely our fascination/repulsion with aspects of our socioeconomic milieu that we prefer to shut our eyes to but also to our fascination/repulsion with the most haunting depths of ourselves.[29]

Munby sees the gangster as providing a view into our world from a different perspective: "If there is a problem the society is worried about or a fantasy it is ready to support, odds are it can be located in the gangster."[30]

Recent work on blackface minstrelsy can be applied to the study of the gangster to help explain the rise of the figure in American entertainment in its first stage of development, for it is not long after the waning of the blackface minstrel show in the late nineteenth century that the Italian replaced the African as a subject of imitation in popular culture. Eric Lott, in his brilliant study *Love and Theft,* writes, "The black mask offered a way to play with collective fears of a degraded and threatening—and male—Other while at the same time maintaining some symbolic control over them."[31] This is precisely what happened to Italians in the gangster films of the 1930s. Another dimension that the gangster figure shares with the blackface figure is overt sexuality. Lott notes, "Bold swagger, irrepressible desire, sheer bodily display: in a real sense the minstrel man *was* the penis, that organ returning in a variety of contexts, at times ludicrous, at others rather less so."[32] Again, Lott provides a key perspective: "What appears to have been appropriated were certain kinds of masculinity. To put on the cultural forms of 'blackness' was to engage in a complex affair of manly mimicry."[33] It is this mimicry of masculinity that is the greatest function of the gangster figure.

Early gangster representations, enacted by Jewish actors such as Edward G. Robinson and Paul Muni, also convey a sense of projected fantasy: "Minstrel characters were simply trash-bin projections of white fantasy, vague fleshly signifiers that allowed whites to indulge at a distance all that they found repulsive and fearsome."[34] This minstrelsy stage as it applies to Italian Americans is notable for its distortion, if not disfigurement, of Italian culture, ostensibly for plot purposes, but actually as a means of maintaining power over the attraction of the foreign, including the repression of women in Italian culture and the replacement of the mother–son paradigm with the father–son paradigm. As will be shown, this aspect is actually picked up and utilized in the second stage by Italian-American artists. This first stage also distorts the communal aspect of Italian culture, replacing it with the American stress on individuality.

As Jack Shadoian points out in his study *Dreams and Dead Ends,* the gangster film can make us "see things that would otherwise be hard to see. It locates an underworld, a world beneath the surface and shows it to us—a literal embodiment of those things that exist but are difficult to see in American life."[35] Shadoian finds the gangster embodying "two fundamental and opposing American ideologies—a contradiction in thought between America as a land of opportunity and the vision of a classless, democratic society."[36] The gangster functions as the scapegoat for the obsessive desire for self-advancement, and unrelieved class conflicts are played out in the films. The gangster is also a guide to the underworld, taking audiences places that they might never go on their own. Other themes surrounding the early depictions of the gangster include the disintegration and destruction of the family, the substitution of a "false family"—the gang—for the real family, and a son of the New World rebelling against a father from the Old World. In the wake of the success of these early gangster films, however, came stricter Hollywood censorship and World War II, both of which contributed to decreased interest in gangster storylines. When the gangster returned to popularity in the second stage of development, he would have his greatest impact through the work of Italian-American artists.

The second stage of the gangster's trajectory begins with Mario Puzo's novel *The Godfather* and the three films based on it. At this stage, the Italian-American artist uses an accepted and profitable public vehicle, the gangster film, to tell a story that is personal. The mother–son paradigm employed by Puzo in *The Fortunate Pilgrim* is exchanged for the father–son paradigm in *The Godfather*. (In one of his last interviews, Puzo admitted that he had modeled Don Corleone after his mother.) This is repeated in most of the films that derive from the Puzo/Coppola oeuvre, and also in the work of Martin Scorsese.

The third stage, the parody or renunciation of the earlier figures by Italian Americans, begins with a television series, *The Sopranos*, which has become to America of the new millennium what *Dallas* was to the 1980s. In this respect it reveals that the Italians have finally, after more than one hundred years of living in this country, assimilated sufficiently to capture enough prestige to warrant a prime-time cable soap opera. But people miss the mark when they try to limit interpretation of these characters to their Italian-American speech and visual styles. This hit series signals a major change both in what the gangster represents and in what is happening to the American way of life. The original American gangsters represented a traditional, patriarchal sense of manhood that came from an old European model. Violence was used to acquire and sustain honor, and for this type of gangster, the swarthy, "European-looking" Italian offered instant identity with the type; after all, America has always compared itself to Europe to determine its difference.

ITALIAN-AMERICAN MASCULINITIES

The Italian-American man is the result of the interaction of centuries of Italianate masculinities coming into contact with the variety of masculinities that have developed into the American man. Descriptions of

Italian masculinity go back as far as Roman times. As we know from the writings of Cicero and Tacitus, a man was expected to protect the honor of his family by controlling his women. A woman's purity—the chastity of a daughter and the faithfulness of a wife—reflected a man's public esteem. Men devised ways of restraining women's desires, monitoring female behavior, and rectifying violations. The mere suggestion of a family's dishonor, or *ingiuria*, required a response: some type of action, often violent, against the female family member (daughter, wife, or sister) and the man who led her into dishonor. Not only was honor-saving violence expected, it was legally sanctioned until only recently by Italian law.

Since the fall of the Roman Empire, Italian manhood has been an ever-changing distillation of all the cultures that have invaded and occupied the Italian peninsula. Codes of behavior put forth in Baldassare Castiglione's *The Book of the Courtier* and Niccolò Machiavelli's *The Prince*, originally intended to instruct the nobility, eventually touched all levels of Italian society. A man was expected to be able to handle his own problems with coolness and detachment. In Italy, it has always been important to control one's public behavior, evident in the phrase *fare una bella figura*, "to cut a good figure." Self-control, moreover, has to look effortless, an achievement called *sprezzatura*. The Italian word *omertà*, said to be a version of Spanish *ombredad* ("manhood") has come to mean "silence," but it actually refers to proper male behavior. Italian masculinity is typically expected to be displayed through actions rather than words: "*Le parole sono femmine*," goes an Italian saying, "Words are feminine"; but "*i fatti sono maschi*," "actions are masculine."

Because Italy was so often invaded and ruled by foreign powers, the Italians found social stability through *l'ordine della famiglia*, the order of the family. The father is the head of the family, the rest defer to his authority. But the Italian mother, who ruled within the home, had a relationship with her male children quite different from the mother–son bond of other cultures. This mother–son relationship is reflected in religious as well as secular representations throughout Italy. Mass emigration during the late nineteenth and early twentieth centuries threatened this long-standing order and brought Italian notions of masculinity into contact with those of the United States.

Most of the earliest Italian immigrants were men who came to make money and planned to return to Italy. Many of these men lived with fellow Italian workers or boarded with Italian families. Americans were fearful of the early Italian immigrants, who were characterized in newspapers and literature as dark, dirty, dangerous strangers. Newspapers were filled with accounts of urban crime attributed to Italian immigrants. It was felt that without the refining influence of women, and lacking the traditional social controls that modified male behavior, the men would not only become corrupted, but also turn their corrupting behavior toward American women. Such thinking led to the characterization of the Italian immigrant man as a brute, and it would not be until Italians mastered English that alternative representations would appear. Even Henry James, an Italophile, disassociated himself from Italian immigrants, characterizing them once as "gross aliens to a man."[37] However, most of these men proved to be hard workers, much in demand by employers.

In Italy, physical affection between men was quite common and these displays continued in the United States. A higher degree of homosocial affection is accepted in Italian-American culture than in mainstream American culture. Greeting people of the same sex with hugs and kisses on the cheeks or sometimes even on the mouth is not regarded as homosexual behavior. In many religious festivals, the men who share the burdens of carrying statues, and sometimes huge platforms and towers, hug, kiss, and cry in each other's arms. With separate roles for men and women, these community events serve as opportunities for gender training. Young boys selected to participate are able to demonstrate their manliness by enduring pain and suffering with other men.

In spite of public displays of often intense affection between men, however, a great deal of homophobia exists within Italian-American male culture. Homosexuality, though more accepted in the Greco-Roman–based culture of Italy than in the northern European culture of United States, represents a threat to the family order because it does not contribute to the strengthening of the family though procreation. However, as Italian-American culture becomes more assimilated, many Italian-American homosexuals have gained acceptance from their families, who become supportive of their sexuality and invite their contributions to the family.

Traditionally, the world outside the home was considered a manly domain, while the domestic front was controlled by women. In American cities during the early part of the twentieth century, different ethnic groups controlled different neighborhoods. Movement could be dangerous when crossing the street meant entering a neighborhood patrolled by a hostile group. Consequently, Little Italies across the country became stages for the public display of manhood as Italian-American men protected their home turf from invasion, and these neighborhoods were breeding grounds for street gangs.[38] Social organizations and labor unions also served as sites for displaying masculinity, especially during labor conflicts when working men asserted their rights and fought for improved pay and working conditions.

The all-consuming nature of American popular culture presented opportunities for men like Joe DiMaggio and Frank Sinatra to project Italian-American manliness onto a national screen and to become role models for American men. One way of proving unquestionable masculinity, as well as loyalty to the new country, would be performing military service during World War II; nearly 500,000 Italian Americans served in the armed forces, a higher proportion than in any other ethnic group. As Italians assimilated and moved up the economic ladder, they left their urban enclaves for the suburbs.

By the mid-twentieth century, traditional notions of American manhood began to be challenged by feminism and gay liberation. The Italian-American man evidences a traditional patriarchal sense of manhood derived from a European model that confronted an American model of manhood. Therefore, he made a good foil for these new ideologies. The idea of using violence to establish and maintain honor was still clung to, even as the efficacy of patriarchy was disappearing. This is one reason why films like *The Godfather* had such an effect on American culture of the 1970s, and it continues to be culturally relevant today.

The Italian-American man has usually signified nothing but trouble in American culture. From the sweaty workers in the Boston Common who frightened Henry James to the exotic Rudolph Valentino's sensuous strides across the silver screen into the hearts of American women, from the cocky strut of dapper gangsters across television screens to the gold-chained disco dude played by John Travolta, the Italian-American man has been called on whenever a breach of status quo civility needed to be displayed, especially through the body. Not until the third stage of the gangster representation is there a redefinition of the Italian-American man.

The Sopranos, if it has anything to teach us, is about the emasculation of the traditional Italian-American male. Like many male baby boomers in the throes of middle age, Tony Soprano is trying to figure out who he is and why he does what he does. He has come to realize that he is not the man his father was, and that his son will not be able to carry on the family tradition. Trapped between the past and the present, with an unimaginable future, he begins to feel weak and after a couple of incidents in which he loses consciousness, he visits a doctor. When the doctor suggests that Tony visit a psychologist to help him deal with stress, he stumbles on a way of feeling better; but for Tony Soprano it comes at a cost, and that cost is betraying the tribal code of keeping silent, especially to strangers. Tony begins to lose his traditional sense of manhood first by talking about his work and, second, by talking about it with a woman. Hesitant at first, he finds that as he continues to talk, he begins to question the traditional order of things and this leads him to question his role as a husband, a father, a son, and a gangster. After Tony Soprano, there can be no Mafia in the traditional sense. When Tony breaks the code of silence, part of the Old-World notion of *omertà*, he is no longer behaving the way a man should, through actions more than words.

The reason for *The Sopranos'* popularity is that the show, on a superficial level, gives its audience an acceptable bad guy whose job it is to uphold an alternative way of life that lives off capitalism without contributing its "fair share." Unlike the operatic *Godfather* films, *The Sopranos* features typical American family qualities, radiated by the Soprano family. They function in the everyday world of middle-class America, but maintain an Old-World sense of structure and obligation that separates them from their neighbors. And while the patriarchal mode of that world is weakening, its matriarchal foundation is surfacing. Whether through Tony's wife, his mother, or his psychiatrist, the power of Italian-American women to change the order of things is featured as never before. Coppola offers the feminine power of Connie Corleone, who essentially mimics the violent ways of her brothers, but *Sopranos* creator David Chase presents the strong women of the Soprano family wielding power and shaping events through their hearts and minds. A trajectory, started in the early episodes of this series, suggests a development of this gangster unlike any past representation. Italian America has now created a gangster who can speak beyond the confines of the ethnic ghetto, and about issues beyond cops and robbers.

Tony Soprano is the last of the wiseguys, and he is a pivotal figure in the development of wise men. This entails developing the skills to gain knowledge and use it instead of violence to solve problems. It is by using one's knowledge, not physical force, that boys become men, and wiseguys become wise men. In the third stage, then, the gangster represents the unraveling of traditional Italian-American culture and a sincere attempt to make sense of the influence of Italian culture on American culture by questioning the status quo and constantly seeking further knowledge.

Whether Tony Soprano represents a degeneration or a regeneration of the gangster remains to be seen. Actually, this is not as important as the fact that he has come to signify the postmodern American who struggles to fashion an identity that reconciles an ethnic past with a multicultural present. Perhaps it is the gangster who will lead the United States into a post-multicultural period in which Old-World chauvinism succumbs to acceptance of New-World diversity. In the hands of American artists, especially those of Italian descent, the gangster represents the last stand for patriarchy in America, and a chance for Americans to relive a known past as they head into an unknown future.

2

THE GANGSTER AS CULTURE HERO: MARIO PUZO AND FRANCIS FORD COPPOLA

Whenever the Godfather opened his mouth, in my own mind I heard the voice of my mother. I heard her wisdom, her ruthlessness, and her unconquerable love for her family and for life itself, qualities not valued in women at the time. The Don's courage and loyalty came from her; his humanity came from her.[1]

—Mario Puzo

The gangster has been an attractive figure in popular culture ever since his arrival on the screen in the early 1930s, but it was not until Mario Puzo created Don Corleone that the figure achieved iconic status. One reason for this is that Don Corleone is the first fictional gangster who is not presented as a psychopath.[2] Earlier depictions led Robert Warshow to write:

The quality of irrational brutality of rational enterprise become one. Since we do not see the rational and routine aspects of the gangster's behavior, the practice of brutality—the quality of unmixed criminality—becomes the totality of his career. At the same time we are always conscious that the whole meaning of this career is a drive for success: the typical gangster film presents a steady upward progress followed by a very precipitate fall.[3]

Puzo did not employ this formula for *The Godfather*, though Francis Ford Coppola used it in the film versions. When Puzo's Vito Corleone commits a crime, the reader is right there with him and knows the thinking that precedes the act and the emotional responses that follow. Corleone is not a ruthless gangster who kills simply to defy authority, like Rico Bandello in the film *Little Caesar*, or to advance his own career, as does *Scarface*'s Tony Camonte. Corleone is not a dirty old man; he is "straitlaced about sex,"[4] he never so much as flirts, and he exhibits only the most wholesome behavior around women and men alike. At the end of Puzo's novel, Vito's son Michael does not have the fall that Coppola would give him in the second film. Puzo leaves Michael Corleone at the head of the family, in a respected position of authority.

Puzo's humanized depiction of Don Vito Corleone has inspired dozens of imitations in subsequent novels and films, and it has influenced both artists and cultural critics to think differently about Italian culture in the United States. For example, Camille Paglia, in a 2002 forum presented by the National Italian American Foundation, held Puzo's and Coppola's versions of the Italian-American gangster to be far superior to others, such as David Chase's creation of Tony Soprano, because of the way they depict "the dignity of the Italian-American male."[5]

This chapter looks at the novel, *The Godfather*, to determine how Puzo revises earlier notions of the gangster as social deviant to create in Don Corleone a gangster who can arguably be considered a bona fide culture hero. Typically, culture heroes play a role in the creation and discovery of processes or contribute to conditions that enable a civilization to be born, saved, or develop further. In Greek mythology, for example, Prometheus steals fire from the gods for human use; he is divinely punished, but humans gain a new tool. The very lives of culture heroes can describe how a culture originated and can also model behavior that is deemed appropriate in that culture. Often of divine or exotic birth, culture heroes come to a human world to contribute something that fundamentally changes the way humans view that world. The gangster figure as developed by Puzo functions in these and other ways. An Italian-American culture hero should show Italian immigrants how to use the best of Italian culture to survive in the new world. Even though assimilation to mainstream culture may be inevitable, if it happens on the immigrant's terms, it can be less traumatic and more rewarding, especially if that immigrant profits by utilizing what he or she can from the source culture. An Italian-American culture hero, then, should defy total assimilation.

The critic Robert Viscusi, author of *Buried Caesars and Other Secrets of Italian American Writing* (2005), helps shed light on the possibilities of divine birth for the gangster. In his essay "Professions and Faiths: Critical Choices in the Italian American Novel," Viscusi states that the Italian-American novelist "brings to an American theme an orientation that is particularly Italian ... The American theme is professional life, and the Italian orientation grows out of the imaginative form that Christianity takes in the culture of the Southern Italian."[6] Viscusi identifies an Italian-American suspicion of the idea of middle-class professionalism which he attributes to a "special brand of Christianity." This suspicion manifests in the writing of Italian-American authors through their portrayals of working-class characters who enter professions and turn their backs on their ancestral communities. One example Viscusi uses to illustrate his point is the character Dr. Emile Gardella in Guido D'Agostino's *Olives on the Apple Tree* (1940), who changes his name from Emilio and ignores the needs of the Italian community as he attempts to build his practice and enhance his standing in the WASP community. Emilio's sister, Elena, is the suspicious character who tries repeatedly to get her brother to remember his roots and responsibilities to his people.

In a later essay, Viscusi introduces the idea that the "allegorical destiny of Italian-American heroes [is] to endure ritual death and processional re-identification in the process of becoming divinities."[7] It is the children of working-class martyrs who become culture heroes of Italian America, such as the character of Paul in *Christ in Concrete* by Pietro di Donato. After the death of his father, Geremio, Pietro becomes an antichrist figure who leads his family away from dependence on organized religion. Viscusi explains, "It was clear to the discourse [of Italian-American literature], if not to its explicators that no other role was open to Italians in the American imagination except that of divinities. The Puritans had preempted the role of moralists, [what R. W. B. Lewis called the "American Adam"] and the Blacks the place of the victim."[8]

Like the life of Pietro di Donato's Geremio, Vito Corleone's life becomes a sacrifice that enables his children to realize better lives in the United States. *The Godfather* (1969) tells the story of an Italian immigrant and his family's experience in the Americanized version of the Sicilian Mafia. But unlike that of Geremio, Vito's life becomes a model for his children to emulate rather than overcome, one that enables imitators to thrive in the new land.

The prototype of the immigrant worker turned gangster and eventually culture hero also can be found in the character of Larry Angeluzzi, in Puzo's second novel, *The Fortunate Pilgrim* (1964). Also in this novel is the source of the feminine traits that humanize Don Corleone, making him a gangster that the reader can love as well as hate. This chapter focuses on *The Fortunate Pilgrim* and *The Godfather*, with additional reference to Puzo's later gangster novels, *The Sicilian* (1984), *The Last Don* (1996), and *Omerta* (2000), as well as to Coppola's film version of *The Godfather*, to illustrate how Puzo's gangster figure has permeated the U.S. cultural imagination and set the benchmark for subsequent (re)presentations of the gangster.

MOURNING BECOMES MAMMA

The Fortunate Pilgrim opens with Lorenzo (Larry) Angeluzzi riding the railroad tracks on a horse as a "dummy boy," a young man who warns people when a train is coming through. Puzo describes Larry as an urban cowboy: he "spurred his jet-black horse through a canyon formed by two great walls of tenements"; he is watched by children "in silent admiration" riding "straight and arrogantly as any western cowboy."[9] Along the way he waves and makes his horse "rear up for the people."[10] These feats demonstrate that Larry is well on his way toward manhood, since in order for a young boy to become a man, he must perform masculine feats in public.

Just what is masculine behavior in Mediterranean culture is examined in David Gilmore's *Manhood in the Making: Cultural Concepts of Masculinity*. Gilmore claims that there are "three moral imperatives" relating to the ideals of manliness in the Mediterranean: "first, impregnating one's wife; second provisioning dependents; third, protecting the family. These criteria demand assertiveness and resolve. All must be performed relentlessly in the loyal service of the 'collective identities' of the self."[11]

Larry also must overcome the failures of his father, Anthony Angeluzzi, who "carelessly let himself be killed in one of those accidents that were part of the building of the new continent."[12] Anthony's death and consequent loss of control in the family is seen as his failure as a man. He had been "the master, but a chief without foresight, criminal in his lack of ambition for his family, content to live the rest of his life in the slum tenements a few short blocks from the docks where he worked."[13] A good man must have ambition not only for himself, but also for his family. In typical Italian fashion, in the father's absence, the father's responsibilities fall to the oldest son. Therefore, Larry must begin contributing to the family's welfare at a young age by providing for the family through his railroad job and by protecting his brothers when they get into trouble on the street. When he falls short of providing the customary protection for the entire family, his mother, Lucia Santa, must step into a family position of power traditionally reserved for men.

Even before she is forced to take on traditionally male roles, Lucia Santa expresses doubts about a man's ability to perform masculine work: "That men should control the money in the house, have the power to make decisions that decided the fate of infants—what folly! Men were not competent. More—they were not serious. And she had already begun to usurp his power, as all women do, when one terrible day he was killed."[14] Anthony dies in a work accident on the docks, crushed in the mud of the river by a fallen load of bananas. After properly grieving her husband's death, Lucia Santa remarries Frank Corbo, a man who ignited her passion and presented her with a practical solution to her problem of providing for her children. From the beginning, though, Lucia began to assert her authority over Frank both in public and in the bedroom. When he made love to her, "she had been the master."[15]

Judith Halberstam, in *Female Masculinity* (1998), sees female masculinities "framed as the rejected scraps of dominant masculinity in order that male masculinity may appear to be the real thing."[16] The women Halberstam studies "long to be and to have a power that is always just out of reach."[17] As Halberstam explains:

> I have no doubt that heterosexual female masculinity menaces gender conformity in its own way, but all too often it represents an acceptable degree of female masculinity as compared to the excessive masculinity of the dyke. It is important when

thinking about gender variations such as male femininity and female masculinity not simply to create another binary in which masculinity is not simply the opposite of female femininity, nor is it a female version of male masculinity ... very often the unholy union of femaleness and masculinity can produce wildly unpredictable results.[18]

Puzo does present us with something quite different. From the outset of *The Fortunate Pilgrim*, Puzo develops female masculinity through the figures of Lucia Santa and her daughter, Octavia, in ways that suggest that the women are enacting masculine roles quite naturally to fill voids left by the men in their lives, who ultimately present masculinities that have failed to perform. Halberstam's idea of female masculinity (though she directs it toward "queering masculinities") can be applied first to the construction of the Italian immigrant mother, and then to the construction of the Italian-American gangster. A later chapter in this book uses Halberstam's ideas to read Louisa Ermelino's creation of the female gangster, but for now female masculinity can be understood through the interaction of mother and son.

Lucia's oldest boy, Larry, the "dummy boy," is introduced as "a good son" who "always gave his mother the pay he earned ... True, he now kept some money for himself, stashed it; but after all, he was seventeen and a young man in America, not Italy."[19] This notion of a behavior acted out in the United States that would not be acceptable in Italy marks the beginning of a sense of two worldviews coming into conflict through the Italian-American characters, and it shows how America has changed the traditional Italian mother–son dynamic.

Larry is quite a ladies' man, but he is also responsible for helping to maintain the traditions of his community:

Famous for his conquests, he was the neighborhood Romeo, yet popular with all the old ladies of the Avenue. For he had Respect. He was like a young man brought up in Italy. His good manners, which were as natural as his pleasantness, made him always ready to help in the countless mild distresses of the poor.... . But most important of all, he took part with real zest in all the events of communal life—marriages, funerals, christenings, death watches, Communions and Confirmations; those sacred tribal customs sneered at by young Americans.[20]

Larry's behavior conforms not only to the expected public performance of Italian masculinity, but also to an American public performance of masculinity represented by the cowboy: "People would think of him with respect, as a man to be wary of, yet not mean or vicious. He was the hero in the cowboy pictures, like Ken Maynard, who never struck a man on the floor."[21] Puzo continually refers to the cowboy, a popular figure in films of the late 1930s and early 1940s, a type of admired, public masculinity that boys of Larry's era imitated. The cowboy figure conveys a strong and stable sense of masculinity, an appropriate symbol of American independence. But this American figure of masculinity does not maintain the family, and so Lucia must take on that male role.

Lucia's first major act in this "masculine" role in the novel comes when Larry's public activities begin to overstep the bounds of expected Italian male behavior. Larry is cuckolding his boss, and this, at least publicly, puts Lucia in a difficult situation. She confronts the family for whom her son works, the Le Cinglatas, taking on the public role of the father. She must defend the reputation of her son and her family. When Larry doesn't show up for Sunday dinner with his family, she believes he has violated the family honor: "The eldest son, the shield and buckler of a fatherless family, had not shown the respect due his blood or his mother."[22] This lack of respect is a violation of the Old-World notion of a son's proper actions toward his mother, and it forces Lucia to take action that moves her from her home, the site of traditional female power, outside into the public world, the place where traditional male power is exercised. She heads to the Le Cinglata family with the thought, "America or no America, seventeen years old or not, working or not working, he would obey his mother or feel her hand on his mouth. Ah, if his natural father was alive there would be real blows— but then, Lorenzo would never had dared leave a paternal roof."[23]

As she ascends the stairs of the Le Cinglata home, she thinks, "No son of hers would be a gangster, a criminal sucked-out jellyfish to an older woman without shame."[24] In a role uncharacteristic of women in the old country, Lucia Santa confronts husband and wife. Larry, shamed by his mother, strikes at her and then recoils in shame: "His image of himself had been shattered. He had actually struck his mother and shamed her before strangers. And for the sake of people who had used him then sent him away."[25] The realization of this behavior turns into a shame that binds Larry to future service to his mother, and he begins to do the work of the man of the family.

When Larry later rescues his brother from a police chase, he becomes a good man in the eyes of everyone in the neighborhood, except his mother, and in her thoughts, we come to see the weaknesses of such public performances of masculinity:

> Lucia Santa was happy, but a little irritated by all the fuss about the fight, the masculine pride and hoopla, as if such things were really of great importance. Now she wanted to hear no more of it. She had that secret contempt for male heroism that many women feel but never dare express; they find masculine pride in heroics infantile, for after all, what man would risk his life day after day and year after year as all women do in the act of love? Let them bear children, let their bodies open up into a great blood cavern year after year. They would not be so proud then of their trickling scarlet noses, their little knife cuts.[26]

This understanding of constructive pain leads Lucia Santa to dismiss the destructive pain caused by male behavior.

When Lucia's second husband, Frank, suffers a nervous breakdown, major cracks begin to form in the once powerful facade of Italian masculinity that Puzo has created for his characters: "It was always the men who crumbled under the glories of the new land, never the women. There were many cases of Italian men who became insane and had to be committed, as if in leaving their homeland they had torn a vital root from their minds."[27] That "vital root" is none other than the traditional performance of masculinity that limits the Italian male in the United States in ways he was not limited in Italy. In order to provide for his family, Frank had to leave home for a long time, which kept him from making love to his wife and protecting his family. In his absence, his wife and stepdaughter had to take control of the home, and they do this quite well:

> Everything was running smoothly; they were both in rapport—the daughter a faithful but powerful underling; the mother undisputed chief, but showing respect and admiration for a clever and faithful daughter's help. It was never said, but the father's banishment had relieved them of a great deal of ten-

sion and worry. They were almost happy he was gone, and their rule now absolute.[28]

In fact, their rule is so strong that it gives Larry the opportunity to abdicate his responsibilities toward the family as oldest son when he further disgraces his mother by running off and getting married. As his sister Octavia surmises, "This was the real reason for his marriage, that the mother had ruled with too iron a hand, taking most of his pay check, restricting his freedom, so he had chose this means of shedding his bonds. And now that the family was in trouble, Larry could see no future in it."[29] With his new family's needs to consider, Larry becomes less dedicated to the responsibility of being the oldest son in his mother's family. He continues to provide for his mother financially, so he begins thinking of how to earn more money. This takes him to Mr. Di Lucca, also known as Zi' Pasquale.

Zi' (uncle) Pasquale is the first instance of a Puzo gangster. He is "Italian, but dressed American, with no trace of the greenhorn; hair trimmed close, tie skinny and plain and solid colored."[30] When Larry is offered a job, he feels he cannot even ask what the job would entail for fear of insulting the man, so he agrees. Mr. Di Lucca, as it turns out, hires him as a collection agent for the bakery union. The baker who sets him up for the job remarks, "Now you will learn what the world is and become a man."[31] Larry goes on not only to collect dues but also to enforce union power through strong-arm tactics. He becomes a gangster, albeit one connected to a legitimate business. An editor asked Puzo to build his next novel around the character of Larry. When he wrote that book, it was Larry's mother who became the model for the most famous gangster in American fiction.

Although we know from the author's statement that the model for Don Vito Corleone is Lucia Santa, we can begin to see the power of Puzo's later gangsters expressed in his portrayal of one other woman in *The Fortunate Pilgrim*. The public persona of the gangster as one who instills fear and respect comes through Teresina Coccalitti, "the most feared and respected woman on Tenth Avenue. Tall, rawboned, dressed always in black she wore for her husband twenty years dead, she terrorized fruit peddlers, grocers, and butchers; landlords never dared scold her for late rent, home relief investigators allowed her to sign necessary papers and never asked a single embarrassing question."[32] Coccalitti teaches Lucia Santa to save money by buying food and clothing from "eloquent hijackers" who "dealt more honestly with you than the shopkeepers from Northern Italy who roosted on Ninth Avenue like Roman vultures."[33] Through this friendship, Lucia learns how to survive in the world without the help of men. However, both Coccalitti's and Lucia's worlds change when each loses a son.

For Lucia Santa, the death of her son, Vincenzo, Larry's younger brother, is unbearable. At Vincenzo's wake, Larry helps the doctor anesthetize his mother to spare her the physical expression of her grief. This is a grief expressed twice earlier, after the deaths of her two husbands, so the stifling of it this time is particularly telling: "Dr. Barbato was holding a needle in the air. Larry was gripping his mother with all his strength to keep her from bucking up and down in convulsions."[34] Lucia Santa is sedated to keep her from feeling the full effects of her grief—in essence, to keep her from mourning. This is the American response to grief. The Italian response is unrestrained, and it can lead to madness when not expressed appropriately through ritualistic mourning.

This expression of grief that leads to madness is presented in the shortest chapter in the book. Chapter 25, just over one page long, is dedicated to Teresa Coccalitti, whose three sons are killed in World War II. Coccalitti wanders the streets, calling out " 'Aiuta mi! Aiuta mi!' Screaming for help against the ghosts of her three dead sons, Teresina Coccalitti ran along the edge of the sidewalk, her body tilted strangely, her black clothes flapping in the morning breeze."[35] Why does Puzo devote a whole chapter to such a short scene? The conclusion of that chapter should help the reader understand:

> Who would have thought that fate would dare to strike such a blow against Teresina Coccalitti? Kill three of her sons in one year of war, and she such a cunning sly person, always secretive and capable of any treachery for her own advantage. Did nothing help then? Was there no escape for anyone? For if evil cannot prevail against fate, what hope is there for the good?[36]

This penultimate chapter sets up a stark contrast between the Old World and the New. In America, the natural feelings of mourning are not allowed to escape. They are curtailed, stifled, repressed, drugged, and kept from surfacing. When grief is not stifled, yet allowed to get out of hand rather than performed in a proper traditional way, it leads to madness, a madness connected to the evils of the world. The bottom line for the immigrant is "Americanize or go crazy."

In the final chapter of *The Fortunate Pilgrim*, Lucia and her family move to the suburbs. This is a sign of the immigrant's assimilation to American culture, but it also suggests a loss of Lucia's power. Puzo, in essence, kills Lucia's dominance by moving her away from her power base, the ethnic community, where her native language could still be used to further her causes, where her friendships could aid in providing for and protecting her family. The move to the suburbs also symbolizes the turning over of power to the next generation, especially to the males. Long Island, a promised land for New York City's Italian immigrants, becomes the home base for the family in Puzo's next novel, *The Godfather*, in which Lucia Santa is transformed into the most famous fictional gangster the world has ever known.

Lucia Santa as Don Corleone

What a surprise it must be to all those who modeled their manly American literary, film, and television gangsters on Don Vito Corleone to find out that his character was really based on a woman! Women have always had a hand in fashioning the gangster identity, but in *The Godfather*, novel and films, the great American gangster was humanized in ways never before imagined.

Puzo's novel opens with undertaker Amerigo Bonasera (whose name means "Good Evening America," symbolically signaling nightfall in the American empire) sitting in a New York City courtroom, where he has come for justice, American style, only to be served something that falls far short of his Italian expectations. For true Italian justice, he must go to Don Corleone, in the suburbs. A look around the suburbs today makes it clear that they are no longer the utopian havens that once promised wealthy urbanites refuge from the ills of city life. Some are quickly succumbing to the same overcrowding and pollution that led to their creation. The suburbs, as we have come to know them, appear to have been simply a phase—what Robert Fishman calls "the point of transition between two decentralized eras: the preindustrial rural era and the postindustrial information society."[37] Fishman calls the new developments "technoburbs" that have "renewed the linkage of work and residence"[38] that once characterized the earliest city life, the very quality the suburbs were created to negate.

The earliest suburbs, going back to Chaucer's time, were where "robbers and thieves instinctively huddle[d] secretly and fearfully together."[39] But modern suburbia not only restructured people's relationship to work and family, it also expressed "a complex and compelling vision of the modern family freed from the corruption of the city, restored to harmony with nature, endowed with wealth and independence, yet protected by a close-knit, stable community."[40] All this begins to change when gangsters find their way in.

With the creation of the suburbs, the home becomes the main sphere of female power. Work and home, integrated in urban life, are separated as the suburbs become home and the city work; men's sphere of influence thus belongs to life outside the home and women's inside the home. In 1841, Catharine Beecher, author of five influential books dealing with domestication, wrote that "the 'cult of true womanhood' is linked to the home with piety and purity."[41]

This, Fishman suggests, was inherent in the creation of the earliest suburbs:

> The city was not just crowded, dirty, and unhealthy; it was immoral. Salvation itself depended on separating the woman's sacred world of family and children from the profane metropolis. Yet this separation could not jeopardize a man's constant attendance to his business ... . This was the problem, and suburbia was to be the ultimate solution.[42]

Although the suburbs generally imply a degree of emasculation of the traditional male, Don Corleone, who conducts most of his business from his city office, does use his home on the day of his daughter's wedding to strengthen connections between his family and the outside world. Neighbors and community members are invited into the home for the wedding, bringing the outside world into the family space. His daughter's marriage to Carlo isn't the traditional marriage of a child of the powerful, intended to protect and expand family power. However, Vito Corleone's daughter's wedding does serve as the suburban backdrop for his continual expansion of his family's power, demonstrated by granting favors to those in his service. These are favors that will ultimately strengthen his ties to the grantees. If the home is the place where the family is nourished and strengthened, traditionally through acts performed by women, then Vito Corleone represents a male version of this role, just as Lucia Santa in *The Fortunate Pilgrim* was a female version of a man's role. Vito Corleone's central place in the home is especially telling because Puzo's Italian women play minor roles in *The

Godfather. Christian Messenger, in his brilliant study of Puzo's works, explains the minimal role Mama Corleone plays in *The Godfather*:

> The infusion of maternal power and vitality into the silent, strong patriarch who always guides his family, who "reasons" with his enemies, who is "very strait-laced" in sex is yet another cross-gendered sleight-of-hand in the American popular culture whereby the role of a strong woman character is recast into that of a "domestic" and "multiple" male character.... *The Godfather* needs no true female characters since Puzo's mother, alias Lucia Santa, recycled into Don Corleone, is in firm control of the family's destiny.[43]

Puzo does go to some wild extremes portraying the masculinities of Don Corleone and his fellow Mafia leaders. They are depicted as heroic male figures, hypermen or supermen who "refused the dominion of other men. There was no force, no mortal man who could bend them to their will unless they wished it. They were men who guarded their free will with wiles and murder."[44] The Don speaks of the hard life of the gangster, fostered by the continuation of traditional Italian family collectives that proved to be formidable enemies for American law enforcement. The extremes that these mafiosi go to as they protect their families mirrors the energy that Lucia Santa employs in *The Fortunate Pilgrim*, yet *The Godfather* falls short of the drama created in the earlier novel in this regard because it continually draws our attention away from the female core of Vito Corleone's masculinity.

From the very opening of *The Godfather*, it is apparent that an Italianate sense of masculinity cannot survive transplantation to the United States. Recalling Gilmore's three roles, which have defined masculinity in many of the world's cultures—the ability of men to procreate, provide for, and protect their families—fulfilling these roles becomes a challenge to the Italian immigrant males in *The Godfather*. The problems that these men face wouldn't arise in Italy, or if they did, the men wouldn't have to face them alone. They would have their family members for support. To solve these problems in the United States, they must go to see Don Corleone, the head of the symbolic larger family.

Don Corleone asserts himself as the mediator of traditional Italian masculinity in America when he confronts his godson, Johnny Fontane, a singer who can't provide for his family:

"You can start by acting like a man." Suddenly anger contorted his face. He shouted, "LIKE A MAN!" He reached over the desk and grabbed Johnny Fontane by the hair of his head in a gesture that was savagely affectionate. "By Christ in heaven, is it possible that you spent so much time in my presence and turned out no better than this? A Hollywood 'finocchio' who weeps and begs for pity? Who cries out like a woman—'What shall I do? Oh, what shall I do?' "[45]

The word "finocchio" is equivalent to English "faggot," and the finocchio is identified as one who uses words instead of actions and is therefore effeminate. Once the Don sets up this definition of what is not a man, he can proceed with his instruction as to how Johnny can regain his respect and his manhood: "A man who is not a father to his children can never be a real man. But then, you must make their mother accept you."[46] The Don says Johnny's wife takes advantage of him because he showed her he was soft: "Because you acted like a 'finocchio.' You gave her 'more' than the court said. You didn't hit the other in the face because she was making a picture. You let women dictate your actions and they are not competent in this world, though certainly they will be saints in heaven while we men burn in hell."[47]

Book One of *The Godfather* sets up the background of the story and gives an overview of how one should be a man in the United States. The story of Michael Corleone, Vito's son, becoming a man comprises the rest of the novel. In order for Michael to become a man, he must demonstrate the ability to exert power over other men; he must perform his masculinity publicly, for others to see. In order to sustain this power, the other men must see him as someone who has the power to take life. Michael Corleone becomes recognized as a man in his family the day he kills the police captain, McClusky, and the drug trafficker, Sollozzo. Michael is in his mid-twenties when this happens, much older than his father was when he was considered to have achieved manhood.

When Vito was twelve, growing up in Italy, his father was murdered. Everyone, including his father's enemies, assumed that Vito would seek revenge because he could use a shotgun despite his youth, so he was forced to flee to the United States for his own protection.[48] As Puzo writes, "The Don was a real man at the age of twelve."[49] There is nothing about Don Corleone's American entry into manhood in the novel; it is said only that that he went to work in a grocery store, and that at the age of eighteen he married. A few years later the couple had their first child.

When Don Fanucci, a neighborhood bully, threatens the Corleone family's welfare by insisting that Vito's employer hire Fanucci's nephew, forcing Vito's layoff, Vito must find another way to support his family. Vito harbors an intense anger toward Fanucci for the loss of his job, but in true Mediterranean fashion, he never displays his anger publicly, opting instead to wait for revenge. In the meantime, Vito finds work in thieving. He decides that he must get rid of Fanucci, and when the time is right, he does. It is this act of revenge that makes him a "man of respect" in his neighborhood. After that his masculinity is performed publicly, but no longer through violence or overt threats. Instead, Vito helps others in his neighborhood, although underlying each of his actions is the implied consequence of what might happen if one crosses a man who is capable of murder.

From this point on in the novel, Vito's sons become the ones displaying qualities of masculinity—the Don has nothing left to prove. A powerful sexuality is revealed in his oldest son, Santino (Sonny), who is described as "generous and his heart was admitted to be as big as his organ."[50] Second-born Fredo has sensitivity but lacks "that personal magnetism, that animal force, so necessary for a leader of men."[51] And finally there is Michael, the youngest, whose masculinity the Don once worried about, "a worry that was put to rest when Michael Corleone became seventeen years old."[52] As soon as the Don finds out that his son has had sex with a woman, he is satisfied that Michael is masculine.

A deeper look at Michael's character reveals that he has a propensity for violence his father does not have. This could be because Michael Corleone doesn't mature, and so he doesn't separate from his mother. The psychotherapist Christina Wieland, in *The Undead Mother: Psychoanalytic Explorations of Masculinity, Femininity, and Matricide*, observes that matricide "has been the Western, culturally sanctioned means by which separation from mother has been achieved."[53] This matricidal solution, she argues, is responsible for the inability of men truly to separate from the mother, creating only "the semblance of separation, by violent means."[54] Wieland argues that a murder serves to bind victim and victimizer forever, and that the only way to change the destructive bent this Western behavior has instilled is to enable men to not kill the mother, but instead to place that loss in its proper place, to mourn it. If we assume that Don Vito Corleone is a subconscious mother figure, then Michael, as his son, is little more than a mama's boy. Vito is, thus, a mother-based gangster, the mother of modern gangsters.

MICHAEL CORLEONE IN THE OLD WORLD

The word "mafiosi," when referring to the traditional Sicilian mafiosi, means " 'men with a belly,' meaning, figuratively, power and courage; and literally, physical flesh, as if the two went together as indeed they seem to have done in Sicily."[55] In order for Michael to gain the power and courage of his father, he must be reborn in his father's homeland.

In *The Godfather*, Sicily becomes for Don Corleone what the planet Krypton is to Superman: a legendary place of origin, the experience of which elevates him to the status of a hero. This is exemplified best through the character of Michael Corleone, the one son who is closest to total American assimilation. Michael is sent to Sicily to hide out after avenging the attempted assassination of his father and to unlearn the American behavior that is incompatible with his family's life. For example, during his sister's wedding reception he breaks the old country's code of silence by telling his girlfriend stories about the "more colorful wedding guests," such as Luca Brasi. Michael also explains to his girlfriend what is going on at the meetings held inside his father's study and interprets the ambiguities that she, as an outsider, is incapable of reading. When his father is shot, Michael returns to the family house, and "[f]or the first time since it had all started he felt a furious anger rising in him, a cold hatred for his father's enemies."[56] This fury drives Michael back into the family fold and leads him to avenge his father's shooting. Until he does, he has been as sheltered and innocent as the women in the Corleone clan. In fact, he attempts to dismiss his girlfriend Kay's fear that he will be the target of the same violence that almost took his father's life by saying, "I'm known as the sissy of the Corleone family. No threat."[57] This all changes after he murders the police captain and Sollozzo, the man who orchestrated the hit on his father. This act becomes the public performance of masculinity that certifies Michael's manhood and gains him the respect that comes from fear. His ancestral culture's code demands vengeance for his father's blood, and Michael acts accordingly.

After the murder Michael flees to Sicily, that otherworldly ground of his being and his subconscious. There he meets the characters who embody the new condition of his soul, which is now marked physically by his disfigured face, the result of an earlier beating by the same police captain. Through Dr. Taza, a local professor and historian, "He came to understand his father's character and his destiny ... to understand men like Luca Brasi, the ruthless *caporegime* Clemenza, his mother's resignation and acceptance of her role. For in Sicily he saw what they would have been if they had chosen *not* to struggle against their fate."[58] The education Michael receives during his exile in Sicily enables him to take command of his father's kingdom in the United States and ruthlessly rule it in an Old-World manner. In the almost feudal system of Sicily and southern Italy, peasants could not aspire to a better life by challenging the forces that controlled them. As a result, they focused on what could be controlled, the family unit. This poverty and lack of control were why so many families emigrated to other lands, especially the United States. The world into which so many immigrants came was one built on the myth that, through political liberty, each person could become whatever he or she wanted, with enough work. This Puritan work ethic and the built-in reward system did not require that the family stick together, and indeed often led to the breakup of a nuclear family. Thus, the central conflict of *The Godfather* is how to keep the family together and "Sicilian" for its own good in a land that has lost its dependence on the family unit for survival. It is in Sicily that Michael gains his father's Italian sense of masculinity, which enables him to return to the United States and take over the reins of the Corleone family.

Besides learning the importance of family and the need for allies to help a man protect his family in Sicily, Michael is exposed to old-fashioned notions of manhood through incidents like seeing his bodyguard Fabrizio's tattoo: "a husband stabbing a naked man and woman entwined together on the hairy floor of his belly."[59] This notion of Sicilian honor rationalizes and justifies the use of violence in the protection of what is considered to be one's property; if his wife (his property) cheats on him, her murder and that of her lover is completely accepted as natural and justified. In Sicily Michael also meets Apollonia, the woman who will become his first wife: "He understood for the first time the classical jealousy of the Italian male. He was at that moment ready to kill anyone who touched this girl, who tried to claim her, take her way from him."[60] After their marriage, "That night and the weeks that followed, Michael Corleone came to understand the premium put on virginity by socially primitive people. It was a period of sensuality that he had never before experienced, a sensuality mixed with a feeling of masculine power."[61]

While Michael is away, Don Vito is busy planning for his youngest son's return. During a meeting with the other Mafia leaders, he reminds them of the qualities that make up manhood: "I am being prudent, I've always been a prudent man, there is nothing I find so little to my taste as carelessness in life. Women and children can afford to be careless, men cannot."[62] Thus, the wise man, the saintly man, is one who acts judiciously and prudently, more calculating than his son Santino, more confidently than his son Fredo. Santino dies because of his inability to control his temper and Fredo proves too inept to defend his father. This leaves Michael as the only possible heir to the Don's sense of manhood, and, thus, control of the family. The film version of *The Godfather* shows Vito sitting as he utters those words. Behind him is a portrait of an English gentleman in which the head of the portrait is not visible, suggesting the head of Vito takes the place of the original subject's head. The lights behind Vito create a halo effect.

FRANCIS FORD COPPOLA'S *GODFATHER* MOVIES

For the most part, Coppola follows the direction of Puzo's novel, but the choices he makes when changing the story are made from a perspective that reflects the generational differences between Puzo, the son of immigrants, and Coppola, the grandson of immigrants—a perspective that reflects attitudes toward masculinity that had changed drastically in only one generation.

Beginning with the choice of Marlon Brando to play Don Corleone, Coppola showed that he would be creating a completely different kind of gangster film. Brando, the former symbol of rough, tough, rebellious American masculinity in the 1950s, conjured a significant and unmistakable male presence. Thus, by casting an icon of American masculinity as the lead, Coppola enabled the melding of Italian and American masculinity in ways that earlier portrayals had never attempted.

The film version explains that Vito's father was murdered for an insult, whereas in the novel Puzo writes, "The father refused to knuckle under and in a public quarrel killed the local Mafia chief."[63] The film adds that Vito's older brother took to the hills swearing revenge and was subsequently killed. Vito was, thus, placed in the position of having to defend himself. In the second film, *The Godfather Part II*, it is explained that Vito Andolini's name was changed to Corleone by an ignorant official at Ellis Island. This is not the way it was presented in the novel: "And in the new land he changed his name to Corleone to preserve some tie with his native village. It was one of the few gestures of senti-ment he was ever to make."[64] In altering this detail, Coppola adds to the victimization of Vito Andolini. By increasing the insults that Vito must confront, he increases the viewer's sympathy toward the acts that Vito commits later on. Coppola takes this to a higher level when Vito witnesses his mother's murder in the second film. She is killed by the bodyguards of Don Ciccio, after failing to reason with the Don to save her son. In the novel, "his mother sent the young boy to America to stay with friends."[65] Coppola simply piles up a number of reasons why Vito must demonstrate his manhood in order to right wrongs committed against him and his family.

Vito, in the novel, never avenges his father's murder, but he does kill a man who threatens the livelihood of his family—Don Fanucci. Vito murders Fanucci during the feast of San Rocco, a saint who helps the sick and afflicted. From this time on Vito acts to take "care of his world, his people."[66] Unlike Fanucci, Vito becomes a beneficent feudal lord: "Don Vito Corleone helped them all. Not only that, he helped them with goodwill, with encouraging words to take the bitter sting out of the charity he gave them."[67]

In *The Godfather Part II*, Vito kills Don Ciccio on Palm Sunday. This action, not in the novel, emphasizes Vito's connection to Old-World notions of justice, of vendetta. When Michael hides out in Sicily in the first film, he notices that there are very few men in the town of Corleone, prompting him to ask, "Where are the men?" He is told that they are all dead from *vendette*. The reality would be that they all left looking for work in Germany and other more industrialized areas of Europe. Again, this exaggeration is used to strengthen the Old-World ways that are the foundation for the behaviors that Coppola and Puzo portray as Sicilian customs.

The proper man is one who works and does not waste time play-ing. When Michael begins taking over the family business, he visits Las Vegas and walks into a party which he thought would be a meeting. "Who are the girls? Get rid of them. I'm here on business," he admon-ishes Fredo, as his father has admonished Sonny earlier in the film.

Coppola goes to extremes to establish Fredo's lack of the mascu-linity required for him to assume command of the family. Fredo, the second oldest after Santino, should be next in line to inherit the patri-archy. However, he is continually placed in positions where his fail-ure to be a man is featured. When his wife dances suggestively with another man and falls in a drunken stupor, he turns to his brother and says, "I can't control her, Mikey." Coppola goes on to exaggerate the differences between Michael and Fredo in ways beyond the novelized version. For example, he shows that the characters are opposites by their clothing: Fredo in bright colors, Michael in blacks and grays. Fredo slurps banana daiquiris and is obsessed with sex, Michael sips straight whiskey or club soda and is never seen even leering at women. When Fredo is killed, which doesn't happen in the novel, he is reciting the Hail Mary, something that strengthens his identification with the females in the family (the ones who do the praying), again reinforcing his lack of masculinity.

One of the major differences between the novel and the films is in the figure of Kay, Michael's girlfriend and, later, wife. At the end of the novel, Kay has become Michael's silent, supportive Italian-American wife who takes communion at daily mass where "[s]he emptied her mind of all thought of herself, of her children, of all anger, of all rebellion, of all questions" before she says "the necessary prayers for the soul of Michael Corleone."[68] In the second film, Kay is not the passive, supportive woman from the novel. Toward the end of the film, she confronts Michael and reveals that she aborted her pregnancy: "You are blind. It wasn't a miscarriage. It was an abortion, like our marriage." She goes on to explain that the fetus was a boy, and that she stopped him from becoming a gangster, "[b]ecause this all must end. I knew there would be no way you would forgive me." This difference again is generational. The character of Kay from the film reflects Coppola's awareness of contemporary women's fight for equal rights, while Puzo's woman is stuck in the past. This difference becomes even more obvious in the third film.

In *The Godfather Part III*, Michael is knighted *commendatore* in the Order of St. Sebastian, an organization modeled after the historical Knights Templar of Malta. His knighthood is based on his philanthropy and the hefty gift of $100 million for Sicily's poor. It is against this backdrop that Michael continues to deal with changing notions of manhood. Michael does not want his son to be an artist, an opera singer. He wants him to be a lawyer or a business man. Michael says things like, "I spent my life protecting my family," as though he needs to justify what he has done. However, when Vincent, the illegitimate son of Michael's brother Sonny, comes to him looking for a place in the family business, he says to his nephew, "I don't need tough guys." Coppola replays an earlier scene between Santino, Don Vito's oldest son, and Vito using Vincent to play Santino to Michael's Don. When Michael tells Vincent, "Never let anyone know what you're thinking," we are reminded of the lesson that Don Vito tried to teach Santino. Michael attempts to pass wisdom to Vincent because he doesn't need wiseguys, he needs wise men. But it is soon clear that wisdom can't settle affairs until violence is stopped. And even when violence is stopped in the *Godfather* movies, it is turned inward for a generation and it surfaces in depression and anger.

In *The Godfather Part III*, Coppola's use of food and the place where food is prepared becomes significant in showing how the roles of men have changed. Men begin to take over the role of maintaining food traditions. This is best seen through the character of Vincent, Sonny Corleone's illegitimate son. Vincent courts his cousin, the daughter of Michael Corleone, and they wind up in the kitchen of the restaurant he runs. When Vincent asks her if she knows how to prepare gnocchi, she laughs and tells him she can't cook a thing. Her instruction in the art of shaping the pasta soon turns into foreplay, and the two make love in the kitchen. It is important that the man is seen as master in the commercial kitchen, not the domestic kitchen, but the gender shift is on. Real men know how to cook.

Lest anyone think that there is even the hint of gender revolution in the story, Coppola tunes in to the deep underground of stereotypical Sicilian male behavior when Michael's son, Anthony, performs the lead role in the opera *Cavalleria Rusticana*, an opera in which one man kills another for sleeping with his wife. The echo here to the novel is to Fabrizio's tattoo and to the puppet show from the first film, in which a father kills his daughter for dishonoring her family. It is this scene of the puppet show that Finucci says he couldn't watch any more—it was all too violent for him. At the end of the opera, as they are walking down the stairs of the opera house, there is an assassination attempt on Michael, and his daughter is killed. Michael in a sense has killed his daughter, for it is she who takes the bullets meant for him. His sins killed her. When Michael does die, at the very end of the third film, he dies wearing the clothes of his father; but unlike his father, he dies in the fashion of the great Italian curse, "come un cane," alone, as a dog, with no one to watch his death, no one to mourn his passing.

The depiction of the gangster in *The Godfather*, both Puzo's novel version and Francis Ford Coppola's three films, has much to say about how Italian-American culture fares. As a culture hero, the gangster figures as a romantic type. A romance, according to the *American Heritage Dictionary*, is first of all "a long medieval narrative in prose or verse, telling of the adventures of chivalric heroes." This is certainly something that Puzo has accomplished and Coppola has equaled, if not bettered, with his films. But it is not until definition number 9 of the word "romance" that the real explanation emerges of *The Godfather* as a romance, for it is definitely "a fictitiously embellished account or explanation." *The Godfather*, as many critics have pointed out, tries to explain many things: American capitalism, American imperialism, Italian traditions, and more. But along with those themes, *The Godfather* looks at the changing notion of American masculinity as it has been affected by changes of the 1960s, the rise of feminism, and the fall of the traditional American he-man. For it was after this period that Americans learned that the strength of a man was more than muscles, that the Marlboro man could die of cancer, and that fathers didn't always know best. Against this tempest of change stand the Corleone dons, tragic and violent versions of Peter Pan, upholding all that was traditionally manly for men who were afraid of becoming feminized.

Representations of Italian-American masculinity in popular culture continue to reflect stereotypes, but they nonetheless provide useful windows on ethnicity and masculinity in contemporary American culture. In films of the 1970s, figures following Don Vito Corleone include Rocky Balboa (*Rocky*, 1976) and Tony Manero (*Saturday Night Fever*, 1977), along with many other who exhibit physical power and aggressiveness, criminality, and overt sexuality. These are attempts by Hollywood filmmakers to marginalize troublesome characteristics of traditional patriarchy that were under feminist attack by associating them with Old-World ethnic cultures. During this same period, other Italian-American artists tried to demystify such notions by realizing the gangster figure through writing and film. The journalism of Gay Talese and the films of Martin Scorsese offer excellent examples of attempts to move the gangster figure out of romance and into reality.

II

Realizing the Gangster

real, *adj.*
1. Being or occurring in fact or actuality; having verifiable existence;
2. True and actual; not illusory or fictitious; 3. Genuine and authentic; not artificial or spurious.

realize, *v. tr.*
1. To comprehend completely or correctly; 2. To make real or actualize.

3

THE TRUTH ABOUT GANGSTERS: GAY TALESE AND BEN MORREALE

The media gangster was an invention, much less an accurate reflection of reality than a projection created from various Americans' beliefs, concerns, and ideas about what would sell.[1]

—David Ruth

In everything I write I'm trying to get close as I can to a fuller truth, using real names, real situation, not falsifying or fabricating.[2]

—Gay Talese

This chapter analyzes Gay Talese's nonfiction exposé *Honor Thy Father* (1971) and his memoir *Unto the Sons* (1992) to demonstrate the great attraction the gangster had to the typical Italian-American man as a model for manhood during the 1960s and 1970s. It also examines other realized versions of the gangster figure presented by Ben Morreale's novels from the same period, *A Few Virtuous Men* (1973) and *Monday, Tuesday … never come Sunday* (1977).

45

Go "Figura": the Gangsters of Gay Talese

Gaetano "Gay" Talese is often mentioned as one of the early practitioners of the "New Journalism" that emerged in the 1960s. Tom Wolfe, Hunter S. Thompson, George Plimpton, and Truman Capote were other New Journalists, turning out literary news and feature stories on underground groups and unsavory characters. Talese moved from news and feature writing to authoring a number of best-selling books, including *The Kingdom and the Power* (1969), an insider's history of *The New York Times*; *Honor Thy Father* (1971), the true story of gangsters Joseph and Salvatore "Bill" Bonanno; and *Thy Neighbor's Wife* (1980), a personal look at sexuality in the United States during the 1970s. His unique personal approach to creating investigative books and magazine articles secured Talese a reputation as an American original.

When the definition of *bella figura* finally appears in English dictionaries, a photograph of Gay Talese ought to accompany it. Talese, seldom seen without a tailored suit, and rarely in the same one twice, is the perfect embodiment of *bella figura*, which Gloria Nardini explains is "a central metaphor of Italian life." Nardini defines this Italian code of public behavior as "a construct that refers to face, looking good, putting on the dog, style appearance, flair, showing off, ornamentation, etiquette, keeping up with the Joneses, image, illusion, esteem, social status, reputation—in short, self-preservation and identity, performance and display."[3] The phrase *fare figura*, "to cut a figure," defies simple definition, but it deserves consideration in any discussion of things Italian and Italian-American. Essentially, *figura* refers to the public presentation of self in both appearance and behavior. *Figura* creates an impression and a *figura* is a beautiful or good impression; *brutta figura* a bad or ugly one. *Figura* is central to any discussion of the performance of masculinity, and it must be considered when realizing the American gangster of Italian descent.

Talese is one Americanized Italian who holds on to traditional notions of Italian male behavior. He uses the word *omertà* (which denotes desirable masculine reserve, but which has been mistakenly translated for years as "the Sicilian code of silence") to explain why Italian Americans don't write good novels about their own culture. Talese's explanations of Italian-American culture are filtered primarily through his own experiences. It comes as no surprise, then, that when he raised the question "Where are the Italian American Novelists?" on the front page of *The New York Times Book Review* (14 March 1993), his attempt to answer it—hindered by his lack of familiarity with the vast body of literature created by American writers of Italian descent—reduced the experience of Italian-American writers to his own, offering explanations that sounded plausible but did not reflect the complexity of the subject. This was a familiar approach for Talese, and the one he took in presenting the first in-depth, nonfiction portrait of an Italian-American crime figure by an Italian-American writer. Talese almost always begins writing about something that piques his curiosity by submerging himself in the same environment that creates and sustains his subject.

When Talese decided to write about the Italian-American gangster, he knew he was onto something sensational, and something that had long been a favorite subject of American journalism. The journalist Tom Ventsias reports that organized crime received more regular attention in the news after the arrival of Puzo's novel and Coppola's film:

> Most big-city newsrooms had a reporter exclusively assigned to the mob beat ... and while these reporters generally stayed within the basic boundaries of journalistic principles, many of the more prolific "mob writers"—scribes like *New York Post* columnist Steve Dunleavy and bestselling author Gay Talese— were known to hang out with some of the shady characters they were writing about.[4]

Talese's own method of reporting was based on "hanging out." Not content just to employ colorful quotes from eyewitnesses, Talese, whenever possible, became the witness of what he reported on—if not of the events that made the subject newsworthy, then certainly the effect that media attention had on the subject. Talese's great impact on journalism was his suggestion that the journalist is not simply a writer reporting facts, or even using fictional techniques such as characterization or dialogue to report reality. Rather, Talese showed that a journalist could make his own experience the subject of his writing: simply put, Talese turned his news stories into autobiography. Ventsias further historicizes the Talese-made gangster:

> In 1971, New York journalist Gay Talese published *Honor Thy Father,* considered by many as the first nonfiction book with a true insider's view of the Mafia. Other manuscripts on the mob had been published, but most dealt with mobsters who had defected and turned government witness—à la Joe Valachi

and *The Valachi Papers*—or criminals who were already dead and forgotten. Trading upon his Sicilian ancestry and employing remarkable reporting and research skills, Talese detailed the life of Bill Bonanno, heir apparent of major New York Mafia boss Joseph "Joe Bananas" Bonanno. The book was an immense success and would further whet the appetite for an American public eager to embrace all-things-Mafia.[5]

Gay Talese was nothing if not a creator of controversy. As a journalist for *The New York Times*, he knew what it took to sell words. Talese apparently saw the story of Bill Bonanno as more a story of the relationship between a father and son than a criminal investigation. Talese's own experiences with his father, recounted in his later memoir, *Unto the Sons*, gave him great insight into the father–son relationship of the Bonannos. He applied his own father–son experiences to one of the earliest descriptions of Bill's relationship to his father: "It was obvious that he was awed by his father, and while no doubt had feared him and perhaps still did, he also worshipped him."[6] Talese's relationship with his own father was quite similar, especially in terms of the son's showing unquestioned obedience and respect to the father. By concentrating on the Bonanno family dynamics, Talese created the story of a relationship to which any American could relate. Inside the story of the gangsters Bonanno, Talese found the story of his own family.

Most of the reporting on the gangster, from his earliest media appearance through Al Capone, was done by outsiders looking in. Since the 1920s Americans have read second- and third-hand stories by reporters such as Ben Hecht, who doubled as a journalist and a screenwriter (*Underworld*, 1927; *Scarface*, 1932). When Talese sees Bill Bonanno in the federal court building in Manhattan, on January 7, 1965, he sees not a gangster but a guy who could easily have been his friend: "I wondered, not for the first time, what it must be like to be a young man in the Mafia. Most of what I had read about organized crime in newspapers and books was obtained through sources in the federal government and the police."[7] In fact, over the course of writing the book, Talese does form a friendly relationship with Bonanno and his wife and sees himself as a conduit through which members of the family can relate to one another: "I had become a source of communication within a family that had long been repressed by a tradition of silence."[8] No other writer had been able to make such a personal connection with a gangster.

HONOR THY FATHER (1971)

Honor Thy Father is an *apologia pro vita sua* on behalf of a gangster by a writer who realizes that this easily could have been his own story. Talese's account of the gangster becomes very personal here, as evident in the book's dedication to the children of Salvatore (Bill) Bonanno "in the hope that they will understand their father more, and love him no less."[9] Following the dedication is an author's glossary which Talese uses to introduce the people and language of the book. In the 1992 reprint, Talese added an "Author's Foreword" in which he explains that the origins of the book were connected with his father: "This book evolved out my father's embarrassment—my Italian-born father's embarrassment over the fact that gangsters with Italian names invariably dominate the headlines and most television shows dealing with organized crime."[10] Organized crime became an embarrassment that Talese took on himself to uncover and explain in order to expose the humanity behind the headlines—as though in some way he was coming to the aid of his father. Written the same year that his memoir *Unto the Sons* appeared, this foreword reflects an even stronger awareness of the role of the father–son relationship in Italian-American culture than the memoir does. In the foreword, Talese also recounts how Bill Clinton referred to Mario Cuomo as a "mafioso," proving that the association of the gangster with Italian-American men has not been left in the past, but instead continues to haunt the contemporary Italian American.

Most people who looked at Bill Bonanno in the 1970s saw a loser, a gangster. When Talese looked at Bill Bonanno, he saw a family man. Much as Mario Puzo saw his own family in the Corleones, Talese recognized aspects of his in the Bonannos. Identifying too closely with your subject is dangerous, though, especially for a journalist, who is expected to uncover and report the truth. To his credit, Talese never "goes native" with his subject by joining forces with the mafiosi. However, some critics objected that he "dressed up" his subject and whitewashed characters everyone else had dismissed as hopeless criminals. Talese, being Italian American, could see something that other writers could not. However, he did not realize exactly what he had seen in that encounter until much later in his career. In an interview with the director Michael Corrente just after the release of Corrente's film *Federal Hill* (1994), Talese asks Corrente, "Could it be that in the 'correct' 1990s, when masculinity is not well defined and when old-style 'virility' and separateness is an affront to feminism, the Italian-American actor is the only type that can satisfy some filmgoers' fondness for 'men who are men'—crude, aggressive, macho—while not indicating male society as a whole, because Italian Americans are marginal people?"[11] Significantly, Corrente cannot answer the question, for his own film depends on the very type that Talese questions. What Corrente can't see, and Talese, twenty years after his own portrayal of this type was beginning to see, is that the role of the tough, macho Italian-American man is the very role the gangster has been playing ever since the rise of second-wave American feminism and the downfall of the John Wayne version of the American tough guy.

Early in *Honor Thy Father*, Talese sees Bill Bonanno and one of his fellow gangsters, Frank Labruzzo, as men who are not in tune with their time. He envisions the whole crime business as a revised version of feudal culture. Referring to these two men, Talese writes: "It seemed both absurd and remarkable to the two men that they had never escaped the insular ways of their parents' world, a subject that they had often discussed during their many hours of confinement." He also calls Bonanno and Labruzzo soldiers in a "feudal war."[12] Bonanno's 1956 marriage to Rosalie Profaci, the niece of Joseph Profaci, another gangster leader, is reminiscent of a feudal matrimonial contract designed to connect two powerful families. Talese uses the story of the couple's Sicilian honeymoon to give us some historical background on the family and the place of the Mafia in Sicily. In many respects, this sequence is reminiscent of Puzo's description of Michael Corleone's trip to Sicily. In both cases, the visitors come to a better understanding of their family and their own places in it.

Honor Thy Father opens with the suspected kidnapping of Joseph Bonanno. Upon hearing of his father's abduction, his son Bill goes into hiding. At this point Talese begins describing Bill's boyhood, explaining that Bill's first personal involvement with his father's "business" occurred when members of the Federal Bureau of Investigation visited his high school and questioned him, in front of his school's principal, about his knowledge of the murder of Vincent Mangano. Although he handled the questions well, he came out of the experience quite disturbed. "He felt the eyes of the other students on him, but he did not face anyone as he took his seat; he felt separated from his classmates in a way that he had not felt before."[13] This is the beginning of a sense of shame about his family that Bill inherits from his father and must hide from the rest of the world. It becomes the fundamental basis for the development of Bill's gangster behavior. This experience creates a dual existence that challenges his identity in ways that most people never have to face. Bill sees his attempts to gain an education as pulling him away from his father. Talese points out that this duality leads him to infer his father's demand for loyalty: "At certain times, particularly when his father seemed to be at odds with other bosses or to be hounded by federal agents, he [Bill] had felt both a desire and a responsibility to stand by his father, to lend verbal and emotional support even though his father had not requested it, saying instead he wanted Bill to remain in school concentrating on his studies. And there were times when Bill's interests seemed to be centered entirely around the campus."[14] This alienation from mainstream American life, Talese argues, is the result of being "born of such foreign fathers and ... remain[ing] loyal to them throughout one's lifetime."[15]

Talese is adept at bringing out the rationalizations that Bill uses to remain connected to his father even though he does not wish to take on his father's problems or be identified as a gangster. For Bill, it becomes a matter of defending the family against threatening outside powers. In the course of that defense, Bill comes to see his father as a Christ-like figure:

> He also did not want to separate himself from his father's circumstances or feel apologetic or defensive about his name, particularly since he did not believe that his father was guilty of crimes against society. Sometimes the reverse was true; society was using such men as Joseph Bonanno to pay for the widespread sins in the system. In any case, no matter how damaging the consequences might be to himself, he could not turn against his father, nor did he really want to. His emotional link with his father was very strong, exceeding the normal bond of filial fidelity. It was more intense, more unquestioning, there was a unity in the tension they both shared and a certain romanticism about the risk and dangers involved, and there was also a kind of religious overtone in the relationship, a combination of blind faith and fear, formality and love ... during their months apart, Bill's youthful imagination and memory had often endowed his father with qualities approximating a deity, so impressive, absolute, and almost foreign was the elder Bonanno in person.[16]

Bill begins to learn from his father that to protect himself from the potential harm that outsiders can cause, he will have to keep his true feelings to himself. The practical aspects of survival as a mafioso's son are accompanied by family stories that will become mythic as time passes and will fuel the young Bonanno's sense of identification with a noble past:

> A kinship of sorts probably did exist between these men and the legendary American cowboy of the Old West and certain stories he had heard as a boy involving gun battles between mounted Mafiosi in the hills of western Sicily. He had heard that his grandmother in Castellammare sometimes packed a pistol in her skirts, a kind of Ma Barker, and the Sicilians of that region today still honor the memory of the bandit Giuliano, a leader of a gang of outlaws who shared what they stole with the poor.[17]

Bonanno sees himself as a link in a lineage of historical figures who lived outside the law.

But Talese does not allow Bonanno to become a myth from the past, nor does he provide us with an opportunity to dismiss Bonanno as a boy trapped in a fantasy. He dares to compare Bonanno's service in a Reserve Officer Training Corps camp and in the Army Reserves with the Mafia experience: "He memorized the United States military code, which in principle was not dissimilar from the Mafia's, emphasizing honor, obedience, and silence if captured. And if he had gone into combat and had killed several North Koreans or Chinese Communists, he might have become a hero. But if he killed one of his father's enemies in a Mafia war, where buried in the issues was the same mixture of greed and self-righteousness found in all the wars of great nations, he could be charged with murder."[18] Without further comment, Talese leaves the question in the reader's mind: Mafia, U.S. Army, what's the difference? (It is important to remember that at the time he wrote this book, the United States was involved in the unpopular war in Vietnam.)

Bill does get the experience of being in a Mafia war, and in Part II, Talese prefaces the war stories by detailing the Bonanno family's roots in Sicily. He compares the control they had over farming jobs with the power wielded by "ancient princes and viceroys before them, taxing their subjects for services rendered, services that included the arbitration of neighborly disputes, the recovery of stolen property, personal assistance in all family problems, personal redress for wrongs to one's honor or one's wife."[19] As Talese suggests, this behavior is what is expected of men: "They were spoken of in hushed tones by other men but never called Mafiosi. They were usually referred to as the *amici*, friends, or *uomini rispetatti*, men of respect."[20] What Talese does so well is set the scene for the justification of Mafia power by suggesting it was simply a means for men to survive in an unjust environment:

> They believed that there was no equality under law; the law was written by conquerors. In the tumultuous history of Sicily, going back more than two thousand years, the island had been governed by Greek law, Roman law, Arab law, the laws of the Goths, Normans, Angevins, Aragonese ... and no matter whose laws it was, it seemed that it favored the rich over the poor, the powerful over the weak. While the law opposed vendettas among villagers, it allowed organized brutality and killing by government guardsmen or king's arms.[21]

So the Mafia rises as a defensive strategy that enables the protection and perseverance of family over time. These are explanations not offered in other journalistic portrayals of organized crime, such as Peter Maa's *The Valachi Papers* (1968).

Talese spends most of his time examining the gangster from the male perspective, but he does turn at times to the effect that the gangster figure has on women. However, he focuses nearly all such attention on Bill's wife, Rosalie, leaving Bill's mother in the background. As far as Talese is concerned, the most interesting relationship here is that between father and son, not mother and son. When he does bring women into the story, it is usually to show how they serve as a way of measuring a man's honor. Real gangsters do not have outside affairs without serious repercussions to their family's public reputation and honor. When Bill has an affair, therefore, it "represented his first blatantly rebellious act against the Sicilian family structures that had shaped him and sometimes sickened him. When Rosalie proposed they separate, he said firmly that he would not let her go."[22] Bill sees his relationship with another woman as just something men, especially those who provide well for their family, can and should be entitled to have. But to the older members of the family, Bill has ventured into territory that borders on disgrace. In typical patriarchal fashion, the man who took over the Profaci family after the death of Rosalie's uncle

Joseph steps in to try to ameliorate the situation by demanding that Rosalie return to her husband: "Magliocco was an old-style Sicilian. He believed that a man's wife was his property. But Sicilians also greatly respected wives, regarded them as objects of honor, and any husband in Sicily who had been as indiscreet as Bill would undoubtedly have been shot to death long ago."[23]

Talese also investigates the role that gangsters play in the U.S. economy. A key to realizing the gangster is to portray accurately his relationship with the economic system that enables both his existence and his success. In chapter 9 of *Honor Thy Father*, Talese explores the business of the Mafia and the massive investment by local, state, and federal governments in the 1960s in investigations conducted by many agencies to try to eradicate the Mafia. What Talese uncovers is the role played by everyday people in providing the gangster's income. He reports that an estimated 75 percent of the money taken in by organized crime was contributed by gamblers.[24] This connects the everyday man to the gangster in ways that previous media portrayals did not suggest.

Realizing the Mafia life also means deromanticizing the gangster. Talese is careful to show that the life of the gangster is more boring than media portrayals might suggest:

> When the average American citizen thought about the Mafia, he usually contemplated scenes of action and violence, of dramatic intrigue and million-dollar schemes, of big black limousines screeching around corners with machine-gun bullets spraying the sidewalk—this was the Hollywood version and while much of it was based on reality it also widely exaggerated that reality, totally ignoring the dominant mood of Mafia existence: a routine of endless waiting, tedium, hiding, excessive smoking, overeating, lack of physical exercise, reclining in rooms behind drawn shades being bored to death while trying to stay alive.[25]

His attention to the dull details of everyday life enables Talese to realize the gangster as no previous writer had, and to deprive him of much of his romance.

Talese demystifies the notion that crime is somehow inherently connected to the Italian version of family. By continually presenting Bonanno's obligations to his wife, children, and extended family members, he depicts a depth of humanity in Bonanno unequaled in previous gangster portrayals. The business of organized crime is not fundamental to family life, he explains, but in many ways it is affected by traditional family dynamics. In "Part III: The Family," Talese brings the reader deep into the experience of Bill's wife, Rosalie, as she begins to deal with the justice system. This aspect of gangster life would not be seen again until David Chase's *The Sopranos*.

One of the more interesting moments in *Honor Thy Father* occurs when the reality of Bill's experience as a gangster meets the romanticism of Puzo's novel. Bill finds Don Corleone "a believable character"[26] with aspects of Vito Genovese and Thomas Lucchese,[27] whose actions remind him of organized crime connections to the Kennedy family. Bill also says he "identified" with Michael Corleone: "As Bill continued to read the book [*The Godfather*], he became nostalgic for a period that he had never personally known."[28] This is a mood also felt by Tony Soprano in one of his sessions with his analyst, when he laments that he "came in on the end of something."

Success for the gangster figure was a double-edged sword, especially for gangsters who grew up in America. To stay in power, one had to deflect attention away from one's activities. Real gangsters definitely needed to live with *bella figura* in mind, and they also needed to avoid the attention the United States gives to celebrities. But in a modern world in which technology makes surveillance nearly invisible, one might become a celebrity just by being seen or heard on government tapes; the extra attention makes avoiding detection almost impossible. The challenge was to obtain some attention, but not too much. To prove he was a success in organized crime, a man had to display masculinity publicly:

> It was essential, if one wished to succeed in the secret society, to at least give the appearance of prosperity and power, to exude confidence and a carefree spirit; although in doing so, the Mafia man's life became more difficult for him in the larger world where government agents were watching him, tapping his phone, bugging his home, seeking to determine the source of his illegitimate income so that he might be indicted for income tax evasion. The Mafia man was consequently forced into an almost schizophrenic situation—while he was pleading poverty to Internal Revenue and was attempting to conceal his resources, he was also attempting to impress his friends by

picking up checks, driving a new Cadillac or Lincoln, and by otherwise living beyond his means.[29]

Living beyond their means would be the price paid by American gangsters for pursuing the code of *bella figura*, a twist that the lawman and Mafia investigator Remo Franceschini noticed soon after the appearance of the *Godfather* films. Franceschini did intelligence work for the New York City Police Department and became an expert on organized crime. While promoting his book, *A Matter of Honor: One Cop's Lifelong Pursuit of John Gotti and the Mob* (1992), Franceschini told how he noticed that lower-ranking gangsters started acting more like the Hollywood gangsters after they saw these films. The new generation of gangsters wanted to be like John Gotti: "They like the exposure, the expensive suits, the fast talk. Movies glorifying the Mob, like *The Godfather*, have made kids want to go in."[30] This focus on image, on the way they are perceived by others, especially those not involved directly with crime, is a far cry from the origins of mafioso behavior, and it helped contribute to the eventual downfall of the gangster.

Talese points out the U.S. fascination with the Italian-American gangster, seeing it as comparable to other sociopolitical persecutions in U.S. history that arise whenever a scapegoat is needed by society to encapsulate its evil:

> The Mafia in the sixties, like Communism in the fifties, had become part of a national illusory complex shaped by curved mirrors that have an enlarged and distorted view of everything it reflected, a view that was widely believed because it filled some strange need among average American citizens for grotesque portraits of murderous villains who bore absolutely no resemblance to themselves.[31]

This is a pattern that dates back to the persecution of Native Americans and the enslavement of Africans, but Talese sees the attack on the Italian-American element of organized crime as a means of ennobling not the criminal, but the crime fighter. When Congress requested millions of dollars to fight organized crime, it did so to increase the sense of protection Americans felt they needed from such a terrifying giant, for "to diminish the size of the antihero was to diminish the size of the hero."[32] With the Mafia as a national symbol of sin and Satan, those who rose up to defend the citizens would be guaranteed hero status. One need only glance at the list of politicians who made their way to the top by chasing gangsters—from Thomas Dewey to Robert Kennedy to Rudolph Giuliani—successful prosecution of gangsters has often served as a path to greater political power.

As Talese writes about Bill's court case over his using a stolen credit card, besides going through the details of the trial, he tries to understand the experience from Bill's perspective as a father. Talese imagines how Bill will explain everything to his children and comes up with the conclusion that Bill "saw his father as a misplaced masterpiece of a man who had been forged in a feudalistic tradition, but had been flexible enough to survive and prosper in mid twentieth-century America, albeit not in the manner of which Judge Mansfield would approve."[33] Talese also imagines how Bill would explain his interpretations of the democratic system of government: "He wanted them [his children] to understand that the law was created for the majority of people, and that there were those who committed acts that the law opposed and so those people were penalized; but he also wanted them to know that the law often changed, that what was disallowed now might be permitted a few years from now."[34]

Talese takes time at the end of the book to present the case of the gangster Joseph Colombo, Jr., and his attempt to unify the nation's estimated (at that time) twenty-two million Americans of Italian descent into the Italian-American Civil Rights League. Italian Americans, not known for their propensity to protest discrimination publicly since the repression of the worker movements of the early twentieth century, put on a powerful show of strength, with more than forty thousand in attendance at a rally held in New York City's Columbus Circle on 29 June 1970, Italian-American Unity Day. Some anxiety-prone Italian-American historians and activists saw the shooting of Colombo at the rally as an assassination akin to those of Malcolm X and Martin Luther King, Jr., and as part of what Richard Capozzola refers to as "ethnic genocide."[35] The work of the League did, however, catch the ear of the government long enough to prompt Attorney General George Mitchell to send out a memo ordering all government agencies to stop using words like "Mafia" and "Cosa Nostra" in their communications.

Talese concludes with an "Author's Note" in which he explains that, in writing *Honor Thy Father*, he was most interested in "how the men passed the idle hours that no doubt dominated their days, about the role of their wives, about their relationships with their children."[36]

After initially making contact with Bonanno, Talese had a number of encounters with the gangster that drew them closer. In one such incident, Talese sees Bonanno during an afternoon after Bonanno has been attacked. Talese sends a tip to a newspaper editor friend of his who puts Bonanno's story in the paper, something Bonanno wants.[37] By helping out here and there, Talese is able to participate in the gangster life. He later meets Bill's father, Joe Bonanno, who at first is skeptical about the book. Ultimately, Talese realizes that he, as author of the book, plays the role of mouthpiece for Bill:

> While my initial proposal to write about him might have been flattering, particularly since he then felt so misunderstood and had gone through life being his father's son, I do believe that later I served as an instrument through which he could communicate to those closest to him. He could reveal through me, who respected and understood him, thoughts and attitudes that he did not wish to personally express to his family, to his father.[38]

What Talese points out, but doesn't quite understand until later in his life, is that by communicating feelings this way, Bill Bonanno is able to maintain a public sense of *bella figura*. This sort of communication leads to the creation of a "culture of indirection," a culture in which the intermediary serves as a "godfather" of sorts. Thus, Talese becomes an emotional godfather to Bill Bonanno through the writing of *Honor Thy Father*. There are echoes of the culture of indirection in Gay Talese's own family's history, *Unto the Sons*.

UNTO THE SONS (1992)

In *Unto the Sons*, Talese turns to the story of his own family's coming to the United States, and in the process he tries to capture images of the history that shaped modern Italy and America. He retells the ancient myths of Saint Paolo di Francesco's miracles, as well as accounts of the evil eye, and combines these with excerpts taken from of his uncle Antonio Cristiani's diary, interviews of living relatives, and a number of published sources.

The early chapters of *Unto the Sons* focus on Talese's youth as an "olive-skinned" kid in "freckle-faced" Ocean City, New Jersey during World War II. Talese introduces the conflicts that second-generation Italian Americans know all too well: "There were many times when I wished that I had been born into a different family, a plain and simple family of impeccable American credentials—a no-secrets, non-whispering, no-enemy-soldiers family that never received mail from POW camps, or prayed to a painting of an ugly monk, or ate Italian bread with pungent cheese."[39] From this introduction he moves into his father's story in Maida, a village in the toe of the Italian boot, and on to his father's emigration to America. The story then shifts back farther to his great-grandparents. Toward the end of the book, Talese becomes a character himself. The book ends by circling back to the opening, a move that prepares the reader for a sequel. Talese ends *Unto the Sons* by saying that his next book will follow his personal history from college through to his stint in the Third Armored Division in Germany, where he served as public information officer for Creighton W. Abrams.

Unto the Sons opens with a first-person point of view, as a traditional autobiography, and then shifts almost imperceptibly into the third person, where it stays even through the author's own birth and childhood. By remaining in the third person, Talese suggests to readers that people are not who or what they were in their past. He also suggests that one's representation of that past is, in fact, a "fiction" in the true sense of the word: a conscious construction, susceptible to interpretation and revision.

Talese has been attacked by critics for his emphasis on the stories of his male ancestors at the expense of his female relatives. However, he believes that Italian women are central to men's ability to do what they do. He demonstrates this in *Unto the Sons* through his stories of the "white widows," the wives left behind by emigrating "birds of passage." Further evidence of Talese's respect for the power women have comes through the story of his mother, Catherine, who took over her husband's business while her husband brooded over the conflict between his native and adopted countries during World War II.

Throughout *Sons* there are also profiles of historical figures such as Garibaldi, Napoleon, and Mussolini, which, while connecting the family's stories to the larger fabric of history, also serve as vehicles for exploring and criticizing the Italian character. Talese's interpretation destroys the stereotype of the cowardly Italian soldier and explains why Italians, "individualistic in the extreme," never organized into a strong sociopolitical force in America. He explores Old-World notions of fatalism, and then re-creates the lives of immigrants who defied "destino" to renew their lives in America.

Talese began his life feeling as though he did not belong in the United States:

> I felt different from my young friends in almost every way, different in the cut of my clothes, the food in my lunch box, the music I heard at home on the record player, the ideas and inner thoughts I revealed on those rare occasions when I was open and honest.
>
> I was olive-skinned in a freckle-faced town, and I felt unrelated even to my parents, especially my father who was indeed a foreigner.[40]

This sense of difference became a shame that Talese covered by assimilation into American culture and mastery of the English language. Yet no matter how American he became, he was still rooted to his ancestral culture through his father: "To me he could confess his anxiety and, possibly, guilt, or at the very least expose a side of himself that his tailor's taste for appearances would prevent him from revealing beyond the walls of this mirrored apartment."[41] Just as Bill Bonanno did, Talese learned lessons from his father about how to present oneself in public.

As Talese explores his father's history, he cannot help but retell the story of the Sicilian Mafia, even though his father's birthplace of Maida, in Calabria, sixty-five miles northeast from Messina, Sicily, is more connected to the story of the Calabrian criminal element known as 'Ndrangheta. Perhaps he is drawn to the Mafia of Sicily because it is better known to the American public. Whatever the reason, he connects his family's story with the Mafia and presents it as a story his father told him: "In addition to King Peter's [Peter of Aragon's] army, many of the noble families of Sicily and southern Italy supported the cause of the mob, which had meanwhile organized itself into secret groups led by underground chieftains who, according to my father, were the first 'godfathers' of the Mafia. This, my father insisted, is how the Mafia began—as a revolutionary resistance dedicated to the overthrow of such tyrannical foreign despots as Charles d'Anjou."[42] He explains that the Mafia went on to become "a political weapon" that helped those powerless peasants who showed their loyalty to it: "While my father never condoned the Mafia, he always said he could well understand its continued existence."[43]

Talese also includes an account of his family's own gangster:

> My mother had a cousin in Brooklyn who was a member of
> the Mafia, or so I always assumed because, although he never
> held a job, he invariably arrived at the Brooklyn home of my
> mother's parents for holiday dinners driving a big new car and
> wearing silk suits and shirts adorned with diamond cuff links
> and stickpins—and tilted forward on his head was a black bul-
> let proof hat, a bowler, that was lined with steel.[44]

Later he says that his mother refused hospitality to this cousin when
he dropped in unannounced to spend a few days with them on the
shore. His father, unhappy that she "had been inhospitable to a 'mafi-
osio,'" contemplated that the fallout could possibly lead to a vendetta.
His American-born mother was unconcerned and went about her
business.

I suggest that this story is included in the narrative of Talese's life
because to many Italian-American men, the gangster represents an
attractive way of being a man in a world where following the rules is
safe but often boring. As a child, no doubt Talese was impressed with
his mother's cousin who was such a flashy, free-wheeling guy. Finally,
men are attracted to gangsters because there is something quite heroic
about standing up for one's dignity in the face of oppression, even if
that oppression is incurred through one's own criminal behavior. It is
this doomed heroism that often seems to ennoble the traditional masculine qualities of the gangster, even as the definition of masculinity is
challenged as never before.

MORREALE'S VIRTUOUS MAN

At the same time that Puzo created the Corleones and Talese was writing about the Bonnano family, Ben Morreale was bringing his own realistic version of the gangster to fiction. Unlike Mario Puzo's romantic
depictions of the gangster, the mafiosi of Ben Morreale's novels come
from his own observations of Sicilian and Sicilian-American life. Morreale has often complained that Puzo had no idea what he was writing
about, and that, in fact, Puzo's Mafia was nothing like the real thing.
He also complains that Talese applauded Puzo's novel *The Sicilian*, saying that only a true Sicilian could write that story. Evidently Talese
assumed that Puzo was Sicilian, when his family actually hailed from
Naples. It is Morreale's insistence on realism that makes his gangsters
particularly worthy of attention.

In *A Few Virtuous Men (Li cornuti,* 1973), Morreale shows readers his version of the real thing. The novel takes place in Racalmora, a fictional name given to Racalmuto, Morreale's ancestral commune. There the mafiosi are known by various names, including "the men with moustaches" and "the virtuous men," and in the town there is order. Everything is *sistemato,* well arranged, in its place. The character Pantaleone, a local writer and historian fashioned after the real Sicilian writer Leonardo Sciascia, explains that *sistemato* comes from a Greek word meaning, "ensemble, together, a state of relationships."[45] Bill Bonanno echoes this years later when he tells his own story in *Bound by Honor* (1999): "Mafioso is, first and last, about the nature of relationships. Unless this most essential and traditional point is understood, nothing else about who we are and where we come from, what we have done, and what has eventually become of us here in America is any way comprehensible."[46]

A Few Virtuous Men is told through the eyes of a priest, Father Buffa, who is given the *injuria* or nickname Juffa, after the great fool of Sicilian folklore. Father Buffa is presented as a reliable, rather pathetic narrator. That Morreale should use a priest to reveal the "system" set up by the gangsters might seem strange to those outside Italian culture, but an insider knows that there are two professions that can turn the head of any Italian in a room quicker than any others: the gangster and the priest.

Juffa is the pastor of a church in Racalmora built "to honor a statue of the Virgin Mary found in North Africa by a party of penitent brigands."[47] The statue, originally a black Madonna, was whitewashed over the years. The gangsters with whom Juffa comes in contact are not the swaggering types seen earlier in depictions by Puzo; they resemble more closely the old men of Bonanno's experience. Morreale creates Don Raphaeli Petrocelli, known as Don Tarralla because of the lemon-scented cookies he carries with him. Tarralla usually responds to requests for help by saying, "I'm a nobody in this town. I close my eyes and most of all my mouth because Your Honor knows how things are done here. So I know very little and can do even less."[48] In other words, Morreale's "real" gangster employs the ancient practice of *sprezzatura,* the art of downplaying one's power and making the impossible look easy. Morreale's characters represent the genuine reactions of the gangster struggling to preserve the order that enables him to exert control over his environment. To Taralla, "order was more important than money. He had learned that to disturb the harmony of society, to break its laws, the order of things, is to destroy what little beauty and meaning there is in this life."[49] Morreale's gangsters work within what they see as a sense of the world's balance, although often this balance must be forced into being through violence.

In the gangster's world, masculinity and respect are often gained through violence. For example, in *A Few Virtuous Men*, Pepi, a friend of Don Tarralla, escapes to the United States. The villagers in Racalmora all "expected great things of Pepi when he had gone to America because, 'hadn't he knifed cops in broad daylight right here in the village just because they rubbed him the wrong way?' "[50] In this world, actions speak louder than words, but a few well-placed words in the right ears have their own power: "Little confidences, softly spoken, became another of the privileges the circle of the virile and virtuous men permitted themselves. From that phrase 'ci la ficiru—they put it to him '—one would know how someone died."[51] That knowledge could be imagined by many, but proven by few.

Don Tarralla disappears from the village as fascism gains control of western Sicily, and he returns only when the American forces have occupied the island after World War II. Morreale's Don warns others that there will be problems from those who would establish a legal system for postwar Italy: "Look out for men of virtue who want to make the law. I'm not well educated, but wherever there is a revolution you'll find men who think themselves virtuous, men who think that they are better than others. Because you know 'who commands, makes the laws' and if you make the laws you're not bound by them."[52] But again, the Don's speech is strategic in that he publicly protests the very system that supports his lifestyle.

Many Italians, even Sicilians, in the United States had never heard the word "Mafia" until it was publicized by the U.S. news media. Morreale reflects this reality in his novel when he writes: "Every once in a while a son of these immigrants would return and ask, 'Tell me, what sort of thing is this Mafia?' Most people shrugged their shoulders honestly, for they knew nothing about it although they understood things. But the questions continued."[53] The villagers eventually begin to see that there are benefits to encouraging the proliferation of the idea of Mafia: "So many of these questions were asked by such rich and intelligent people who could read and write, who indeed wrote in magazines and books about this Mafia—some even said that Racalmora was a town of "Mafiosi"... Eeh. One had to take a certain pride in all this. One was spoken of in America."[54] Even Don Tarralla sees the publicity as bait for tourists and does nothing to stop it.

Morreale offers an explanation for Sicilian male behavior through Pantaleone: "These virtuous and virile men became 'more virulent' as Pantaleone said. He reasoned that the Mafia was a state of mind in Sicily that had been fed by the imperialism of Greece, Rome, and the Normans, but most of all by the colonialism of the Spaniards ... . Tarralla was the answer to a thousand years of colonialism."[55] Pantaleone goes on : "Certainly, for the historian this Mafia does not exist because there are no documents, no witnesses, no records of any kind that can be nailed down by footnotes. Therefore, for the historian, the scholar, the Mafia is something beside time, that runs parallel to history. In a hundred years there will be no bibliography on the Mafia ... . And yet actions take place, things happen. What are we to make of them?"[56]

Pantaleone insists that the true Mafia exists only in the United States: "Is it an accident that of all the countries where Sicilians have gone, only in America has this Mafia taken hold?"[57] He compares Richard Nixon with the mafiosi of Sicily, finding them all to be virtuous men. He comments, "It was a stroke of genius when Fellini in his *Satyricon* went out of his way to choose a face to play the role of Trimalchio who was Richard Nixon as an old man."[58] What characterizes Trimalchio is that he is fat, showy, and given to excess, very unlike Morreale's slim, wiry Sicilian gangsters. The real gangster, as portrayed by Morreale, is the epitome of a gentleman on the surface, no matter what violence he has been accused of. Indeed, when Tarralla dies in a car explosion, his *figura* is preserved: above his coffin is a black banner displaying the words "He Was a Gentleman." Men like Tarralla, who control so much in Sicily and yet slink in the background, are brought to the United States in Morreale's novel *Monday, Tuesday ... never come Sunday* (1977).

The protagonist of this coming-of-age novel is Cholly Carcelli, loosely based on Morreale himself. Although the novel's gangster is not the main character, his presence affects most of the men in it. Lu Zi Luigi is the head of the "men with mustaches." "They had a lot of names for these men," explains the narrator, " 'Maffiusi, Camurista,' or the men of the 'Manunira,' The Black Hand ... No one spoke of Mafia."[59] When Cholly's father decides that the only way for the family to survive is for him to go to work for Zi Luigi, Cholly's mother refers to the gangsters as *malantrini* ("bad boys"). The new association of Cholly's father with these men is marked by a change in his dress: "He got a black overcoat that looked very tight on him. Every time he wore it he seemed out of breath. He bought a white, white hat with a black band, like somebody had died. It had a very small brim, but it was high, like one of my mother's pots. On his shoes he wore spats buttoned on the side by little pearl knobs."[60] The association even changes his father's behavior:

> In the evening after supper my father would take a long time to get dressed up in his new clothes. As he put on his striped shirt, he'd snarl at the mirror and then laugh. When he'd put on his jacket, he'd hunch his shoulders a few times and twist his mouth to the side as if he was saying "yeah" silently. Then he'd hitch up his pants, pat his breast, frown and then walk over to the closet. There, out of a large yellow box, he took a forty-five automatic pistol, stuck it close to his head and hunched his shoulders again. And all the time my mother cried on her bed in the dark.[61]

When Cholly's father, who acts more as a collection man than a muscle man, is arrested, the philosophy behind the need for the gangster in American society is explained. Lu Zi Luigi has the political clout to find a lawyer—not a very good one, but he "did know … the people who made the laws. And that, Lu Zi Luigi said, was the important thing. But then Lu Zi Luigi came from Sicily where the poor didn't stand a chance in the courts against those who made and judged the laws."[62] In America, justice, as in *The Godfather*, comes only through the strength of relationships. Ultimately, though, Luigi understands that his career as a gangster is merely transitional. As for the Bonannos (and as Bill Bonanno argues, for the Kennedys), the gangster life is simply a means to move his family into a better life. Lu Zi Luigi explains: "I have done many things. Now I have a lot of money. I have land. My children will go to fine schools. And you know, Mimi, I have no pleasure. I feel no pleasure in it. They will never know the pain I had to gain all that they will inherit. That money will have no meaning for them. And I'm sure they will soon be ashamed from where that money came."[63] Lu Zi Luigi is able to die naturally in old age because he is not a gaudy dandy who draws attention to his actions, or worse, the evil eye through envy, which would have attracted the attention of both the government and rival gangsters. He is honored with a grand funeral. Cholly's father never recovers from the experience of having been a gangster and goes insane.

Gay Talese and Ben Morreale have fashioned their gangsters out of old world notions of *omertà*, and their attempts to capture the "real" gangster constrast sharply with the cinematic gangsters of Martin Scorsese and Michael Cimino.

4

ROUGH BOYS:
THE GANGSTERS OF MARTIN SCORSESE
AND MICHAEL CIMINO

Both Martin Scorsese and Michael Cimino stay close to personal encounters and historical subjects in their attempts to realize the gangster through their films. Both filmmakers also reflect period notions of "tough guy" masculinities in their male characterizations, proving that although the gangsters they portray may contain clues about masculinity, they are mired in stage two of the development of the gangster figure—appropriation. They have not yet realized how to be wise men.

The films of Martin Scorsese counter the romantic view of the gangster in Coppola's *Godfather* films through Scorsese's use of techniques derived from the French New Wave Italian neorealism, and cinema verité. In many respects, Scorsese's gangsters are more similar to Talese's, in that each author offers his own vision of reality. Scorsese grew up on Mulberry Street in Manhattan's Little Italy. His own experiences, combined with journalistic accounts, helped him create the composite characters of the gangsters in his films. Scorsese's gangsters grow up in the streets away from the watchful eyes of fathers who work, and mothers who, if they don't work, stay home and remain nearly invisible. These gangsters start off as rough boys who continually try to prove their manhood. The cultural critic Pellegrino D'Acierno observes that Scorsese's films comprise "a cinema of the sons," while those of Coppola form "a cinema of the fathers." D'Acierno means that Coppola attempts to portray a sense of traditional Italian manhood in his works. Scorsese first establishes a sense of that tradition in his films, then shows that as the more Americanized young men break away from that traditional sense of manhood, they remain impatient boys. D'Acierno characterizes the cinema of sons as "a cinema [that is] generated from previous cinema and is characterized by a recycling of previous styles, by the hybridization of genres and narrative modes, by fragmented citations and the general strategy of intertextuality."[1] This cinema is characterized by Oedipal struggles with ethnic or cinematic fathers. These struggles can be seen in the style and stories of Scorsese's films.

Mean Streets (1973), *GoodFellas* (1990), and *Casino* (1995) together established Scorsese as the maker of gangster films par excellence. In each film Scorsese achieves a striking sense of realism that comes from the sources of his stories: *Mean Streets* was based on his own life experience and *GoodFellas* and *Casino* on nonfiction books by Nicholas Pileggi.[2] Scorsese's films all move chronologically, following the rise and fall of the gangster. In this way, they reflect the reality of the documentary rather than the romanticism of fictional drama.

Many of Scorsese's films are about redemption in the Roman Catholic sense of the word, in which one achieves salvation by overcoming the temptation of sin and living a virtuous life. However, there is a deeper sense of redemption possible for men which transcends any religious context; that is achieving a wholeness of self by developing the human qualities wrongly attributed only to the feminine. The notion of a man's being redeemed through a woman's love or sacrifice is a very old cliché. The deeper sense refers to the redemption of the *human*, and this is something one needs when one has fallen from grace. It can be said that in order to be a man in modern American society, one must necessarily fall from grace. Until a man comes face to face with the need for redemption and achieves awareness of the means to reach it, his "feminine" side, he will remain an immature boy, stuck in the gangster's world, forever trying to prove his masculinity by distancing himself from what is considered feminine, beginning with his mother and then all the other women he encounters in his life.

MARTIN SCORSESE'S *MEAN STREETS* (1973)

Mean Streets, Scorsese's second major film, plays more like a documentary than a drama, primarily because of the way it is shot and edited. Scorsese uses special effects and lighting to create drama while he also emphasizes the realistic aspects of his gangster. The opening montage introduces the characters through scenes from black-and-white home movies. The characters play to the camera as subjects did in the early days of home movies: the camera remains still and the people pose and then move. In those days few people thought of moving the camera and, so, many early home movies depend on the subjects to provide any motion on the screen. Scorsese refines this technique by wielding a hand-held camera throughout much of the film. This helps to create a sense of reality, making it seem as though the audience is seeing the action through the eyes of an individual participant.

Another Scorsese touch that helps set the scene is his use of music contemporary with the action. The opening song, "Be My Baby" by the Ronettes, evokes the 1960s, when the action takes place and doubles as a comment on the immaturity of the boys about to be introduced. These boys are all trying to find their own way to manhood in their neighborhood, which in its insularity mimics the Italian villages of their ancestors.

Mean Streets is essentially a coming-of-age tale. Since the young men in the movie are trying to prove their manhood without many positive role models, the influence of the traditional ways of becoming men, including the performance of machismo, is still very strong. Franco La Cecla, in *Rough Manners* (2000), writes: "One becomes a man only by strenuously working to escape maternal influence. Adolescent males face an extremely difficult and painful passage. They must erase from their bodies the 'effeminate' influence of their mothers and the other women of their community, replacing them with 'rough manners.' "[3] Thus, the rough play of childhood gives way to the toughness of manhood. La Cecla theorizes that because the state of grace is perceived as feminine, the young man must find a way to be, in a sense, "disgraced"; this state of disgrace must be achieved alongside and in front of other men.[4] In brief, masculinity is a public performance, and until a young boy displays his manhood, he is considered a boy. La Cecla elaborates:

In the absence of a clear and easy distinction, men avail themselves of rough manners. Males, in order to show that they are real men, must produce rowdy noise and make scenes—the roar of a Harley-Davidson, popping wheelies on a Vespa, a certain tone of voice. Otherwise, their "sex" remains invisible, dangerously neuter. Machismo, from this point of view is a "negative construct." As a Mexican proverb points out, either you are a macho or you are nothing: "*El macho vive mientras el cobardo quiere* (the Macho lives while the coward wishes he could)." This is to say that there is no zero degree of masculinity; it is always excessive, hypertrophic, emphatic. Machismo then, is the only way that men can be seen.[5]

The public show of machismo becomes a game of one-upmanship that often escalates from play into violence. La Cecla suggests that the origins of machismo can be found in Mexican culture. The Latina scholar and writer Ana Castillo explains: "The word macho means to be male or masculine. Machismo then is that which is related to the male or to masculinity. Machismo, as associated with Mexican culture for the social scientist, is the demonstration of physical and sexual powers and is basic to self-respect."[6] These are the very powers that Scorsese's rough boys struggle to demonstrate—to achieve not just self-respect, but the respect of others. However, the more they exercise these powers, especially when not following the guidance of a wise man, the further they distance themselves from the possibility of achieving a healthy maturity. In almost all cases, rough boys must separate themselves from the world of women in order to earn the label "man," and yet once they enter this world of men, they seldom develop skills that can move them beyond simple survival in a material world. This limited development manifests itself in the growing distance between men and their feelings. Castillo sees this separation reflected in social division throughout the world: "When we speak of machismo, we immediately refer to a division of power between male and female, between a world power and colonized nations."[7] She elaborates:

Machismo has divided society in half. It divides the world into the haves and the have-nots, those with material power and those who are rendered powerless. It has divided our behavior into oppositions, our spirituality regards Catholicism in dualistic terms of good and evil and an economic world politic based on brute might. The feminine principle is not the opposite of machismo. "The feminine" may be generally termed as the *absence* of machismo—all the qualities that have been negated, denied, denigrated, and made to be essentially valueless by our society. Machismo has served to distort our perceptions of humanity, which includes the feminine.[8]

Castillo traces Mexican machismo back to Arab influences in Spanish culture: "The ancient culture of the Maghreb originated in North Africa, spread throughout the Mediterranean, and as a consequence of the conquest of the Americas via the Spaniards, to the Southwest United States, Latin America, and the Caribbean."[9] Castillo locates the notions of women as a man's property, male honor, and the "vendetta" in the Maghreb culture: "What is the purpose of the vendetta? Usually to save family honor; that is, to regain some material loss; women are counted as a man's material property. The male members of a family are responsible for a vendetta; in the case of an absent father, the task usually falls on the eldest brother."[10] When this notion of manhood is tied directly to a capitalist economy, it makes it nearly impossible for a young boy who wants to be considered a man to avoid acquiring capital at any cost. Again, Castillo perceptively connects this notion to social ills: "There is no justification for machismo. Morally there never was, although given the economic system that civilization developed, society depended on patriarchy to uphold its political and economic principles of change. Machismo has lost its raison d'être."[11]

Mean Streets is a platform for boys to display their machismo as gangsters. Thematically, the opening sequences of both *The Godfather* and *Mean Streets* dramatize attempts to be a man in the United States. The opening of *The Godfather* presents three men attempting to do what is expected of a man—the baker to make his daughter procreate, Johnny Fontane to provide for his family, and Amerigo Bonasera to protect his family. And *Mean Streets* opens with scenes of three young men attempting to do the same. First, the character Tony finds a young man shooting heroin in the bathroom of his bar and throws him out. It is his way of protecting the neighborhood from drugs. Next, Michael is trying to buy a hijacked shipment of camera adapters, attempting to earn a living. Finally, the story's protagonist, Charley, first seen in a church praying before a statue of the Madonna, is later shown weaving his way through Tony's bar, strutting like a rooster, flaunting his sexuality by jumping onto the stage to flirt with a topless dancer. All three of these young men, wearing stylish suits, are doing what they think is expected of a young man in their society, and they are a striking contrast to the character of Johnny Boy, who, wearing a leather jacket and a silly hat, is first seen blowing up a U.S. mailbox, a senseless adolescent prank that does nothing to establish his manhood. Each of Scorsese's rough boys has the desire to become a man, but in their attempts to realize this desire they never reach maturity, at least not within the confines of the film's chronology.

There is nothing organized about the crime that occurs in *Mean Streets*. Scorsese presents neighborhood guys who do what they need to do to make a living. They are everyday, ordinary guys. The closest character to a mafioso is Charley's Uncle Giovanni, who settles neighborhood disputes without flamboyance and generally takes care of business through talk instead of violence. Against this display of maturity is set the behavior of the young men, who fight at the drop of an insult, even one they don't understand, as when one of them is called a "mook" (street slang for "black"). What they are fighting for is a sense of honor that they believe can be assaulted in any number of ways, including verbal attacks.

D'Acierno perceptively sees Scorsese's boys as the losers and *lazzaroni* they really are—the type that is referred to by older Italian Americans as

> *morti di fam'* (literally, "those dying from hunger," but, in fact, a derogative [*sic*] term without any connotations of pity that is applied contemptuously to "losers," those who have not mastered the system and internalized the law of the family). Scorsese does not mythologize them [these boys], nor does he view them with ironic detachment from the superior position of the bourgeois author. Rather, he becomes one with them, using cinematic language to establish a cultural, psychological, and linguistic equality with them and their milieu—the culture of violence, Scorsese's own culture before it was mediated by cinematic culture.[12]

Here D'Acierno alludes to Scorsese's portraying the culture of masculinity as a struggle to negotiate one's place in a society that expects its men to be strong and tough enough to handle life on the streets. It is out on the streets that money is made and protection of the family is enacted. For example, the rough city boys separate themselves from suburban kids by ripping them off when they venture into the city to buy illegal fireworks. Being a man requires becoming what the Italians call *furbo*, "sly" or "slick," and one of the things that separates the "boys" of the suburbs from the "men" of the city is the ability to tell the believable lie—and, of course, to determine when a lie is being told. It is through the sins of lying and stealing that rough boys fall sufficiently from grace to be called men in the world of their neighborhood.

La Cecla speaks of masculinity in Sicily during his youth:

> Masculinity at that time and in that place … expressed itself as a strange combination of boldness and isolation … . One became a male "jerkily," reacting to and never escaping the physical embarrassment of adolescence. A real male is a bit awkward, rough, tough with his body. If he remains graceful—Peter Pan, who could fly—or rounded in his movements, then he would remain in sweet childhood, dream in his mother's lap. He must lose that "grace"; he must become "graceless," "disgraceful".[13]

Peter Pan is a boy who fantasizes his masculinity and never tries to prove it in the real world; the gangster is the boy who tries to realize his masculinity through his fantasies.

Those fantasies are played out in male spaces, often spaces to which "respectable" women are denied entry, such as bars, men-only clubs, and strip joints. Tony's nightclub is such a place: there are topless dancers and the jukebox plays songs like Jimmy Roselli's famous version of "Malafemmina," ("Bad Woman"), a song about a beautiful woman as sweet as sugar with a face like an angel who only makes men cry, essentially turning them soft and feminine. This song is typical of the Madonna/whore symbolism inflicted on women in the world of the gangster. There are the mother and the wife and then there is what Charley calls the "cunt"—for example, his neighbor and secret lover, Teresa. He takes her out, sleeps with her in hotel rooms, and yet never has a thought of marrying her, simply because she lets him have sex with her. The other woman Charley "plays" with, reinforcing this division between the respectable Madonna and the disrespected *malafemmina*, is the black topless dancer from Tony's bar. Charley makes a date to meet her, but when his cab comes by the corner where she is waiting, he has the driver keep going because he's worried about how being seen with her will affect his *figura*: "All I need now is to be caught in the village with a *mulinjan*"—*mulinjan* is slang for an African American, from Italian *melanzana*, eggplant.

It is in this man's world of the bar, a place devoid of respectable women, that male acts of honor and dishonor are carried out. One example from *Mean Streets* is a vendetta. A drunken gangster gets up from the bar and makes his way to the bathroom, where he is shot by a boy who believes this man killed his father. In an interesting twist, Scorsese has this young man follow the drunk into the bathroom. There the boy undoes the collar of his coat, revealing long, silky hair, which might cause viewers to think he is a woman. Until the gun comes out, this confrontation could also be a homosexual encounter. But when the young man pulls out his gun, there can be no mistaking his intentions, yet his motivation is still not clear. Charley's Uncle Giovanni explains the situation later, during a conversation with the young man's uncle. The drunk, the epitome of *brutta figura*—for real men don't lose control even when they are drunk—is executed by the young man, who does what he believes he must do to assert his manhood—kill the man who has killed his father. In Italian culture, one way to become a man by default is to have a dead father. Thus, the young boy, as a new man, must avenge his father's murder to effect his transition from boy to man. The hint of homosexuality in this scene foreshadows the young gangsters' later interactions with homosexuals. Homosexuality, even the hint of it, becomes a strong threat to one's identity as a heterosexual man, so heterosexual men in the gangster world must distance themselves from homosexual behavior. In the film, two homosexuals from the neighborhood who have fled with the boys from the bar after the shooting and piled into a car with them, start yelling out sexual catcalls from the car to men on the street. The boys hit them and throw them out of the car.

Another possible threat to one's identity as a heterosexual male is a strong identification with nature, which in the world of the traditional gangster can be read as feminine. Being too close to the feminine threatens one's masculinity, so Charley continually tries to distance himself from the very things that attract him—the female stripper and sex with Teresa. To admit that he cares for either of these women would weaken his standing among the gangsters. Charley, in spite of how he feels about Teresa as a possible wife, has developed a certain intimacy with her that he does not have with his male friends. He is able to speak about his unconscious life with her. He tells her about a dream in which he experienced an orgasm, but instead of sperm he ejaculated blood.

This dream, which goes unexplained in the film, signifies Charley's inability to see sex as a natural function of keeping the family bloodline going. What happens in the dream is unnatural, and it implies that Charley's attitudes toward sex and his sexual behavior go against the natural functions of intercourse. Later, when he and Teresa take a walk along the beach, he goes out of his way to distance himself from nature. He tells Teresa he hates the ocean, the beach, the trees; what he likes is spaghetti and clams, John Wayne, and Francis of Assisi. This distancing of himself from nature should be read as a typical male move toward the hard-edged, unfeeling masculine. The juxtaposition of the American icon of masculinity, John Wayne, and the Italian icon of kindness, Francis of Assisi, bring up an interesting dichotomy involving Italian and American notions of masculinity. There are few, if any, American male role models for sainthood, but Italy abounds in male saints who gained honor by living exemplary lives and became role models and namesakes for children.

Uncle Giovanni tries to teach Charley how to be an honorable man: "Honorable men go with honorable men," he tells Charley when he warns him about the trouble with the loose cannon, his cousin Johnny Boy. "I know we are *compari* [related by coming from the same region] with them [Johnny's family]," he says, but in spite of their family relationship, and in spite of the fact that Johnny Boy is his namesake, Giovanni warns Charley to be careful. Charley must negotiate the right way of handling the fact that Johnny Boy is his cousin; because of kin ties he does have some responsibility for Johnny's wellbeing, and also for the fact that Johnny Boy is a *morte di fame*, a troublemaker who takes no responsibility for his actions. Johnny Boy looks to Charley for help, but he cannot imitate Charley's way of being a man. Johnny Boy thrives on the thrill of violent pranks and aggressive displays of daring. In one scene he is on the roof of a neighborhood building with a gun and starts shooting into the sky, as though aiming at the Empire State Building. This defiance of neighborhood norms represents the struggle of men against the power of the world outside the neighborhood.

Charley, by virtue of his intimacy with Teresa, is able to control himself better and to feel for Johnny Boy in a way that Johnny Boy could never feel for Charley. Charley, unlike Johnny Boy, has developed a sense of honor, fostered by his relationship with Giovanni. Giovanni acts as a surrogate father, something most gang leaders do, as D'Acierno has perceptively pointed out. Giovanni attempts to keep the traditions alive into Charley's generation, but as the film's ending suggests this might not be possible. As D'Acierno writes: "Scorsese narrates the breakdown of the third-generation Italian-American family and the failure of its traditional culture, particularly the Church, to maintain its integrative function."[14] Not only has the Church failed Charley, but so have Don Giovanni and the world of traditional Italian masculinity.

The ending of the film highlights this break of tradition brilliantly, as Johnny Boy runs away from Michael. Charley has borrowed Tony's car to take Johnny Boy away from the streets. Michael and other neighborhood boys catch up with them in another car and shoot everyone in Tony's car. Michael, the gangster with the *figura*, or street reputation, must make a public example of Johnny Boy if his manhood is to be honored by others. In the end, it is Charley's inability to solve the problem of how to take care of Johnny Boy and himself that gets him wounded. Scorsese casts himself in the role of the shooter at the end of the film, playfully naming this character Jimmy Shorts, a silly name that comes from a male locker-room joke. Tony's car crashes into a fire hydrant, which baptizes the bloody scene, suggesting a simultaneous cleansing. Out comes Charley, bleeding from his wounds, falling to his knees as though in repentance. Their neighborhood world has yet to reckon with this incident; Giovanni is seen watching television, minding his own business, and out on the streets the Italian *festa* continues, as though, in a strange way, tradition has found a way to encompass this juvenile violence. In his next gangster film, Scorsese revisits the world of the rough boys, but this time he approaches the gangster from a less personal perspective, based on nonfiction accounts by the journalist Nicholas Pileggi.

MARTIN SCORSESE'S *GOODFELLAS* (1990)

Nicholas Pileggi's riveting account of organized crime, *Wiseguy*, serves as the basis, and in many places the actual script, for Scorsese's second gangster film, *GoodFellas*. The book tells the story of Henry Hill, a real gangster turned informant. Pileggi wrote *Wiseguy* from interviews with Hill and other people, and in many cases he simply presents actual transcripts of those interviews, so Hill's voice comes through strongly. From the film's opening, in which the voice of Ray Liotta as Henry Hill says, "As far back as I could remember I always wanted to be a gangster," to the very end of the film, which finds Hill lamenting the boring life he must live as a participant in the federal witness protection program, *GoodFellas* emphasizes Hill's attitude toward the manly life.

As a young boy, Hill is dazzled by the glamour of the gangster life-style. Accepting this glamorous view of gangsters, Hill constructs his view of how to be a man based on what he sees and what he thinks he knows about gangster culture. He is unable to imagine any other way of being a man. Hill starts working with the local gangsters while in his early teens. Thus, he spends his formative years in the company of the men who run the neighborhood. He witnesses these men using violence to establish their authority. La Cecla's comments on southern Italy are equally appropriate to describe Hill's exposure to lessons in masculinity: "After weaning or at the threshold of adolescence, they [young boys in southern Italy] are taken from their mothers, and they are placed in the house of the men, chambers where identity is forged. Here, adult men will subject them to violent and humiliating rituals."[15] This is the experience that Scorsese re-creates from Pileggi's book.

If the clothes make the man, then Scorsese realizes gangster man-hood through the costuming of his characters. His gangsters' cloth-ing, often ostentatious displays of shimmering sharkskin suits, knitted sport shirts, or button-down shirts with tented collars, constitute a uni-form that separates the gangster from the rest of society. La Cecla com-ments on the relationship of the uniform to masculinity: "Men's cloth-ing serves to 'cover,' not 'uncover,' the male; it serves to conceal him in the regularity of the uniform, which establishes him in a brotherhood of other males and in the silence of the outfit."[16] The masculinity pre-sented by Scorsese's gangster is meant to be consumed by other men, more than by women. Again La Cecla informs on this point: "Mascu-linity, even collective masculinity, is not something to be put on show. It is meant to be consumed strictly in the interior of the group."[17]

The neighborhood in *GoodFellas* is run by the Ciceros—Paulie, the boss, and Tuddy, his brother. Hill soon learns that the real function of the Ciceros is to provide "protection for people who can't go to the cops." They create a system for organizing the neighborhood and teach Hill his place in that system. They warn Hill, "Never put your name on anything!"[18] They tell him that what is important in life is to earn the respect of others, and that one does that by finding his place in the system and staying there. But before Hill can find a place in the gang-ster system, he must leave his place in his family's system. Hill has no problem with this. He doesn't see his father's life as a model for his own:

"My old man's life wasn't going to be my life. No matter how much he yelled at me, no matter how many beatings I took, I wouldn't listen to what he said."[19]

Before long, Hill stops going to school: "There was something ludicrous about sitting through lessons in nineteenth-century American democracy when he was living in a world of eighteenth-century Sicilian thievery."[20] Being a wiseguy, he learns, is not so much about using violence as about "getting over" on other people, often by stealing and using stolen credit cards for nights out on the town. The use of stolen credit cards, which got Bill Bonanno his jail time, reflects the trickster aspect of the gangster figure. As Hill explains, "If you knew wiseguys, you would know right away that the best part of the night for Paulie came from the fact that he was getting over on somebody."[21]

Hill learns that the two rules of wiseguy life are: "Never rat on friends" and "Always keep your mouth shut." He proves to the gangsters that he is worthy of trust and worthy of being called a man, when he is jailed and still keeps his mouth shut about what he knows. Jail becomes a ritual of manhood, and when Hill exits the courthouse after his trial he is greeted by the other gangsters with: "You broke your cherry," a phrase usually referring to a woman's loss of her virginity.

In a number of other instances, men in the film challenge each other's masculinity. The character who best exemplifies this is Tommy DeVito, played by Joe Pesci. Tommy constantly tries to prove his manhood, perhaps because he is shorter than the other men, but as La Cecla explains, a young boy is often pushed to the limit to do this: "Aggression, ridicule, physical contact on the brink of homosexuality, as if to push the others to the extreme limit—where it is up to them to escape embarrassment; all of these things serve to 'roughen' young men, to teach them manners that would clearly show that they were not female."[22]

In one scene Tommy DeVito is ridiculed by Billy Batts, a gangster who has just served time in jail and is celebrating his return to the neighborhood. Batts is a "made" member of the mob, meaning he has been inducted into the Mafia. He's been gone so long, he only recalls Tommy as a boy who used to shine shoes. Tommy cannot take the teasing and eventually beats Batts to death. When Tommy is not shown the proper respect by Spider, a young boy who is serving him his drink during a card game, he shoots the boy in the foot. Later on, when Spider tells Tommy, "Go fuck yourself," Tommy's friends laugh at him, and Tommy pulls out his gun and kills the boy.

In a subtle way, which only those who know Sicilian culture can really appreciate, Scorsese uses humor to refer to masculinity. This happens when Tommy brings Henry Hill and Jimmy Conway (played by Robert DeNiro) to his mother's house to get a knife. Tommy's mother (played by Scorsese's own mother) serves the guys a meal and tells them a story about a man whom everyone referred to as *cornuto contento*, the "contented cuckold," a man who knows that his wife is cheating on him, but never says a word to anyone about it. He's always very quiet around others. One day someone makes a comment about his silence, and his wife responds that he never says anything. The cuckold then says, "What am I supposed to say, that my wife is fucking somebody else?" His wife responds, "Shut up, you're always talking!" The story is funny only to Tommy and his mother, so they both try to explain it to Hill and Conway. Beyond the humor is the comment that life is sometimes better when certain things are left unsaid. The cuckold exposes himself by talking, publicly acknowledging his emasculated status. The moral of this story is that those who talk too much risk losing their masculine reputation.

As in the *Godfather* films, there are a number of scenes in *Good-Fellas* in which an older man shows a younger man what men are expected to do. When Henry and his wife are having problems, Paulie steps into the family dispute to instruct Henry: "No divorce," he says, "we're not *animali.*"

The film ends with a version of Paul Anka's song "My Way" performed by punk rocker Sid Vicious. This punk version blasphemes the song Frank Sinatra made famous, which became an anthem for the Italian gangster. Vicious, who does the song "his way," defies the glamour and class of the Sinatra version through his off-key singing and offbeat sound. Scorsese's mission is to destroy the glamorous illusion of gangster life presented in earlier films, and this ending leaves no doubt that the reality of gangster life is something else entirely. As D'Acierno perceptively states:

> It is clear that Scorsese's intention is to de-romanticize and demystify the figure of the Mafioso, an intention made explicit at the narrative level by the terminal breakdowns experienced by the three primary members of Paulie Cicero's crew at the film's conclusion: Hill, whose gangster high has become a cocaine high, turns stoolie to save himself, ingloriously entering a Witness Protection Program to live the rest of this life as

a "schnook"; the out-of-control Tommy DeVito whose gangster high expresses itself routinely in psychopathic blasts of violence and cruel displays of power, [and who] goes so far over the edge that the mob has to exterminate him … Jimmy Conway, "the kind of guy," as Hill's voice narrates, "who rooted for bad guys in the movies," winds up enclosed in a total paranoia.[23]

Although Scorsese's gangsters, portrayed as losers, show that the gangster life is not as romantic as otherwise thought, *GoodFellas* does not comment on alternative versions of manhood. Scorsese's *Casino*, based on another Pileggi book, deals with the real-life figures of Rosenthal and Tony Spilotro and basically repeats the story of the gangster as loser. Not meant to be the morality plays of Coppola's trilogy, Scorsese's films simply record what he sees as the reality of gangster life, and he realizes the dark side of that life, the side that Coppola chooses to symbolize more than show. Gangster life, Scorsese implies, is not a metaphor for what is wrong or right with the United States; it is simply the way these men have chosen to live . Unlike Coppola's gangsters, they do not represent larger issues, other than a sense of an Old-World notion of manhood that has trapped men in the macho mode of existence. D'Acierno observes: "Scorsese's characters are subpolitical: they are 'morti di fame' in the Gramscian sense of the term, members of a parasitic underclass that has no political or even class identity, marginals without a history and doomed to permanent underdevelopment … . They exist in a cultural vacuum from which the laws of the father and the mother have receded."[24]

Scorsese's gangsters are shown as men trapped forever in an immature stage—physically adult, but behaving like boys. Because Scorsese has chosen this simple realization of the gangster figure, he has not presented a way for us to imagine a gangster-free masculinity. This absence of an alternative presentation of masculinity persists in his films even to *Gangs of New York* (2002). The films of Scorsese serve as models for many subsequent gangster films: Michael Cimino's *Year of the Dragon* (1985) and *The Sicilian* (1987), Abel Ferrara's *The Funeral* (1990), Quentin Tarantino's *Reservoir Dogs* (1993), and Michael Corrente's *Federal Hill* (1994). The following section concentrates on one film by Cimino, because it is based on a novel by Mario Puzo and involves an Italian-American director realizing another Italian American's fiction.

MICHAEL CIMINO'S *THE SICILIAN* (1990)

Michael Cimino, best known for directing the Oscar-winning film *The Deer Hunter*, came under critical fire for directing *The Sicilian*, based on Mario Puzo's novel of the same title. The novel is a spin-off from *The Godfather*, set during Michael Corleone's exile in Sicily, and continues Puzo's use of Sicilian culture to explain "Mafia" and "mafioso" behavior. The Sicily that serves as the antithesis to the United States in Puzo's *The Godfather* becomes an even stranger place in his novel *The Sicilian*. As Don Croce explains to Michael Corleone, "Sicily is a tragic land. … There is no trust. There is no order. Only violence and treachery in abundance."[25] At a later point in the film, the narrator also explains, "For the Sicilian believes that vengeance is the only true justice, and that it is always merciless. On this Catholic island, with statues of a weeping Jesus in every home, Christian forgiveness was a contemptible refuge of the coward."[26]

Set in a transitional period of Sicilian history, the years 1943–1950, *The Sicilian* tells the story of the real-life Sicilian bandit Salvatore Giuliano, who robs from the rich, conservative landowners to give to the poor peasants, who in turn hail him as their savior. Giuliano fights both the ancient traditions of the Mafia and the post–World War II Italian democratic government. Depending on the account, the actual Salvatore Giuliano, who lived in western Sicily from his birth in 1922 to his assassination in 1950, was either smart or stupid, a savior or a scapegoat, an egotist or a servant of the people, a fool or a wise man, a Mafioso or a *cafone* ("stupid one"). While the sources debate on what he might have been like in real life, they do agree that he was one of the most interesting personalities to emerge from the postwar years in Sicily.

The story of Giuliano's life has become a modern legend that rivals the old English story of Robin Hood. The truth will forever be debated, but the story has become the source of a number of literary, musical, and dramatic works. From Francesco Rosi's film *Salvatore Giuliano* (1962) to a contemporary Italian musical by Dino Scuderi (first staged in 2002), the Giuliano story offers a way of examining postwar Italy, just as the assassination of John Kennedy became a way of reading postwar America.

The Sicily of Puzo's novel, an extension of the land of *The Godfather*, is not the Sicily that winds up in Michael Cimino's film. Although Cimino's *The Sicilian* is based on the novel, Cimino does not follow through with Puzo's story line. The character Giuliano, in the hands of Cimino, becomes a spokesperson for the Italian-American experience. At the time he was making *The Sicilian*, Cimino was working his way out of a professional exile resulting from his box-office disaster *Heaven's Gate* (1980). His next film, *Year of the Dragon* (1985), was not a total failure, but it still did not fulfill the promise of his brilliant debut, *The Deer Hunter* (1978). Perhaps Cimino selected a Puzo novel for his next project because it had commercial potential similar to the novel that brought fame and fortune to his contemporary, Frances Ford Coppola.

There was no need for Cimino to re-create the Giuliano story for his audience because Francesco Rosi's documentary had already presented the story. More to the point, the elements of the story that contributed to making Salvatore Giuliano a household name in Italy had little or no relationship to American culture during the Ronald Reagan era. The true story of Salvatore Giuliano begins with the immigration of Sicilians to the United States. Giuliano's parents were immigrants who achieved a small level of success in America and were able to return to their hometown of Montelepre, Sicily, with enough money to buy a house.

During World War II, the Italian fascist government severely repressed the local Mafia forces formed earlier by the *gabbellotti*, the caretakers of the estates of absentee landlords. In 1943, the Allied invasion of Sicily ousted the Fascist rulers and Mafia power was resurgent. From 1943 until after the war, the Italian economy suffered and the black market was the norm. Giuliano biographer Billy Jaynes Chandler notes that as much as 70 percent of urban food distribution was accomplished through the black market.[27] Giuliano found himself caught up in this system, and on 2 September 1943, he killed a *carabiniere* (a state policeman) trying to arrest him for smuggling food. Giuliano then went into hiding. A few months later, he killed another solider as he watched his family being rounded up. Because he acted as they might have acted, and as they believed a true man should in protecting his family, the community helped him when he went into hiding.

Giuliano took to the mountains and lived as a bandit in the manner of Robin Hood. During this time there was a growing political movement in Sicily to divorce the island from mainland Italian control. In the spring of 1945, Giuliano sided with those in support of an independent Sicily and became a colonel in the movement's army, shifting from bandit to rebel leader. Therefore, Giuliano was much more involved in

Sicilian politics than either Puzo's novel or Cimino's film depicts. As Chandler notes, "Giuliano's commitment to the separatist cause was genuine. He fought for it harder and longer, and with considerably more skill and success, than did anyone else."[28] Giuliano, "a republican of liberal leanings ... favored [Sicily's] annexation to the United States as its 49th state."[29] Thus, as a pro-American and anticommunist, he ultimately became a pawn in the hands of local Sicilian and national Italian political forces; some say even the United States was involved, working behind the scenes to keep Italy from becoming communist.

Cimino's portrayal of Sicily revises the mother–son paradigm dominant in Sicilian culture into the father–son paradigm dominant in American culture. This emerges in a comparison of the historical reality of Giuliano's life with Cimino's adaptation of Puzo's fictional portrayal. Understanding the Giuliano story takes familiarity with southern Italian family dynamics, especially those of the mother–son relationship. The local politicians in Sicily harassed Giuliano's mother, his sister, and his father in an attempt to get to the son. In response, Giuliano sent messages designed to remind bureaucrats of this dynamic. One of them stated:

> If you yourselves love your mammas and your country, refuse to fight this fratricidal war ... Do not be deceived by the propaganda of the press and your superiors, who call their war "a war against delinquency," because the war that they make against me should be called "a war against motherhood." Perhaps the reason for my success against this vast effort is due not only to my expertness but also to the Divine Hand whose aim is only one: To rein in those false prophets who want to destroy the greatest love that He defends for us, the most precious thing of our lives, our mammas.[30]

Giuliano sees his persecution as a public siege against the sacred mother–son relationship, a fundamental building block of Sicilian culture. This Italian mother–son paradigm is one that fosters community instead of individuality. It stresses self-connection, a son protecting his mother. In contrast, the emphasis in the United States on self-invention comes from a dominant father–son paradigm, a son rebelling against his father and possibly becoming reunited with the father as a returning prodigal. Gaetano Cipolla points to the centrality of the mother in Sicilian culture:

The mother's role, shaped by thousands of years of history, continues to our day almost unchanged. She nurtures physically and psychologically, she performs social duties in observance of time-worn formulas, she sacrifices her whole life to her family, denying herself in the process and becoming a victim of her dedication to others. Her devotion to her family is so complete that as a Sicilian proverb has it, *"La matri senti li guai di lu mutu"* (The mother feels the troubles of the mute). Inevitably, however, in the battle between the children's desire for freedom and the mother's desire to maintain the status quo—for this reason Leonardo Sciascia considered Sicilian mothers a cause of the stagnation in Sicilian society—conflicts emerge and mothers begin to consider themselves victims, adopting what may be called a martyr's syndrome. In a recent article ... Angelo Costanzo suggested that Sicilian women everywhere eventually end up conforming with the image of the *matri addulurata*, that is, the sorrowful mother who grieves for the loss of her son. It is not a coincidence that in Sicily, out of all the possible scenes of the Madonna's life, the most pervasive is certainly that of the grieving mother.[31]

This is how Giuliano was portrayed in local versions of his story. In the real-life events, the Italian government basically held Giuliano's home town, Montelepre, under siege, enforcing a virtual military occupation of the town through which they terrorized those citizens whom they had not already locked up.

While Cimino's earlier films show the effects of the oppression and exploitation of the American working class, he reaches for a more simplistic representation in *The Sicilian*. The critic Ben Lawton asserts:

The Sicilian is no more about Sicily and the bandit Giuliano than *Heaven's Gate* was about the Johnson County war, and thus should not be evaluated as such. Cimino has said that this film, like all his films, is about the desire for America, the longing for the dream. For Cimino, America is both a dream in its natural state and in its potentiality, and a nightmare in the sociopolitical reality of the country.[32]

Lawton concludes his argument by pointing to the liberating message behind Cimino's use of Sicily as the setting for a movie: "In creating

The Sicilian, Cimino has attempted to rewrite the mythological history of Italian Americans and thus free them from the bondage of an often confusing and contradictory heritage."[33] That is, the Italy that forced migration during the late nineteenth century is no longer there; it is no longer a third-world country where people must emigrate or starve. It has become a place where people can challenge their world, even if they do not change it.

By remaking Sicily as the United States, Cimino, unlike Puzo, has reinvented it to fit his artistic and political requirements, but most of all, he has covered the traditional sense of Sicilian masculinity with a more Americanized version of what it is to be a man. Puzo sees the Sicilian Salvatore Giuliano as what Michael or Sonny Corleone might have become had their father not left Sicily. What separates them is that Michael is the American and Giuliano the Sicilian.[34] Each culture has created a different sense of what it means to be a man and comes up with different expectations for how a man is to act, especially in public. Like most of his fellow filmmakers, Cimino has not explored the unique mother–son relationship that is characteristic of Italian culture, but this theme slowly surfaces in the literature and visual drama of subsequent American writers and filmmakers of Italian descent as they reinvent the figure of the gangster to serve their own storytelling purposes.

III

Reinventing the Gangster

5

QUEERING THE GANGSTER: GIOSE RIMANELLI AND FRANK LENTRICCHIA

This chapter explores how the novelists Giose Rimanelli and Frank Lentricchia use sexuality to undermine the power of the traditional gangster and turn traditional masculine strengths into weaknesses. These two writers reinvent the gangster figure to function as a criticism of Anglo-American and Italian-American cultures. They are both scholars as well as artists, so they have a long familiarity with irony, which they employ to great effect in their depictions of the gangster figure. In different ways, both authors set up the figure of the gangster not only as a target of cultural criticism, but also as a subject who criticizes the very culture that surrounds him. Thus, the gangster becomes a critic of culture as the author criticizes the culture of the gangster. In this way, both Rimanelli and Lentricchia move the wiseguy closer to the wise man.

A second reason for pairing these two is that they both debunk myths created around the Mafia in the United States. In his novel *Benedetta in Guysterland*, Rimanelli plays around with and outright mocks the facts recorded by Talese and romanticized by Puzo. Through parody, he enables us to examine historical "Mafia truths" for the fictions they really are. As Jerre Mangione and Ben Morreale suggest in their historical study *La Storia: Five Centuries of the Italian-American Experience*, the power of the Mafia of Sicily was exaggerated by the Italian government, which sought popular support to eliminate this powerful opposition force.

In his novel *Music of the Inferno* (1999), Lentricchia debunks traditional Mafia myths by having the protagonist "out" a fictional gangster as a homosexual within an old-fashioned Italian-American community. He turns what is stereotypically portrayed as a homosocial community, the gang, into a critique of traditional notions of masculinity through the figure of a homosexual gangster. Until Rimanelli's and Lentricchia's fiction, the gangster was never represented as a homosexual. By queering the Mafia, these authors challenge the narrow definitions of masculinity defined by earlier gangster figures. Both novelists use the gangster's sexuality to draw attention to the absurdity of having the gangster represent an ethnicized version of the iconic John Wayne man. They lead the way toward portraying a more complicated Italian-American masculinity, building the bridge over which the wiseguy travels in order to become the wise man.

GIOSE RIMANELLI'S *BENEDETTA IN GUYSTERLAND* (1993)

In my written introduction to *Benedetta in Guysterland*, and later in my discussion of that novel in my own book *Italian Signs, American Streets*, I offered *Benedetta* as a pivotal work in the development of Italian-American narrative literature. I focused on the place of parody in the growth and increased sophistication of cultural narrative, and I suggested that *Benedetta* was a missing link between modernism and postmodernism and a key moment in the development of a postmodern sense of Italian-American literature. In 1992, when I first considered Rimanelli's novel, I thought of the writer—not the character of the gangster—as a sort of trickster figure. Since then, my thinking has changed somewhat. I thought that I had said all that I could on this complex and sometimes controversial work. However, over the past ten years, I have had a number of occasions to teach the novel, and each time I have learned something new about it through both rereadings and student commentaries. Like many good works of art, *Benedetta* improves with age and continues to offer new readings and elicit new interpretations. I now see the novel as a pivotal work in the evolution of the gangster figure and cultural notions of masculinity, something I did not see as clearly in the early 1990s.

Rimanelli, in the way of all great parodists and satirists, uses an exemplary understanding of the works he plays with to move readers' thinking beyond earlier borders between Italian and Anglo-American cultures, pushing them truly into a new territory called Italian Americana. It is amazing that *Benedetta* was not published until 1993. It was written in 1970, and Giose Rimanelli was an internationally acclaimed writer from Italy who had published seven very successful books, translated into eight languages.[1] He was also a well-known journalist and cultural critic. Since 1961 Rimanelli has been a tenured professor in American universities, including Yale, appointed on the merits of his writing and not by virtue of his academic credentials. *Benedetta*, to Rimanelli, was simply an experiment in English, his first response to the demands of starting over again as a writer with a new language, a man of the world with a new toy.

Yet while the language was new, Rimanelli's knowledge of world literature and of America was not. North America had entered his imagination long before his arrival in the 1950s. His grandfather was born in New Orleans and his mother in Canada. Images of America formed early in his mind from family stories, and when he landed in the United States, he used his first English writings to record the divorce from the native culture that he had chosen to leave. Anthony Burgess notes in an introduction written for *Alien*, Rimanelli's unpublished book of poems, "Rimanelli is one of those remarkable writers who, like Joseph Conrad ... have turned from their first language to English, and have set out to rejuvenate it in a way few writers could do who were blessed and burdened with English as their first language."[2] By often lifting phrases, sentences, and even paragraphs directly out of previous works, such as Gay Talese's *Honor Thy Father*, Rimanelli pays homage to the very works he critiques. It is through his playful critique that Italian-American culture emerges in a new light. In the following discussion, I concentrate on Rimanelli's gangster figures in *Benedetta* and their relationship to what it means to be a man in the United States.

In my first considerations of *Benedetta*, I saw Rimanelli as a trickster in the playful way he created this novel and in the way he toys with the reader, tossing in lines from great literature and U.S. popular culture. That was interesting, but what I did not see was that the gangster was the real trickster in the book, and it is with this in mind that

I offer the following reconsideration of Rimanelli's gangster figures. Rimanelli cannot quite believe that writers like Puzo and Talese take the gangster so seriously. After all, the gangster figure was something that he found quite trivial and amusing in Italian culture. That it was being raised to absurd height in U.S. journalism, fiction, and film deserved to be criticized.

Rimanelli not only uses American culture in his novel, he also brings a number of great literary works to bear on *Benedetta in Guysterland*. A book made of books, the novel tells the story of Clarence "Benedetta" Ashfield, a young woman who encounters the gangster Joe Adonis. Renamed Benedetta by Adonis, who becomes her lover, Clarence is the novel's storyteller. Rimanelli is playing a game with the reader. He has written elsewhere that *Benedetta* was composed as he was learning English during the early 1970s. He refers to and often includes the sources of some of his early encounters with American English. In his dedication he nods to *Esquire* magazine, where excerpts of Talese's *Honor Thy Father* appeared prior to the book's publication. Talese makes an appearance in the novel as Guy Maltese, the biographer of gangster Santo "Zip the Thunder" Tristano (read Joe Bonanno). Rimanelli replaces the word "gangster" with "guyster"—a gangster with a twist. In an earlier draft of the novel, he used the word "gayster."

In *Benedetta*, Rimanelli goes back to the founding of the guyster group in Gela, Sicily, where Santo Tristano was born. Playing on the name of the gangster's hometown, Rimanelli makes Tristano a *gelataro*, or ice cream vendor, and the men who follow him are referred to as the Gelatari. Tristano leaves Gela and goes to Palermiu, the Sicilian dialect form of Palermo, the island's largest city. There he joins a group called Lavanda ("the washer"). The work of *lavanda*, washing clothes, is traditionally associated with women. However, in the novel, the Lavanda are musicians. The word also contains the resonance of cleansing—*lavare* is "to wash, to cleanse," and so there is a sense that Rimanelli is cleaning up the gangster's image through his playful fiction. When the Lavanda come to the United States, they are referred to as "lavenders": "It was not uncommon in those days for Italian lavenders to be working in organizations controlled by other ethnics."[3] With a single play on the word "Lavanda," Rimanelli colors these gangsters with a hue that is often associated with homosexuality. He then extends the gender play by connecting the group with an industry dominated by females and one that has a strong association with gay men: "The 'Lavanda,' now a code name for Italian musical cosmetologists, was not yet the homogeneous syndicate it would become. There were such figures as Arnold Roth-mayer in New York, Charles 'Queen' Sissimon in Boston, and Frank Motherson, also in New York, the latter working closely with Frank Corbello, who was one of the first Italo-American guysters to make a fortune in kissing people during Prohibitionism."[4] Rimanelli's discussion moves deeper into the sexual realm as he substitutes "kissing" for "killing." Through this substitution, Rimanelli brilliantly throws the notion of the gangster's masculinity into question. But more than challenging the traditional macho portrayals of gangsters by equating them with homosexuality, Rimanelli also criticizes traditional notions of masculinity that have established a strong connection between men and violence.

Supposedly incapable of sensitivity, men who are really desensitized through generations of cultural conditioning that has validated the use of violence to uphold honor are also told that having strong feelings and expressing them is a feminine trait. Continued denial of feelings can lead to an absence of feeling altogether. Thus, the perpetration of violence is not difficult when one cannot feel for others, and so many men find themselves able to do harm that more sensitive people could not. It is my contention that this violence, which sometimes requires men to come physically closer to another man than traditional notions of masculinity allow, is a result of the failure of men to find alternative ways of achieving intimacy with each other. I am not talking here about sexual intimacy, although that might enter the discussion at some point. Killing is a perverse form of intimacy and its violence has become a way for men to deal with various inadequacies, not the least of which is the inability to deal with the feelings they do have. To achieve intimacy, then, some men might resort to murder. By substituting the word "kissing" for "killing," Rimanelli suggests this idea and sexualizes the gangster's act of "wasting" someone.

When Benedetta asks Zip the Thunder about murder and its place in the land of guysters, Zip explains the philosophic underpinnings that justify traditional macho-based masculinity:

"You mean kissing, don't you child Benedetta?"
"The kiss of death, yes. Murder, yes."
"The entire economy of the world is based on murder," Zip said.

"Take the war between two bands. How efficient is war! Power proves who is right. If I bleed on this earth, it is mine. Then, when battles are won, peace will walk the land in white splendor, clear calm, in the silence of grass giving no echo back, and we'll … Oh, let peace come up like thunder …"[5]

This explanation rationalizes the violence that is common in macho-based notions of masculinity; the characters' act of kissing other guysters heightens the absurdity of this explanation.

The masculinity of Rimanelli's gangsters is also attacked through their own activities. They all play instruments and belong to bands that perform strange, unmanly acts in nightclubs. In Chicago, there is Scorpione's (read Al Capone's) organization, which makes millions from "recordings," appearances in "transvestite shows," and selling "narco-cosmetics and tailored suits."[6] In New York, the top Lavanda figure is "a short, squat, old-style Southern Italian violinist with a moustache named Joe Crepadio [translated as: Joe May-God-Die—read Joe "The Boss" Masseria, an early mob leader] who was known as Dio the Boss [God the Boss]."[7] One of the clubs in which the New York band performs is La Gaia Scienza, "The Gay Science," the title of the famous Nietzsche book that contains the notion that "God is dead."

When Rimanelli separates the guysters into two groups, the Gaia Societa guysters led by Santo Tristano, and the Normale Societa guysters led by Joe Adonis, he focuses on the key aspect of masculinity of which the guyster/gangster must constantly be observant: sexual orientation. With the gay/normal split, Rimanelli undermines traditional notions of power connected to masculinity and heightens the irony of his novel.

Another way Rimanelli defuses the gangster figure's traditional hypermasculinity is by demeaning, as he desexualizes, the names of real-life gangsters. Rimanelli renames many historical gangsters, but he keeps the name Joe Adonis (the name that gangster Giuseppe Antonio Doto adopted) as it is, because it is a perfect referent to the inherent narcissism of a macho-based masculinity. Rimanelli then gives us Lucky Lu Cane or "Lucky the Dog" (i.e., Lucky Luciano), Vito Failaspesa or "Vito the Shopper" (Vito Genovese), Princess Anastasia (Albert Anastasia), and Frank Corbello or "Frank the Blockhead" (Frank Costello). The narrator of *Benedetta* even refers to Zip the Thunder as being "god-mother" to Joe Adonis.[8] In Scorsese's *GoodFellas*, gangsters constantly challenge each other's masculinity and Rimanelli parodies this when he writes, " 'Joe is worse than anyone I know, for sure,' said Pimple Boy. 'He called me an impotent trombonist once, and I hated him, oh if I hated him … I'll kiss him if he ever shows up again in this territory.' "[9] In this parody, Rimanelli heightens the absurdity of traditional macho behavior. At the heart of Rimanelli's gangster is the penis. Macho men are often accused of thinking with their penises, especially when it comes to issues of love, as we see in a scene in which Santo Zip has sex with underage girls: "As soon as we were left alone, they opened my trousers and took out my heart. They burst out with admiring exclamations about its thickness and its length, the younger one kissed it and they began to revive it with their fingers."[10]

Macho men also see fighting as a way of life. For years it was common and expected for men to fight as a way of proving their masculinity and defending their reputation. One of the things I do when I teach this novel is ask for a show of hands of the males in my class who have had a public fight. This informal annual polling has revealed a steady decline in the number of young men who have had this experience. In my youth, had such a question been asked in class, most likely all the men would have raised their hands, not just because it was more common to have fights, but also because those who hadn't fought would not want to admit it in public. As the character "Fish" explains in *Benedetta*, fighting is something that's a natural part of being a guyster:

> "When I began having my first street fights with a guy two and a half years ago," the Fish said, "I had never thought much about things like 'Mom' and 'Pop,' 'Sins' and 'Sons.' Playing with a guy was something I 'had' to do. I didn't have much choice in the matter. I didn't think about the whole thing and come to a decision. I was driven by needs which I didn't, and to a large extent still don't, understand. All I was aware of was that my needs for physical combat with a guy were both absolutely necessary to my life and contrary to 'everything' I had ever been taught. And that's just my experience."[11]

One of the pitfalls of a guyster is that he is unable to love; this should come as no surprise since if one cannot feel emotionally, one cannot be expected to have feelings for another. This is a guyster fault that Joe Adonis explains:

"Truly, my precious Benedetta, the world does not know its real interests. I shall admit if you want me to, that virtue, just like anything beautiful and sublime, is only an embrace. But if this illusion were a common thing, if all guys believed and wanted to be virtuous, if they were compassionate, charitable, generous, magnanimous, in a word, if everyone were sensitive, wouldn't we be happier? Wouldn't every individual find a thousand resources in society? Shouldn't these resources be applied, as much as possible, to the realization of our embraces, since man's happiness cannot consist in a real thing?"[12]

Rimanelli's guysters are quite immature, and by representing *mafiosi* as boys who never grow up, he pierces the mystique of the gangster as romantically created by Puzo and realistically documented by Talese to reveal that the Mafia and its *mafiosi* are social and historical constructions, anything but natural. Once this is understood, the same can be said about traditional notions of masculinity. This realization comes to Joe Adonis and leads him to found his own group, Normale Societa. Adonis explains to Benedetta: "I found that Lavanda acts as the cause for the degeneration of the formerly confident and opinionated young guy."[13] There is no room for individuality in the guyster/gangster world, just as there is no room for deviance from the norms of traditional masculinity in the world of macho men.

For the norms to be challenged, the world needs a man who sees things differently and acts accordingly. This is Joe Adonis, as Rimanelli renders him through the words of Zip the Thunder:

"He was a guy, then he changed, became a doctor, started organizing his own band. He believes that sexual orientation can be determined with ninety percent accuracy through chemical analysis. He believes that guyness is determined before birth under the influence of society that governs gender. He believes that his results should reduce the stigma attached to guyness and point the way to a possible cure."[14]

Rimanelli's obvious application of the change of thinking about human sexual orientation that occurred in the 1970s to the notion of the guyster/gangster confuses the issue of historical construction of the gangster. Joe's theory of guyster identity was the reason Zip sent him into exile and, thus, away from his lover, Benedetta. As Zip concludes, "In order to maintain our reality as guys, gender identification seems to me to be the goal for all of us."[15] The gangster needs to identify not just with the masculine, but with a macho-based masculinity that enables him to continue behavior that benefits a patriarchal culture and the fraternally organized support system of that culture.

Rimanelli uses the character Joe Adonis to challenge the traditional notions of guysterhood/gangsterhood. In essence, Joe Adonis begins to make the move from wiseguy to wise man. When this happens, he is characterized by the narrator as follows:

> Then suddenly he walked into this mush of unawareness, Joe Adonis, with his physicians of the Bronx; the "Normale Societa" to take care of the "Gaia Societa." And he immediately knew with clarity that it was all a pile of atrocious obscenity.

> A guy in every sense, full, complete, strong with roots and wings, a sense of humor, always there, clarity of vision, of perception, perspicacity—always there. He entered over this world of stagnant pools of trapped women and guysters pretending to be otherwise like moonlight and starlight to frighten owls and mortal eyes. And a purge came.[16]

This purge is referred to as "stage one of the recovery"[17] and is characterized by a purely sexual affair that Joe has with Benedetta's female friend Crystal Baby; it is only after this affair that he and Benedetta are able to exchange a pure and honest love. This change is foreshadowed earlier in the novel when we learn about Benedetta's origins.

Joe tells Benedetta that she must avenge herself on Grendel—a sea monster that "tried to destroy me and bit off my fisher-lover's leg."[18] Rimanelli's reuse of one of the earliest myths recorded in English literature invites commentary on masculinity, especially when one considers the construction of masculinity in *Beowulf*.[19] In the legend, Grendel, a sea monster, kills men. When he in turn is killed, his mother comes in search of revenge. This mother-monster, who also devours men, must be killed. Thus, in one of the founding myths of Anglo culture, men gain identity and project their masculinity by killing a mother figure. This "matricide" is the foundation for what Christina Wieland calls "the unprecedented destructiveness unleashed on the planet and on fellow human beings by the West."[20]

Wieland, in *Undead Mother*, argues that "the boy's dis-identification and separation from mother is not a smooth and easy process, but a violent affair that resembles matricide."[21] She sees this as the core of Western society's psychic structure of masculinity and as responsible for the perpetuation of a culture that sanctions male violence. The way out of this mess is for men to acknowledge their mothers and mourn the loss incurred by their separation from them. Rimanelli's gangsters reflect their upbringing in the way they usually treat the women they encounter. Rimanelli's female characters, notably Benedetta and Crystal Baby, represent the liberated woman of the 1970s, and as such come off as quite aggressive counterparts to Rimanelli's gangster figures; but as Wieland suggests in regard to what she sees as a Western phenomenon, "This 'emancipation' of woman in Western culture, then, should not obscure the fact that it is the 'masculine' psyche—based on the murder of the mother—which prevails in both men and women, and which is manifested in the strong anti-life trend in Western culture."[22] And so, while Rimanelli's gangsters make fun of their literary and filmic ancestors, they do little actually to formulate a model by which wiseguys can become wise men. When Joe Adonis dies, the one man who might have become wise, his obituary reports that one of the businesses he owned was an olive oil importer named "Mamma Mia Importing Company." Behind the guise of this legitimate business, he operated his illegal businesses. Whether Rimanelli fabricated this detail or lifted it from an actual obituary is not important. What is important to the characterization of the gangster Adonis is that this wiseguy operated behind the figurative skirts of his mother.

Another way of translating the name "Benedetta" is "well said" or "well spoken." And what Benedetta, the sometime narrator of this tale, does is speak well in her presentation of how the hoodlum boys have created a playground in a fantasy world where women are objects of their infantile deficiencies and adolescent fantasies. Women, though they may achieve power over men through sexual battles, are actually accepting male control by playing along with men. In the end, the Rimanellian wiseguys may try but can never become wise men. The only wise "man" left at the end of the novel is the narrator, a woman, who shows the folly of basing masculinity on the traditional macho gangster behavior depicted by previous writers. A more telling shift from wiseguy to wise man begins in the writing of Frank Lentricchia.

FRANK LENTRICCHIA AND *THE MUSIC* OF THE *INFERNO* (1999)

The critic, essayist, and novelist Frank Lentricchia was raised in Utica, New York by working-class parents who were the children of Italian immigrants. He was educated at Duke University and began his professional life as a literary scholar, becoming well known in the field of literary criticism. In 1994 he published his first completely autobiographical work, *The Edge of Night*, and from then on he did more creative and less critical writing. Lentricchia's first published fiction was *Johnny Critelli* and *The Knifemen* (1996), two novellas published in one volume. The work reveals the influence of writers as diverse as Mario Puzo, Edgar Allan Poe, and James Joyce, as well as the filmmakers Federico Fellini, Martin Scorsese, and Brian DePalma. There are slight hints of the presence of traditional gangsters in both novellas, but it was not until his first full-length novel, *The Music of the Inferno*, that Lentricchia used fully drawn gangster characters. The late James C. Mancuso, a professor of psychology and amateur literary critic, placed a short review of the novel on Amazon.com in which he wrote, "I continue to be puzzled about one aspect of all of Lentricchia's writings, even after reading *The Music of the Inferno*, which is less sex-infused than are his previous two frankly creative works. I cannot understand his frequent insertion of passages describing outlandish sexual events! I regard those passages as strained and lacking purpose."[23] What Mancuso and other critics have been unable to see is that it is precisely through outlandish sexual acts and the suggestion of sexual perversion that Lentricchia is able to draw attention to what he is criticizing. For no matter how much creative writing he does, Lentricchia is at heart a critic. Whether he is writing fiction or nonfiction, his imagination is piqued by the opportunity to critique.

In *The Music of the Inferno*, Lentricchia presents Robert Tagliaferro, an orphaned child of unknown racial background, who makes a grim discovery of the corpse of a young child, which he respectfully buries in a field, shortly after his eighteenth birthday that causes him to run away from his hometown of Utica, New York. The young man takes refuge in a bookstore in New York City, where he reads his way through the shelves: "In the absence of my father, I acquired knowledge. My knowledge is my memory."[24] Robert's character becomes a composite of all that he has absorbed through his studies. Along the way he keeps notebooks "containing in a minute script illegible to all but himself the fruits of forty-two years of research in the history of Utica and New York State, from the coming of the Dutch to the present."[25] In those notebooks, Robert fortifies himself with the knowledge he will need to overcome the gangsters of his past.

The one thing that Robert is not is sexual. There is no information about his past sexual encounters. He is familiar with human sexuality, but it is hard to tell if it is knowledge gained solely from reading or talking rather than actual experience. Robert returns to Utica at age forty-two to uncover the town's secrets through his knowledge and memory.

The sights conjured in Lentricchia's literary inferno are gruesome and, like those in the great work of Dante, are directly connected to the sinners' actions. The novel presents a vision of darkness that is as exhilarating as it is disturbing; it is the destruction, if not the deconstruction, of the mafioso prototype, and the destroyer is the intellectual, "this curious man, all made of words."[26] Robert has become the cultural critic who has the power to undo the wrongs of the past by forcing men to confront their evil deeds. A man who knows the past, who knows what has been erased, repressed, or forgotten, can be a very dangerous man, especially when he has been hurt by those who created the history he has studied. Robert sees himself as "an ethnic freak in this fair city of such clear ethnic divisions," who has "come back to return the pain."[27]

Going home can be hell, and in this revision of returning home, Lentricchia penetrates the dark recesses of a Little Italy to reveal the sins of Utica's "immigrant merchant princes" who shaped the city's economy, and thus its history. Robert, returned home, begins to change everyone's sense of Utica's past. He meets Alex Lucas, whose name should have been Alessandro Lucca, the grandson of one of the original Italian immigrants to Utica. Alex's grandfather shamed the family enough to make them change their name. Lucas, who in many ways stands to benefit from Robert's knowledge, helps Robert connect to the town's leading Italians. He secures Robert an invitation to the regular dinner meeting of a group which includes men like Albert Cesso, Professor Louis Ayoub, and Sebastian Spina, all descendants of Utica's first Italian immigrants. These contemporary power brokers meet in a cellar restaurant with a gangster boss named Joseph "Our Mother" Paternostra: "slim, spry, ninety years old .... Never called or referred to as 'Our Mother' within earshot, except once. A major mafia *capo* who had controlled for almost sixty-five years the Utica–Syracuse area on behalf of the Don of all Upstate New York (with the exception of that peculiar toilet: Albany)."[28] For most of the novel, Paternostra's sexual orientation remains unclear. Yet when Alex first tells Robert about the town leaders, Robert says that Alex's characterization of the men suggests that "I'd stumbled upon a ring of homosexual gangsters."[29]

Lentricchia, like Rimanelli, debunks the traditional sexuality of the gangster through the figure of Paternostra, the gay mafioso; the racism of Italian Americans through the figure of racist alderman Sebastian Spina, a mayoral candidate; and the pomposity of professionalism through dentist Albert Cesso and Louis Ayoub, a professor of literature. Most of these town leaders have an ancestral link to the founding myths of Utica's Little Italy, and in many ways this is a story about the end of a Little Italy and about how book learning helps to end that world and preserve it at the same time. It is also about the place of modernism in a postmodern world, about the role of facts in history, the purpose of ethnic identity, and the role storytelling plays in claiming and naming that history. The various encounters of Robert and the town leaders in the inferno of Joe's restaurant, where Robert tells his stories over a series of dinners, rewrite the hells of Dante and Milton into the hell of Jean-Paul Sartre, so that "hell" becomes the way the past rests in one's mind after it has been delivered there through other people. Redemption happens only through the revolutionary act of revising the past without reliving it. Robert's dinners, in a sense, represent the afterlife where the gangster awaits the judgment—here, from the cultural critic Robert Tagliaferro. By running away from home as a young man and educating himself, Robert has transformed himself from a potential wiseguy into a wise man.

Robert first attacks the gangster image by invoking the Madonna with the phrase "Our Mother." Everyone in the story knows how Paternostra got the nickname "Our Mother," and that to use it in public is to signal a death wish because it questions the man's masculinity in front of other men. Robert uses the phrase during his retelling of the first sighting of the bay of Manhattan by Dutch explorers, for whom the vision echoes the "originating instant of Greek mythology, the divinization of the earth. The god of all gods, preceding all gods, was a goddess. She was Our Mother, whose womb swelled as the Virgin Mary's would, and from her came everything good, including Our Father, who was questionable."[30] When Professor Ayoub accuses Robert of getting away with speaking "the unspeakable" and of knowing the story of Paternostra's nickname, Robert replies, "A curious footnote, Professor, buried deep in a famous book of the 1960s on the Mafia."[31] Then Robert suggests that Paternostra might suspect that Ayoub knows the truth, but that Paternostra is "a fool beyond our comprehension" because he harbors the "tremendous illusion" that Ayoub is "[t]he man of intellect. The man who has never been fondled by the desire for power"[32] and is, therefore, no threat to Paternostra's power. It is at this point that the reader is finally given the whole story.

As the story goes, Paternostra is running a high-stakes craps game that had been held up a couple of times. He stops by to ensure its security and while he is still there, it is held up again. The robber points the gun at Paternostra and has him strip naked. When he does, Paternostra with "no tone in the pectorals" reveals he has womanlike breasts. The robber responds, "Now you know why Mr. Big Shot is called 'Our Mother' behind his back."[33] Then the robber orders Paternostra's bodyguard, Rosario, to suck on his boss's breast, and when he does, Paternostra achieves an erection and ejaculates. Thus, the nickname is born.

By retelling the story, Robert debunks the traditional macho power behind which the gangster hides and not only reveals the gangster's weakness but also asserts the power of the intellectual to overcome that of the wiseguy. But more than this, Paternostra maintains a homosexual relationship with Rosario, his blond weight-lifter companion. Robert later explains to Alex that "Joseph Paternostra was the Old Don's catamite, a Queen of the Mafia."[34] In this way, Lentricchia turns the homosocial world of the Mafia askew and gives it a glint of homosexuality, undermining its traditional and apparently superficial heterosexual foundation.

Lentricchia, in a truly postmodern move, disrupts Mario Puzo's master gangster narrative. In a direct reference to Puzo's *The Godfather*, the men allude to Puzo as they discuss the founding fathers of Utica:

Ayoub: "Behind every great family lies a crime."
Paternostra: "And a politician."
Alex: "And eventually a writer."[35]

The allusion is to the Balzac quote that Puzo uses as an epigraph to his novel, something that is pointed out by the Professor, who goes on: "Remembered in the lineage of all the great families, legitimate and illegitimate, in the womb of crime, the United States of the Mafia. All wealth is guilty at the source."[36] When accused by the gangster Paternostra of exaggerating everything, Ayoub responds: "The road of exaggeration leads to the palace of fact. Yes, the homeopathic imagination of Mario Puzo, the splendid luridness of his instincts, whose ancestors hid the meaning of their surname by dropping the second 'z,' Mario the novelist with a nose for the disguised stench of all great families. Puzo? *Puzzo*: Stink."[37] Robert goes on to tell the stories of Utica's founding fathers and how they stole their fortunes, to which Ayoub responds:

> "Mario the Stinker has already told your story of swindlers, Mr. Forza, and made a fortune doing so."
> Robert: "As did Mr. Faulkner before him."
> Ayoub: "Yes."
> Robert: "As did Mr. Fitzgerald before Mr. Faulkner."
> Ayoub: "Yes. The American literary history of family gangsterism."[38]

Their litany reveals the connection between American literature and the male powers of history that have come and gone before the Italian gangster.

Along with taking down the gangster in this novel, Lentricchia takes a whack at the silly chauvinism that often accompanies public displays of ethnic pride. Robert also attacks Spina, a racist who may be guilty of a murder in the past; the victim of which Robert believes is hidden under Spina's driveway. Spina represents "blood pride"—a kind of mindless glorying in his identity as an Italian.[39] Robert plans to open an investigation into Spina's past once Spina has been elected mayor of Utica, for he believes "Italian-American pride needs the forum and status of the mayoralty. A great victory comes before the fall."[40] What follows is a series of mock responses given out by Alex and Robert:

> "We are virtuous, because we are Italian."
> "We will support and love each other because we are Italian."
> "It's a privilege to be a fucking Italian."
> "I honor you, my Italian friend, though your values disgust me."
> "The Italian-American people are a very great fucking people."

"The ascension of Spina will trigger epic Italian-American self-cleansing. They will loathe their ethnicity. They will all want to change their surnames to Windsor, Spencer, or Bowles."[41]

Here Lentricchia clears the air of the mindless ethnic boosterism that often pervades the Italian-American identity, especially when ethnic identity is based not on knowledge, but on feelings passed from one generation to the next. Quite often, these feelings, not mediated by knowledge of other ethnic experiences, lead people into unfriendly if not downright hostile behavior that heightens the friction between ethnic groups and leads to "wild in the streets" gangster behavior that kills innocents like Yusef Hawkins (see chapter one, note 37).

Lentricchia subtly introduces a possible antidote to this behavior by recognizing the power that art can have. Alex gives Robert a two-handled burial urn that stands about two feet tall. It is to contain the ashes of Robert's stepfather, Morris. They analyze the urn and discuss its relation to the first representation of the Madonna and Child and the origins of art:

"25,000 B.C. The primal sculptor. He who needs to venerate in mimetic homage the one incontrovertible creative principle. It's the origin of art. The male who needs."

"This has been said before."

"Yes, for 25,000 years. The male emerges from the mother, then spends the remainder of his life trying to represent the mother. A mama's boy. A sissy. *In utero*, forget genital difference. *In utero*, total femaleness. On this earth, when at last a male, he walks but briefly, to and fro, in terrible independence from nature. Don't fuck with me! I am a man! In death, only the female. Back inside her oblivion. Secured forever from tumbling forth. Promise redeemed. Nature. God."[42]

This is the same point Scorsese makes and one that other reinventors of the gangster figure will pick up on: one of the ways a wiseguy becomes a wise man is to contemplate and incorporate aspects of what is traditionally considered female, always at the risk of losing a traditional sense of what is masculine.

At the final dinner, Robert continues his history of Utica, reaching the ancestors of Alex and Cesso and uncovering the sins of their families' past. A fire cuts the meal short and the men run for their lives. Robert takes off for parts unknown, à la Huck Finn, leaving his fortune to Alex. In many respects, Robert Tagliaferro, who has enacted his vendetta by coming "back to return the pain," plays the role of John the Baptist for the coming of the wise man to Italian-American literature. He uses his knowledge both to uncover the macho masquerade enacted by the traditional men of Utica's Little Italy and to right the wrongs of the past. He serves as a moral compass to counter the unchecked behavior of the gay gangster Joseph Paternostra and the crooked politician Albert Spina.

FRANK LENTRICCHIA'S *LUCCHESI AND THE WHALE* (2001)

In his next novel, *Lucchesi and the Whale* (2001), Lentricchia defies traditional and commercial fiction. *Lucchesi and the Whale* is really an anti-narrative—tough reading, but rewarding for the reader familiar with American literature. In his acknowledgments, Lentricchia points to a few academic studies, novels by Don DeLillo, and Herman Melville's *Moby-Dick* as sources of inspiration for his new, macabre tale of a strange academic's search for truth. This section focuses on a small part of the novel which depicts a chance encounter between a gangster who has a name quite similar to that of the novel's protagonist and the protagonist himself.

The center of the fiction is Thomas Lucchesi, an academic wrapped up in his writing. Lucchesi talks mostly to himself, and when he does speak to others, it is as though he is lecturing. This character is a version of a figure common in Lentricchia's fiction: a man alone in the world. Lucchesi observes the fractured bits of his life as they crash into one another, as though seeing his world through a kaleidoscope. This work is among the best of what can be called "anti-novels." There is no plot; this brief (113 pages) fiction is no page-turner. Although it cannot be called a novel, it is a novel approach to writing fiction. What Lentricchia offers is writing that liberates the reader from the tugging leash of a plot. This writing is a story in itself.

Thomas Lucchesi is a man with a peculiar condition: he is with book, as a pregnant woman is with child. When he can't write, he can't breathe, and that is when he seeks inspiration in the strangest places. Sometimes he finds it at the bedside of the dying, mostly his close friends,

but he'll take any dying acquaintance in a pinch. By confronting others' deaths, he denies, if not defies, his own, and in that moment gains
enough power to fuel a few writing sessions. In the section in question,
"High Blood Pleasure," the origins of Lucchesi the artist are presented.
This section also includes a wild "sit-down" with the gangster Thomas
"Three Finger Brown" Lucchese, who functions as the artist's distorted
reflection in an ethnic mirror.

The story of how one writer named Tommy Lucchesi comes to
meet one gangster, Gaetano "Tommy Three Finger Brown" Lucchese,
is told by Geoffrey Gilbert, a friend of the protagonist who is marrying
a female relative of the gangster. Gilbert portrays Lucchese, a year away
from dying of a brain tumor, "like a character they called in Shake-
spearean times a fantastic, more or less a foppish person, who was more
or less a homosexual,"[43] although he goes on to suggest that Lucchese
was probably not homosexual himself. The two Tommys meet in the
gangster's hotel room. The writer has learned "everything there is to
know about Three Finger Brown," and he sees the gangster as a "hidden muse" of his dark writings.[44] Lucchesi the writer was "an English
major who wrote stories full of violence in a poetic style" and authored
such piquant phrases as "the eviscerations of friendship," "the ice-pick
of conversation," "the blood-gouts of time," and "the lacerations of family." In contrast, Lucchese the gangster "actually did violence."[45]

Gilbert and Lucchesi prepare for the meeting by researching the
gangster's biography. They come to the realization that none of their
research can be discussed with the gangster, who "had done 32 murders by the time he was 35."[46] They meet in the hotel room while Three
Finger is watching *The Arthur Godfrey Show* on television. The gangster
asks the writer about his "plans for life," to which Lucchesi replies, "I
want to be a writer."[47] Lucchese responds that he does "a little writing in
my domain, so I sympathize with what you have to go through,"[48] and
then asks the writer to name some writers he idolizes. When Lucchesi
says, "John (the Lung) Keats," nicknaming the poet with an allusion to
his tuberculosis, the gangster says, "I heard of him, but we never met."[49]
They go on to talk about Keats's sexuality. The writer suggests that Keats
was without a doubt heterosexual. The gangster replies, "An associate of
mine once told me that art and sucking cock go hand-in-hand."[50] This
response is a defense of the masculinity that the gangster represents.
Lucchese is in love with the "mouse," or girlfriend, of another gangster, Sam "Momo" Giancana, and she appears on television during the

sit-down. Lucchese openly pines for her in front of the other two men. Soon Gilbert and Lucchesi are introduced to the gangster's bodyguard, a 547-pound man called Frank the Whale. "Three Finger Brown" Lucchese then pulls a move that he suggests is the reason for his nickname. The Whale explains that having only three fingers was a handicap that the gangster turned into an asset when he put them up rivals' asses to "dig around there for the truth."[51]

As in most of Lentricchia's fiction, a dark side emerges in *Lucchesi and the Whale*. Like Edgar Allan Poe, Lentricchia is fascinated with the grotesque, and *Lucchesi* takes us deep into that concept. The scene where the writer meets the gangster is telling in that it shows that educated men and gangsters, wise men and wiseguys, can sometimes be opposite sides of the same coin.

The writer Lucchesi has his whale, too—Melville's novel about a whale occupies, indeed obsesses, his literary criticism. The gangster Lucchese has his whale, the 547-pound bodyguard. Their respective whales protect both men from harm that might come from the real world, a world over which they have little control. The whale becomes the only way to protect someone who has taken supernormal risks. Lucchesi the writer risks his career (and loses his teaching job) when he writes his "secrets in public print."[52] He does not enjoy life outside the page. Lucchese the gangster risks losing a normal life by becoming a murderer, and he cannot enjoy life outside the world of gangsters. Lucchesi the writer advises his students to "live like a no-holds-barred autobiography of yourself, hide nothing so that you'll be freed for serious writing."[53] Lucchese the gangster enacts the experiences that Lucchesi the writer wants without "the consequences."[54] The writer secretly emulates the gangster, but he does not want to live with the possible consequences of a gangster's acts.

In the hands of a sophisticated, highly educated writer, the figure of the gangster can become a powerful site for cultural criticism. Both Rimanelli and Lentricchia create oppositional figures who challenge the traditional representations of masculinity that previous writers and filmmakers have presented.

6

FEMALE MASCULINITY AND THE GANGSTER: LOUISA ERMELINO

Throughout history, the further man moved away from his connection with woman as creatrix, the more spirituality was also disconnected from the human body.[1]

—Ana Castillo

Male authors began to undermine traditional notions of masculinity by playing with the gangster figure's sexuality; this can be attributed to the way that men have traditionally attempted to emasculate each other by attacking each other's sexual powers, and often another's sexual orientation. This occurs because a patriarchal society is built and organized around the performance of physical power. It is a man's physical strength that enables him to have dominance over women, and as long as the world is organized around physical power, men will always have that advantage. One's physical power, then, becomes a likely target for personal attack.

Great advances have been made by women, who can now compete with men in many areas that require physical power. However, such competition still takes place in a world controlled by men. If men have the edge in physical competition, what do women have that might help to organize the world differently? Usually when people speak of women's power, they refer to qualities such as intuition, emotion, and empathy—all facets of psychological power, a power that is exercised through the act of listening, of absorbing information in a situation and then formulating responses based on an analysis of that information. If a man performs his power by speaking (often loudly to gain attention), then, perhaps a woman can be said to perform her power through listening. If wiseguys are ever to become wise men, they should take a look at what men can learn from women and turn speaking into listening.

This chapter shows how Louisa Ermelino creates new notions of masculinity, first in a male character from her novel *Joey Dee Gets Wise*, and then through the female characters of *The Sisters Mallone*. Ermelino takes on the stereotypical notions of masculinity and transforms them, blurring the gender lines. Throughout her writing, Ermelino has been exploring and explaining the places where power lies in Italian-American culture—with the mothers. What earlier male writers have suppressed in their creation of father–son stories, Ermelino uncovers and exploits. Her female characters employ what the critic Josephine Gattuso Hendin has termed "retaliatory violence," a form of violence she sees as peculiarly feminine and one that is characterized by a rationale unique to women.

LOUISA ERMELINO'S *JOEY DEE GETS WISE:*
A STORY OF LITTLE ITALY (1991)

Gender and the proper social place for the Italian-American male and female is the central problem of *Joey Dee Gets Wise*, right from the beginning. In the Prologue, a woman who lives in the Little Italy of New York City's Greenwich Village gives birth to a girl and asks that the afterbirth be taken outside. Alfonsina, the Italian-born midwife, refuses to do that because she believes that the afterbirth must remain in the home, for "the woman stays in the house."[2] The afterbirth of a male child can be taken outside because, as Alfonsina says, "No one wants a man who stays home, a *ricchione*, under his mother's skirts."[3] The word *ricchione* is an important choice here, for it is derived from the Calabrian word *arricchià*, which means "to wish for the *irco* (male goat)." A *ricchione* refers to a female goat in heat; the Italian suffix -*one* is often used to derive a derogatory word. Giovanni Dall'Orto, a self-defined militant gay journalist, writes that the word means "a man that wants to be mounted by another man."[4] Thus, in the Old-World ways, a mother who wanted a strong son would not want him to be associated with the place and work of women. Since the place for the boy is outside the home and the girl inside, Alfonsina believes that a compromise with the mother would be to flush the afterbirth down the toilet, but the mother insists she take it out of the house and bury it somewhere. Alfonsina holds on to the package containing the afterbirth. The mother continues to defy the ways of the Old-World midwife by removing the strips of bed sheet that Alfonsina has used to swaddle the child. "Trouble," Alfonsina says, "You make trouble with this thing. I can tell you."[5]

The mother, who remains unnamed, is in a bad marriage, and on the day of her daughter's birth her abusive husband, Armando, is out drinking away the misery of having sired a "buttonhole." He is found dead that very day by the police, who are unable to determine the cause of his death. Alfonsina returns to the house with the afterbirth, telling the wife she can now flush it down the toilet. The mother demands that Alfonsina hand over the afterbirth and eventually slips it into her husband's coffin and it is buried with his corpse.

By choosing Alfonsina to be her midwife, the mother has risked the ire of Donna Vecchio, the most powerful woman in the neighborhood, "with her powers of *affatura*" (casting spells), who "would be angry that she wasn't called for this baby."[6] When Donna Vecchio arrives to pay her condolences to the woman over her husband's death, she asks about the newborn. When the mother says the baby is well, Donna Vecchio remarks that this is good, but unfortunately the child is not one of "hers." The mother coyly tells her that the child will be named Carolina, after Donna Vecchio, who will be the baby's *gummara* (Standard Italian *commare*, "godmother"). That baby, whose afterbirth was not properly disposed of according to tradition, becomes the catalyst for the story Ermelino creates about how a young wannabe gangster becomes a wise man.

Like Charley in Scorsese's *Mean Streets*, Joey Dee has a fateful relationship with a girl who has a reputation for being strange—Carolina's daughter, Josie. When Carolina gave birth to her daughter, "Donna Vecchio, who could bring lovers back and turn females to males in the womb, was helpless,"[7] and Carolina's husband, Sonny, has to take his wife to the hospital. The birth is difficult and leads to rumors among the neighborhood women that "Josie Magro … would be a little 'pazza' [crazy]."[8] Like Theresa in *Mean Streets*, Josie is viewed as tainted and as quite different from the other neighborhood girls. Joey Dee falls in love with her and tries to keep it secret from everyone.

Carolina has married Sonny Magro, a man whose body is found in the streets one morning as the women head to church. The local mob leader, Fernando "Nicky Mole" Malevento, has had his eye on the beautiful Carolina, and he had his men throw Sonny off a roof so that Malevento can have Carolina for himself. The murder is witnessed by Vito Santero, a neighborhood kid with slow mental abilities, possibly caused by child abuse. Vito is a friend of Joey De Stefano, the novel's protagonist, who feels he is "too grown a man to be in church any-more, even in the back."[9] Vito tells Joey what he has witnessed and Joey warns him, "You go home and you forget about what you saw and you forget you told me anything. Sonny Magro's dead. It don't matter what you saw unless you want to be next."[10] Joey has already learned the les-son of *omertà*—a man doesn't meddle in business that is not his—and will remain silent. Joey is also looking for ways of becoming a man in his neighborhood and not as a "pants presser" like Sonny Magro or a "horse" like his father; both words refer to those who work at com-mon menial jobs. Many Italian-American men in the 1950s and 1960s worked in the garment industry or in the industries represented by the Teamsters Union. Joey Dee feels that he is different, and he is looking for a different life.

Joey Dee's dream is to leave the neighborhood and go to "Vegas, in the desert."[11] Typically, as we have seen in *The Godfather* and in *Honor Thy Father*, the West symbolizes the "real" America for Italian Ameri-cans; is a land of endless horizons, as opposed to the horizonless city where these Italians are born and raised. This is also an element in the plays of Richard Vetere. Worth commenting on at this point is the very lack of visual horizons in the writing and films so far discussed. It is as though the characters have no way of seeing beyond Little Italy. The urban settings in Italian-American works of fiction and film become claustrophobic traps for those who live there. Often the protagonists see traveling west as the best way out.

Joey Dee is reminiscent of Lucia Santa's oldest son, Lorenzo, in Puzo's *The Fortunate Pilgrim*. He is a well-behaved young man, well trained by his mother in the art of social interaction. When he attends the Magro wake, he behaves the way a young man should. He extends his condolences to the widow by saying, " 'I'm sorry for your trouble, Carolina'... It was what he always said at wakes. His mother had taught him."[12] Carolina defies the traditions of Italian widowhood by wearing lipstick and it is this that catches Joey's attention. It makes him think "about Sonny's blood in the street and about Carolina Magro's mouth."[13] As Joey and his friends talk about the funeral, they reveal that Sonny's corpse looks so good because a specialist mortician was flown in. The altar boys have new shoes and Father Giannini has a new chalice in Sonny Magro's name through the generosity of Nicky Mole. Joey Dee knows all this because he is sleeping with Carolina's daughter, Josie. No one else knows about Nicky Mole because "Joey Dee wasn't a guy who talked,"[14] and he "had a reputation for being closemouthed."[15]

Nicky Mole, the leader of the neighborhood wiseguys, had murdered men in the old country and, when he was arrested, was sent to the United States to meet another gangster, Tommy California. "He got rid of everybody Tommy California didn't like and then he got rid of Tommy California."[16] He "had no fears and no weaknesses ... until Carolina Magro."[17] Carolina is not like any of the other women in the neighborhood. She doesn't go to mass and she doesn't mourn her husband in the dramatic fashion the neighborhood expects of a young widow. She is "a wife who wouldn't cook and couldn't manage. So what if she was beautiful? His [Sonny's] mother had told him. What good was it to have a wife that other men wanted?"[18] To have what other people want is to invite the *malocchio*, or evil eye, and, thus, threaten one's well-being.

The other man, besides Sonny, who wants this woman happens to be Nicky Mole, who "did not need women. He would have them if he wanted, but he didn't. From when he was a young man, in the Bassi' of Naples, he didn't. What he wanted was money and the power that went with it."[19] Once Nicky has the power and the money, he still doesn't fall for anyone: "Nicky Mole was too busy for women and the chaos they caused. He saw the men around him with wives and children and mistresses. It weakened them, he thought. It exposed them."[20] When Carolina takes a job cleaning Nicky's office, he "thought she was cheap-looking. Her mouth was too red and her hair was too black. A 'strega,' he thought."[21] A *strega* is a witch. And it turns out that Carolina bewitches Nicky, not with incantations, like Donna Vecchio, but

with her looks. When she knows she has his attention, she stops cleaning and still expects to be paid. He is amazed that she "had no fear,
no respect. Brave men, important men, kissed his hand. This woman
took his money for nothing."[22] In no time she becomes his undercover
lover. Joey Dee knows all this, but he never says a word. He gains the
confidence of women like Carolina by listening, and he never tells others what he learns from them. Talk, in this society, is the province of
women like Joey Dee's mother, who "listened to stories and passed them
on."[23] Joey Dee is a man, and so doesn't talk and "didn't want to listen
to the stories."[24] However, it is the listening—not only to the stories of
the women, but also to their advice—that enables him to work toward
becoming a wise man. Joey also seeks women when he needs protection. Whenever he irritates his father, he runs first to his mother and
then to his father's sister who lives across the hallway.

When Joey Dee doesn't want to do something, or if he doesn't know
what to do, he takes to his bed, where "his mother brought his food
to him and tied a handkerchief soaked in alcohol around his head."[25]
When he finds out that Nicky Mole wants to see him, he runs to his
bedroom. He gets worried because he has no idea what Nicky knows.
Joey Dee runs to the women when he needs sanctuary. And while he
may think he is too old to be going to church, seen as the province
of women ("Sometimes, standing in the back of the church with the
bells ringing and the dollar candles going, Joey Dee believed"[26]), it is
this belief and the guidance of women that keep Joey from becoming a
wiseguy. But before he can make the right decision, he encounters the
top wiseguy.

Joey Dee eventually takes a job offered by Nicky, after meeting with
him and playing pinochle. A little later, Joey's friend Carmine, who is
connected to Nicky Mole, lets him know Nicky wants to see him again.
This time Nicky hires Joey to carry a package to the Magro widow, Carolina, and Joey finds himself attracted to her. The next time he is called
to the Mole's, he is asked to drive a car to pick up the widow. When his
father finds out that he has been hanging around the Mole's café, he
warns Joey not to go back there and tells him to return home from "that
other 'scucciande'," his aunt.[27] The word *scucciande* is a dialect form of
scocciante, which refers to something that is broken, bothersome, or
annoying. Joey Dee's father is frustrated by the women in his world and
claims that his wife ruined Joey "with her babying."[28] Joey listens to his
father and returns home.

When Josie compliments his mother, Joey responds, "Don't let's talk about mothers, Josie. You should shut your mouth when anybody talks about mothers."[29] Mothers in Italian-American male culture are not subjects for public discussion. Josie then runs off, crying, and we learn that Joey Dee actually has feelings: "When Joey Dee couldn't see her anymore, when she turned the corner onto Sullivan Street and she was gone from his view, he kicked the stoop, and if he could have, if it was allowed, Joey Dee would have cried."[30] In contrast to the male behavior in the neighborhood, Ermelino presents the women, a nondescript group who sit on stoops or park benches and serve as the critical conscience of the community. Like a chorus in a Greek play, they see all and, most importantly, they talk about what they see. The women, often referred to as *stregas* or witches by Carolina, create a force to which Carolina's behavior can be contrasted, as she acknowledges in a conversation with Joey Dee:

> "Listen, you think all this is easy for me, that I have no feelings?
> I've got a daughter to raise alone. I've got the 'stregas' on the
> park bench waiting to take out my eyes. They've been waiting
> for me all my life … . There's only one way to do things, from
> the beginning to the end, when Gambino lays you out in a box
> you can't afford. Well let me tell you, I'm not like the rest of
> them. I don't belong here. I never belonged here."[31]

This sense of not belonging is something that begins to develop in Joey. The first clue is that he keeps wishing he could be in Las Vegas. Then Joey begins to understand just what women represent in life and how foreign it is for them to live with such feelings inside male-dominated Little Italy. This happens as Joey begins to notice that he is having feelings, especially for Josie. But while he may be feeling something, he certainly does not understand what those feelings mean.[32]

One day, while searching for Josie, he finds Carolina at home; she does not let him go, and they smoke cigarettes together. She asks him if he takes out her daughter and how he got connected to Nicky Mole. Joey "wanted to tell her that he didn't know and he wished it would stop. He loved her daughter, but he loved her too, in some awful way. And did she know that Nicky Mole had killed her husband?"[33] Joey's confusion leads him to keep silent. Carolina challenges this silence one day when Joey is driving her to see Nicky Mole. " 'You're always so quiet …. You know,' she said, 'you're too sensitive. It won't get you anywhere, believe me. You should grow up. You'll never make it.' "[34] What Carolina means is that Joey needs to become more like the men in the neighborhood if he is to survive there. He cannot let his feelings get in the way of the things a man has to do. A little later, for a second time, he seeks the shelter of his mother's home: "Joey Dee went to bed Sunday night after his cousins left and stayed there. He need time to think. His mother fed him with soup and *pastina* and made plasters to put on his chest. He told her his head didn't hurt and that the alcohol rag made him dizzy, but she tied it around his forehead anyway." Interaction has confused the young man. In many ways, what he wanted, at least at the beginning of the novel, was to become a part of Mole's world. But what he once wanted seems to be slipping away without anything to replace it: "Joey Dee was so cool back then [when he first met Josie]. He had his crew, Mike, Bats, Carmine. They had followed him around back then, did everything he said. Now he was losing everything and going nowhere fast."[35] This illustrates the reasoning that leads Nicky Mole to avoid emotional relationships; a wiseguy cannot afford to be vulnerable in any way.

This time, Joey Dee actually begins to feel sick from staying in bed. His mother diagnoses it as *Mala fattura, malocchio*, saying that someone has given him the evil eye. She decides she is going to call Rosina Scarpacci, the woman who has taken over after Donna Vecchio's death. Joey doesn't want his mother to call her because he is afraid of what his father would think:

> "Ma, the old man hates this stuff. He hates Rosina Scarpacci. 'That witch,' he calls her. You got enemies in this building, Ma. You know who I mean." He moved his head in the direction of Aunt Julia's apartment. "She'd love to get something on you. You know she can't, you're too good, but she'd love to tell the old man you had Rosina Scarpacci up here."[36]

Joey's father might represent a form of oppression, but he is nevertheless representative of the traditional masculinity that Joey is trying desperately to fit into. Men control the objects in their world and do not succumb to spiritual yearnings. Joey sees the weakness of those who are not men, and comes to see that those who are controlled by others are like the pigeons he takes care of, the ones Vito was tending when he witnessed the Magro murder: "Pigeons, Joey Dee thought. We're all pigeons."[37]

These pigeons become an interesting metaphor when one considers the connotation of the word *piccione* in Italian. Similarly to the English word "bird" or the American word "chick," *piccione* can refer to a woman and sometimes is used to refer to the vagina. Carolina has told her daughter Josie a story about how, when a woman wanted her husband to think she was a virgin, she would sneak a dead pigeon into bed with her and squeeze the blood onto the sheets. The pigeon is a recurring symbol throughout the novel, most often in relation to women, but always to those who are controlled by forces outside themselves. For example, Rosina Scarpacci finds "a pigeon sitting on the footboard of her mahogany double bed ... . This was the worst of omens for Rosina Scarpacci who believed in omens. She made her living conjuring spells. Rosina Scarpacci was not Donna Vecchio, but she was still a woman of power."[38] It turns out to be one of Joey's pigeons, and his father demands that he get rid of them. Joey goes on to wonder "if women would always ruin his life."[39]

Eventually Joey begins going up on the roof to get away from his problems when he realizes that taking to his bed as an "act was getting tired."[40] The roof is a place where he begins to imagine possibilities beyond his neighborhood. While he thinks "the roof was not the refuge it had been, the place he could escape the life that was preordained for someone like him,"[41] he does start seeing the horizon, and it is this horizon that represents his ability to imagine beyond the boundaries and limits of his neighborhood. Here, where he has not been since Sonny Magro's death, he finds comfort in flying the birds as he used to. Vito too comes to the roof to be with the pigeons, and he begins talking to the pigeons about how he witnessed the Magro killing. One day he is overheard by Nicky Mole's men. When the news is brought to Mole, Benny Scar asks him if they need to kill Vito. " 'No,' Nicky Mole said. 'Not that. I made a promise to the priest. I swore to God—no innocents. They ain't responsible' ... . Benny Scar knew that when Nicky Mole talked about God or his mother, there was nothing to say. Even the boss had bosses."[42]

In the world of these Italian-American men, actions, not words, communicate their meaning to others. Nicky Mole is a man of few words, and many of the words he does speak are directed to his pet parrot. " 'In the old country,' he told the parrot, 'it was easier to be a man of honor. It was clearer how men should behave.' He petted Santino's beak. 'A black calf, its legs cut off, anyone could understand that,' he said. 'Red and black, blood and mourning, things made sense. Here ... it's different.' "[43] Such signs are the result of actions and not words.

Another symbol of Joey Dee's separation from the men in his community is his penchant for lighting candles in church. Joey Dee no longer sees his bed in his parents' home as a refuge, but he still finds solace in going to church and lighting candles, always "in threes."[44] One day when he goes to church, he finds that the only place where there are three unlit candles in a row is in front of Saint Lucy:

> He never paid much attention to Saint Lucy, a girl's saint, he thought, but he looked at her differently today, at the way she held the brown glass eyes out to him on a plate. Maybe she had saved these three candles for him to light, so he would notice her. Joey Dee lit the three candles and asked Saint Lucy to take care of things, to take care of Vito Santero. She should have a special feeling for Vito Santero, Joey Dee told Saint Lucy. She was the patron saint of eyes and Vito Santero had a messed-up eye.[45]

Later he goes into the church:

> ... full of smoke and flowers ... . A magic show, Joey Dee thought, then checked himself. He didn't like to tempt fate with disrespect. He asked Saint Lucy to intercede for him. He was getting to like her. Chances were good, he thought, that she would come through for him. She was the patron saint of eyes and not much else, and he was giving her all his attention. Joey Dee was partial to the underdog.[46]

The visit to the statue of Saint Lucy marks a turn in Joey Dee's life as he moves away from the traditional dependence on masculine power and toward a new understanding of the power of women. In contrast, Ermelino presents Nicky Mole outside his café as the procession of the feast of Saint Anthony passes by: "Nicky Mole's affection lay not with the underdog but with the man of power, the one carried on the shoulders of other men."[47] Thus, the two powers, male and female, face off and prepare for a showdown. Joey Dee then takes sides with the women, the underdogs, in defiance of the successful and powerful men.

His newfound alliance with the power of women comes alive even in his sleep, as:

he dreams now of the desert, driving in a car with the top down in the desert. The car was always a Cadillac. It was always blue … baby blue, sky blue, powder blue, blue blue. The desert was always in bloom, like in the picture Mikey Bats had shown him in Rocky's barbershop of the naked girl in boots and a cowboy hat. Mikey Bats had pointed to the girl, but Joey Dee had seen the desert and the flowers on the cactus, flowers as big as the breasts of the girl.[48]

The blue that Joey dreams is a color often associated with the Virgin Mary and represents both nobility and the sky. This indirect reference continues when, during the procession for the feast of Saint Anthony, Carolina tells how she used to pin Donna Vecchio's money onto the cloth draping the statue. Joey watches mother and daughter talking and thinks, "They were the dark world of women, lit only by the moon … now she was with her mother and Joey Dee stood alone. 'Stregas,' the ladies said, watching them. They saw everything. They saw Josie Magro not as a girl anymore but as a woman, and their sympathy for her was gone."[49] The moon, in ancient times, was associated with Diana, virgin goddess of the hunt and the woodlands, and that symbol continued to be associated by Catholics with the Virgin Mary. Joey sees now that there is a world of women in which there are untold powers unavailable to him.

When Carmine sees Joey, he tells Joey the guys are looking for him: " 'I don't know, Joey. I don't ask questions. I keep telling you that, but you don't want to hear.' "[50] As long as questions aren't asked, there are no challenges to the status quo of local power. Joey feels that to protect Vito, he needs to take his friend upstate to the motherhouse of the nuns who serve in Little Italy. In confession, he asks the priest about Vito and the local boys; he tries to get Vito to leave and go away to a convent where he will be safe. But this does not happen, and when the bosses find out that Vito witnessed Magro's murder, they silence him. When Joey and Josie go up to the roof to have sex, they find the pigeon coops broken and the rooftop strewn with dead birds. Joey realizes the blood the must be Vito's. He goes to Vito's house and finds that the gangsters have cut out Vito's tongue. Once Joey helps Vito, he goes to church and stays for four masses. "He wouldn't look at Saint Lucy. He thought he would sit there until he was an old man."[51] Joey believes that Saint Lucy failed him, but he still finds comfort in being in the church. He then takes Vito upstate to the convent, where the sisters "almost never talked."[52] As for himself, he returns home and seeks the protection of his mother. "Joey Dee planned to go up to the house and tell his mother he didn't want to see anybody. He knew she would protect him from his father and from the outside."[53] Joey has come to understand the power his mother has to protect him and the power men like his father have to harm him.

Joey decides to confront the men when Carmine tells him he is being hunted. Joey meets the Mole's right-hand man, Benny Scar, who tells him, " 'You're a good kid, but you shouldn't be here … . You should leave the neighborhood is what I'm telling you. Go away for a while. We ain't just pushing you out, though. We want to help you get started someplace. We was thinking of Vegas. Good-looking young kid like you would love it out there. Plenty of action, beautiful girls.' "[54] Their notion of eliminating the possibility of Joey's going to the police is to take care of him and, in a sense, bring him under their control. They send him to see their contact, Fortunata, at the Desert Mirage Hotel. He wants to take Josie with him. When he goes to pick her up, her mother tells him to forget about her daughter because she knows they are not right for each other. Then she has sex with Joey. By sleeping with Nicky's girlfriend, Joey puts the horns on Nicky, turning the Mole into a *cornuto*. In Italian culture, sleeping with a man's wife is a way of getting even with the man for some wrong. Joey is able to fulfill the fantasy that began when he first saw Carolina's red lips and, in his own way, get even for Nicky's harming Vito.

The novel concludes with an epilogue in which Carolina marries Nicky Mole, and Josie is adopted by Nicky Mole and rebaptized with Nicky's last name. Joey Dee learns this when he runs into his old friend, Mikey Bats, outside a Vegas hotel. Mikey tells him that their friend, Carmine, is marrying Nicky Mole's daughter, Josie, and that both Mikey and Carmine now work for Nicky Mole; they have become wiseguys. Joey Dee, on his way to becoming a wise man, is driving a red Cadillac, not the blue one he had always wanted. There is no explanation given for this, but the color red symbolizes the spilled blood that Joey keeps quiet about and, perhaps, also the passion and suffering Joey has endured in becoming a man. The novel ends with Joey Dee driving "far out into the desert. It was in bloom and the cactuses were covered with flowers," [55] just as a traditional western film ends with a cowboy riding off into the sunset. Ultimately he realizes that nothing back home has changed. The novel ends with Josie's and Carmine's wedding, and the neighborhood goes on as though nothing had happened.

So what does Joey Dee get wise to? In a twist on the typical story of boy meets gangster, boy becomes gangster, Ermelino describes a boy who comes to realize that the power of women is quite different from that of the typical Italian-American male and, that in order to live with himself, he must take what he has learned from the women and leave that male-dominated world. Joey has learned that traditional masculinity is constrictive and dangerous.

What the new world he has entered holds in store for a sensitive, wise man in the making is something we can only imagine, yet Ermelino's tale helps us to see that there must be possibilities for the wiseguy to become a wise man.

LOUISA ERMELINO'S *THE BLACK MADONNA* (2001)

In her second novel, *The Black Madonna,* Ermelino explores the power that women have through one of the oldest symbols of female power, the Madonna. The book is set in New York's Greenwich Village. Ermelino tells the story of three mamma's boys through their mothers and captures the claustrophobic, in-your-face reality of what life in Little Italy used to be. Although she does not deal with gangsters per se, the work she does in this novel sets up the twist that she will later play on the gangster figure in her third novel.

The figure of the Black Madonna has a remarkable history that Ermelino does not retell, but it helps to understand its symbolic function in the novel. Lucia Chiavola Birnbaum, in her two books, *Black Madonnas: Feminism, Religion and Politics in Italy* (2000) and *Dark Mother: African Origins and Godmothers* (2002), theorizes the creation of and subsequent attempts to erase early mother-centered cultures around the world, and speculates on survivals in submerged cultures and ritual. Birnbaum claims that the first object of veneration for *Homo sapiens* was a dark mother figure that goes back more than one hundred thousand years. The dark mother's presence can be identified later on in all continents and all religions. Birnbaum traces the evolution of the prehistoric goddess from the dark mother to the camouflaged and often whitened versions that appear not only in churches, but also in points of political uprising throughout the world. She considers Black Madonnas as "a metaphor for a memory of the time when the earth was believed to be the body of a woman and all creatures were equal."[56]

She offers this to explain why there are so many Madonnas in Italian, African, and Asian cultures, and she offers a way of connecting them all into a multicultural mosaic that reflects a basic unity beneath the superficial diversity of the world. By offering explanations of how and why female figures of veneration were replaced with males, she creates new interpretations of such popular cultural mainstays as Santa Claus, who entered European cultural imagination through San Nicola, who, as legends have it, destroyed the temple of Artemis (an analogue of the Roman goddess Diana) because it was pagan. Artemis used to be celebrated on December 6, now the feast of San Nicola. Birnbaum argues that, in essence, the Black Madonna is the Christian version of the ancient earth goddess.

Ermelino's *The Black Madonna* reveals the power that three women have in shaping their sons. The first mother introduced is Teresa Sabbatini. Her story is set in 1948, a time when Italian immigrants earned their American citizenship through serving in World War II. Teresa's husband is a sailor who travels the world, but brings back nothing for his family and inspires rumors in the neighborhood whenever he returns. Their son Nicky loses the use of his legs after a fall. Teresa turns to the Black Madonna of Viggiano, patroness of her ancestral home, for comfort, and the miracles begin.

The second story concerns Magdalena, stepmother to Salvatore, whose real mother dies in childbirth along with his twin. Magdalena is a *strega* from the old country. Sal's father is matched with her when he visits his hometown. Set in 1936, this section traces the power of women through the turbulent time when fascism suppressed any attempt by women to assert power over their own lives and families.

The final section of the novel takes place in 1968, a time of social uprising in the United States, and recounts the story of Antoinette, who gave birth to the neighborhood's largest baby, nicknamed "Jumbo." When Jumbo finally finds love, he needs all the help of his friends to keep his mother from destroying his life.

The Black Madonna features the dark force at work in the mothers as they use their sons defensively, to protect themselves from men who have abandoned them for other lovers and other lives. Through these three mothers, Ermelino connects with the powers of the ancient earth mother known in Greek mythology as Demeter and in Catholicism as the Madonna.

LOUISA ERMELINO'S *THE SISTERS MALLONE:*
UNA STORIA DI FAMIGLIA (2002)

Although *The Black Madonna* contains no significant gangster figures, it is important as a stepping-stone to Ermelino's third novel, *The Sisters Mallone: Una Storia di Famiglia*, in which she writes about male and female gangster figures. Ermelino's concentration on the mother–son relationship returns to an important dynamic introduced by Puzo in *The Fortunate Pilgrim* and later abandoned by him. In *The Sisters Mallone,* Ermelino travels deep into Italian-American culture through the story of three sisters whose immigrant grandfather, born Malloni, finds himself surrounded by the Irish in New York City and does what he can to fit in, even changing his name to Mallone. But as the surface hides the dangers of the deep, these Irish-looking girls are Italian through and through, and capable of heroic acts.

Ermelino is a master at turning the culture of Italian America into contemporary folklore, and the novel is a wonderful old neighborhood tale. The ladies of the St. Ann Society of Mothers form the book's Greek chorus and serve as the community's conscience: "Tragedy was their entertainment. If they weren't mourning its presence, they were awaiting its arrival."[57] Ermelino is hilariously serious in her criticism of the male world of gangsters and mamma's boys, and extremely adept in her dramatization of the natural power of women. Some American audiences are not that familiar with real Italian women who know how to take care of themselves and each other. Led by Anona, their grandmother who raised them when most of the rest of their family died in the great Spanish influenza epidemic of 1918, the sisters learn that men are useful, but not necessary. Anona, an immigrant from the fictional village of Bocca al Lupo near Naples, teaches them to get what they need by giving as little as they can. Helen, Mary, and Gracie all grow up in the Irish-controlled Hell's Kitchen of the 1920s and 1930s. Anona is a devotee of Saint Rita, whose domain of responsibility embraces abuse victims, the lonely, the sterile, the infertile, difficult marriages, forgotten causes, impossible causes, lost causes, parenthood, sick people, widows, and wounds.[58]

Of the two older girls, "Mary was tough, but Helen was flint," and while Mary is the oldest, Helen is the boss.[59] Both take care of their baby sister, Gracie, who marries the pretty-faced mamma's boy Frankie, who doesn't stay home at night. Although there is no Italian-American gangster per se in this novel (in fact, the only gangster figure is Nick

"The Swede" Andersen), gangster behavior is apparent in the actions of Gracie's sisters. Helen hangs around with the boys in Buck O'Brian's clubhouse: "She even dressed like a boy in knickers and argyle knee socks,"[60] fooling many of the boys into thinking she was one of them and earning a job working for O'Brian as a lookout and runner. She even learns how to use a blackjack.[61] One night Helen doesn't come home; it turns out that Buck O'Brian's place was raided by the police and she was sent to Social Services. When Mary and Gracie go looking for her, they stop first at the police station and are told to return in a few days. During an argument with the police, Gracie is told by Anona to " 'Never tell nothing,' "[62] and so the lesson of silence so strongly associated with the male world and traditional *omertá* is shown also to be part of what makes a strong woman.

The one thing that these women do best is listen. Their ability to observe, listen, and process information soon enables them to get what they want without having to directly challenge the men in their world. After the police, their next stop is Buck O'Brian's, where the boys laugh at Mary for asking for help. During the confrontation, Mary spits on the floor at O'Brian's feet and then pulls Gracie out of the clubhouse. Mary pretends not to be afraid and says to her little sister, " 'How are you supposed to tell the good guys from the bad when they're all the same?' " to which Gracie replies, " 'Anona says all men are bad until you teach them different.' "[63] In the process of looking for her sister, Helen, Mary meets up with local gang leader Nick Andersen, whose connections help them find Helen. Nick also falls in love with Mary and begins to lavish gifts on the family.

When Mary and Helen find out that Gracie's husband is seeing another woman, a blond American called Doreen, they follow the two on a date, and then they knock Frankie out:

> Something hit the back of his head … hard. His knees buckled. An arm swung him around and a fist whacked into his mouth. Another punch closed his eye. He tasted blood and thought he heard a woman screaming. He thought it sounded like Doreen, and then he went down.[64]

The sisters employ a form of violence typically associated with gangsters. Frankie never finds out who hit him and assumes it was a man. Helen and Mary abduct Doreen and bring her to Anona's house for interrogation. Once they get the information they need, they force her to take a train out of town. The sisters joke about being tough: " 'We're born man-killers,' [Helen] liked to say, 'We get it from the old lady.' "[65]

Gracie's husband shows that he has not learned his lesson and sometime later he is found to be going out with another woman and even planning to leave town with her. Helen and Mary try to take control of the situation. The sisters discuss their plan in a bar. Nick Andersen, now Mary's husband, wants to know what they're talking about, so she tells him, " 'Nick, you don't wanna know. It's women's work.' "[66] Once again, the women use typical male expectations to disguise their intended, unladylike behavior.

The sisters finagle their way into getting hired on the docks, and one day they come to work dressed as men. What is interesting is that Frankie sees them, but he has no idea who they are:

> He saw the two little guys, the greaser brothers, walking together, coming toward the ship, separate from the pack of men. He couldn't see their faces because their heads were down, their pea caps pulled low against the rain. Christ, they were small. Imagine going through life with your nose in everybody's balls. If he didn't know better, he'd have thought they were girls.[67]

Of course, Frankie's stupidity and his arrogance go hand in hand, and he is soon hit in the back of the head again, and this time pushed so that he stumbles off the edge of the pier to drown. And so the Sisters Mallone get away with the perfect crime, enacting something that, because it has typically been done by men, is never attributed to them.

Even though Ermelino does not actually make the sisters gangsters, they do enact typical masculine behavior that in the world of the novel goes unseen because women are performing masculinity. The crimes enacted by the sisters are witnessed only by the reader, and so the sisters' performances of masculinity do not affect the world in the way that Judith Halberstam's take on female masculinity does (see chapter 2). Thus, Helen, who is marked as possibly bisexual, is not identified as a habitual performer of masculinity in the way a butch lesbian might be. However, what Ermelino brings to our attention in a more obvious way than Puzo does in *The Fortunate Pilgrim* is that it can natural for an Italian-American woman to perform masculinity when necessary. What is interesting is that the sisters do cross-dress when they create the "accident" that is actually the murder of Gracie's husband. The reader is not told what they are wearing during the earlier crime when they knock Frankie out and kidnap his girlfriend, but that they were not suspected suggests that they accomplished the act in a masculine manner. Disguise was mandatory for their murder of Frankie because women would stand out in the man's world of the docks. These women are not only disguised, they act so much like men that not a single man figures them out. The one who comes closest is their victim, but his way of seeing the world keeps him from uncovering them before they kill him. The violence performed by the sisters, while traditionally perceived as being primarily masculine, shows the difference between what we have come to think of as the normal Italian-American woman and what is presented as a highly abnormal representation via the sisters Mallone.

Josephine Gattuso Hendin's exploration of women and violence helps explicate the violence perpetrated by the Mallone sisters. In *Heartbreakers*, Hendin writes that violence enacted by women defies the metaphor of the woman as helpless victim and forces people to envision women outside the usual construct of poststructuralist theory, which she argues is fundamentally antifeminist. Hendin sees the violent women of fiction as;

> masters of logic games and invention, using narrative skill to express their own take on violent action and its meanings. They not only exploit their lives as women and over acts of violence to affirm the immediacy of their agency, but also use their verbal skill to break out of the prison house of linguistic theories of the 'feminine.' They hurl a powerful, experiential art against all their expressive strength.[68]

Her work helps make sense of the role violent women have played and continue to play in the world. Through a carefully constructed and well-reasoned argument, she explains why people should pay attention to real and imagined violent women. Not doing so, in the past, was a way to avoid drawing attention to what could be construed as "politically bad for women."[69] Too often the violence of women, when it has been seen, has been explained away as maladjusted behavior, a woman's acting like a man. Hendin successfully argues that while new developments in violence studies may have improved our ability to realize the impact violence has on contemporary American society, they have not given us "a substantially new way of looking at the role of violent women" sustaining "the silence surrounding the subject."[70] Hendin's take on women's violence helps us see the performance of masculinity by the sisters Mallone as not just an imitation of male behavior, but something that is fundamentally female.

The sisters have learned how to be women from their Anona, who told them the story of how she was able to check her husband's violence by waiting for him to fall asleep, and then hitting him between his closed eyes with a broom handle. When he awoke she told him, " 'The next time, I put a stake through your heart.' " She goes on to tell the girls, " 'Nonno learned his lesson. You gotta make them know what they can do and what they can't. You gotta let them know right from the start.' "[71] Anona is constantly checking the girls when they move too close to the stereotype of the giddy, helpless female. Her sense of femininity encompasses the power typically reserved for males. The violence performed by these Italian-American women falls into the category that Hendin calls "retaliatory violence," which she writes "is most clearly dramatized in intimacy between lovers, in friendship and families. It reverses the interactions between men and women in which women are conventionally victims and involves imposing an alternative value system on apparent deformations of relationships and behavior."[72]

What Anona teaches the girls is not a defensive strategy, or what to do after a man hits them, but an offensive strategy, what to do to keep a man from even thinking about hitting them. What is interesting about the sisters' violence is that it is not defensive; it is not even payback for violence committed against another. The murder of Gracie's husband is retribution for the way he psychologically abused his wife. Helen and Mary decide that this man is no good for their sister. He did not learn his lesson, as Nonno did, and so he must be erased. That he dies on the job entitles Gracie to an insurance settlement, similar to the one that has kept Helen financially independent after her own husband was killed by a beer truck. Not much was made of the fact that her husband was drunk, but some people thought she might have arranged it so he would meet the fated truck while he was inebriated. The older sisters take it upon themselves to decide what is best for their little sister and, thus, determine the fate of her husband. Ultimately, this retaliatory violence "enacts fantasies not only of revenge and power, but of control over one's life and life story."[73] The sisters Mallone slip into and out of male gangster behavior in order to take control of their own lives and the lives of those they love.

No one in their world would even suspect that a woman was capable of committing such a violent and perfect crime.

Ermelino has taken the wisdom that kept Joey Dee from becoming a gangster, mixed it with some of the female power that comes from the Black Madonna, and filtered it through the likes of Saint Rita and Anona to reinvent the masculine gangster performance through the actions of women. The sisters Mallone are much stronger than any of the gangster women in the other works surveyed here because they appropriate traditionally male behaviors rather than limiting themselves to the ways a woman is traditionally expected to behave. Ultimately, Ermelino's reinvention of the gangster through female characters opens up possibilities for the trope to serve Italian-American storytellers in new ways.

7

THE GANGSTER AS PUBLIC INTELLECTUAL:
ANTHONY VALERIO AND DON DELILLO

In this chapter the novels of Anthony Valerio and Don DeLillo are sites for exploring the creation of "the gangster of the intellect." Both these writers exploit the popularity of the gangster as a symbol in order to show new directions in intellectual culture. Tied to their times, both question the gangster stereotypes that have evolved and changed as the power culture of the 1980s evolved into the more introspective culture of the 1990s. Valerio, more than DeLillo, attaches great significance to the gangster, a figure in which he fashions a turning point away from the romanticized wiseguy of the past and toward new ways of seeing Italian-American masculinity.

The critic George Guida has picked up on Valerio's theme of renewing Italian-American masculine identity and calls Valerio a "renovator." Valerio, he writes, "begins by revising the stereotypes of Italian-American men inscribed in *The Godfather*."[1] These stereotypes include the sexual predator represented by the character Sonny Corleone, the "criminal brute" represented by Luca Brasi, and the archetypal patriarch represented by the Don. Guida points to Valerio's work, but he stops short of analyzing just what it is that Valerio has created. Little if anything has been written about DeLillo's use of the gangster figure, especially in his novel *Underworld* (1997). Both Valerio and DeLillo invest the gangster figure with a human sensibility quite like that normally attributed to the artist, and by doing so they invite us to see the gangster from the inside out, as a sort of Everyman.

GANGSTERS MAKE ME LAUGH: THE NEW GANGSTERS OF ANTHONY VALERIO

In *Lefty and the Button Men* (2000), originally published as *Conversation with Johnny* (1997), Valerio presents a sometimes sardonic and always entertaining look at crime and culture. He attempts a literary hit on two stereotypes that have plagued Italian Americans: the gangster and the lover. Although he does not eliminate them, he certainly paralyzes both of them long enough to show that "the cult of *The Godfather* is over." The seed of *Lefty and the Button Men* is a short story Valerio published in 1990, in the first issue of *Voices in Italian Americana*. "The Last Godfather," which appears as a chapter in *Lefty*, sounds the death knell for the gangster as a representative of Italian America and erects the Italian-American writer as a hero in its place. *Lefty* wraps that story in a context that leaps the ghetto boundaries of Italian-American storytelling.

Each chapter of the novel reads like a good stand-up comedy routine. Well timed, each can stand on its own, but they all combine to create a novel that comes together only at the end when the characters merge into another story. The novel is about the balance that must be created between history and imagination so that a culture's history can be used to create art. This is what Valerio achieves in this slightly romantic parable about the relationship between love and friendship. *Lefty and the Button Men* could well be the antidote to the nearly four-decade-long spell cast on Italian Americans by Puzo's *The Godfather*. Valerio's reinvention of the gangster examines three characters placed in the trajectory of wiseguy to wise man: the gangster Johnny, the writer Nicholas, and the professor Ted Nardack, only one of whom is given a surname.

In *Lefty*, Nicholas, whose family has nicknamed him Mootzie, "after mozzarella itself,"[2] is a writer as obsessed with the women he has loved as he is with the stories he must tell. When his latest affair begins to wilt, he decides it's time to get some advice from an old neighborhood buddy who has risen to the position of don.

The gangster character in this novel is called Johnny, bringing to mind the powerful image of John Gotti, and he serves as a confidant to Nick, but also as a straight man off whom Nick plays in order to present his take on the changes going on both in himself and in Italian-American masculinity in general. Valerio writes explicitly about "sexual escapades" rather than reinforcing the "lover/oversexed male" stereotype. Nicholas wants to become an ordinary man and seeks advice on how to stop being a lover. Having sacrificed family for women and writing, Nicholas comes to Johnny, whose overextended family includes the entire Bensonhurst neighborhood, for advice on how to straighten out his life. Over the course of the novel, the two hold a number of dialogues. During the conversations, in which Nicholas confesses the intimate details of his sexual escapades, Nicholas and Johnny pose challenges to each other: Johnny can give Nicholas money and can make him maître d' at a famous restaurant, but it remains unclear whether Johnny can give him what he really needs, such as advice on creating a family or a retirement home for Italian-American writers. Nicholas gives a reading of his story "The Last Godfather" in Johnny's home, and this presents Johnny with a literary model for an honorable way out of his life of crime.

Against Johnny, the pure criminal, and Nicholas, the cultural pioneer, Valerio introduces Ted Nardack, the "Kid Professor," whose name hides his Italian origins and whose behavior in public mocks his true love: his blonde, big-breasted American wife. Nardack, a professor and critic of literature, serves as a foil to both Nicholas the writer/lover and Johnny the gangster. The Kid Professor is a public storyteller of the gangster past through his lectures, readings, and teaching. He is also a private lover who makes fun of his wife in public to elevate his own intellectual work; after all, how can a man who professes love be taken seriously as an intellectual? A strange tension develops between the Kid Professor and Nicholas when the scholarly attention the Kid gives to Italian Americans in crime shadows the development of the very Italian-American culture he is championing. Nicholas asks Johnny to take the Kid aside and steer him straight, away from identifying with crime and toward the development of culture; he wants Johnny to deliver the message that: " 'For the time being, we have to tolerate our crime and our culture, but your job is to promote the culture, not the crime.' "[3] As the Kid Professor needs Nicholas to claim a culture, Nicholas needs the Kid Professor's academic skills to engrave his contribution on the larger society's cultural memory. He needs Nardack's literary history and criticism so that his own writing will become a part of the public record. But he can't allow the Professor to push his work in one breath and tell stories about his own petty criminal exploits in the next.

The novel opens with the narrator, Nicholas, telling about his new girlfriend, a married woman writer he has nicknamed Lefty. She drives him so crazy that he decides he must consult an old friend, the neighborhood don, for advice. Nicholas arrives very carefully, consciously revealing no danger; he's wearing a tight suit so bodyguards can see there are no threatening bulges, and both hands carry gifts—a panettone in one and fresh mozzarella in the other. He wears a smile so that they will realize he has "come on pleasant matters, family matters."[4] Johnny is introduced to the reader as he opens the door for Nicholas, looking "splendid in a green Banlon shirt and yellow cardigan."[5] When Nicholas sees his hairline, he thinks of a barber and that leads him to think of Albert Anastasia, the famous gangster who was gunned down in a barber's chair.

By invoking a legendary American gangster, Valerio invites the reader to compare both Johnny and Nick to the gangster. But when he shifts into the interaction between Johnny and Nick, he shows, through both the characters' actions and the narrator's diction, that these men are moving in a completely different direction than the gangsters of yesterday did. When Nick and Johnny meet, their "first shared look is hard, wildly physical, at the level of the coglioni—this is how Italian men know they are men. Light from our hearts shines up to our eyes when we are with our mothers and our children, and sometimes, after giving them a hard time, our women."[6] Valerio digs deep to find what it is that enables Italian men to feel enough to embrace each other physically in a way that many cultures, especially the traditional American male culture, frown on.

Nick and Johnny are about the same age, but Nick is returning like a kind of prodigal son. He defers to Johnny physically and verbally. He admits that he's been away "from my own" for a long time. They begin their discussion with talk about the past and how a man called Ice, a gangster from the Genovese family "with literary connections,"[7] got Nick a job at the *Police Gazette*, where Nick soon got fired. Nick takes a more dominant stance toward Johnny when Johnny offers him coffee in Italian. The writer orders Johnny to speak English because " 'This is America,' "[8] a gesture that suggests that Johnny still may be strongly connected to the Old World—if not to Italy, then at least the old world of the neighborhood.

Nick tells Johnny that he decided to visit after seeing Johnny's eyes on the cover of *The New York Times Magazine*: " 'I knew they could see into everything, even into my subconscious, and they cleansed it of its penchant for debunking my own, for creating the beautiful lie. Rather than the stereotype, I opted for the beautiful lie. Now I want the truth—what went wrong, Johnny, what went wrong with me?' "[9] The "beautiful lie," which evokes Dante's reference to *The Divine Comedy* as *una bella mezogna*, suggests Dante as a model for Nick to emulate as he overcomes his failure as a lover and moves toward becoming a wise man. Nick then launches into a monologue about how he has become a lover and recounts his past relationships: with his first wife, a Florentine girl; his next love, an Argentinean woman; and now an American Jew, the younger married woman he calls Lefty. Nick is nothing if not passionate and compares himself to his Jewish friend Jacob, Lefty's husband, who has no passion for his own wife. This juxtaposition between the passion of love, at the center of Dante's search for truth and Paradise, and the beautiful lie, or the inability of man to construct truth (being limited to signs pointing toward truth), becomes the focal point of Valerio's reinvention of the Italian-American gangster figure as something that can move a man beyond the adolescence-bound wiseguy and toward becoming the wise man.

The journey is difficult because Nick has to learn to move beyond his traditional ways of reading the world first as a man of the gangster culture. When, after a sexual encounter, Lefty says to Nick, " 'You're my button. You're my button man,' "[10] Nick thinks she is referring to a gang boss's henchman, sometimes referred to as "a torpedo, a shooter."[11] Actually, she is referring to his ability to help her achieve orgasm; the button is her clitoris. To Nick, the button is the connection of a soldier to his gangster boss, and so he is unable to read her figurative use of the word; he even confesses that he's "never killed anyone" nor does he "know certain personages who could have somebody hit."[12] He figures that "She thinks I'm her own private assassin … . I'm willing to murder out of love for her, she believes."[13] His love for her is so strong that he cannot see the metaphor in her use of the term "button," so he takes it quite literally. Eventually he understands what she's saying after she raises four fingers indicating that she is counting her orgasms: " 'You've pressed my button four times. You're my button man.' "[14]

It is through conversations such as this—which are really Nick's monologues about the conversations he and Lefty have as well as most of what happens with Johnny—that Nick formulates and responds to problems of masculinity. One of those problems is that Italian-American men are perceived as being stupid. This notion of being the buffoon, which is constantly addressed by contemporary Italian-American activists, is, according to Nick, something that Italian-American men create to serve a particular purpose: "You and me know that sometimes we Italian men feign that we're slow on the uptake. Especially with family and our women we pretend we're idiots, clinical morons, all for the purpose of eliciting kindness, gentleness. But we're really always a step ahead, aren't we? Fast on all takes—up, down, sidewise, inside-out."[15] Here Nick is referring to a version of cutting a figure, or *fare figura*, noted in earlier chapters. This version is practiced by men like Detective Colombo in the *Colombo* television series, who traps his suspects by making them think he's a bumbling idiot. But placed in the context of Valerio's novel, it appears to be more an excuse than an explanation, and one that enables Nick to avoid dealing with the fact that sometimes he's not as intelligent as he thinks he is.

During their conversation, when Nick presents a metaphysical problem to Johnny, the gangster usually responds physically. For example, when Nick tells Johnny he wants to "make a home with a woman I love,"[16] and then asks Johnny what can he do, Johnny reaches into his pocket and hands him a wad of money. When Nick refuses the money, Johnny tells him he needs a job, and after a quick phone call gets him a job as maître d' at the Club Elegante. As the don, Johnny knows that a man without a job is no man at all. But Nick doesn't want a job. He wants advice; he wants Johnny to tell him what needs to be done; he wants Johnny to straighten him out psychologically. When Nick presents Johnny with one of his physical problems, Johnny doesn't respond. An example of this is Nick's bout of stress impotence. In a chapter entitled "The Paramour," we learn that Nick needs to take a pill before having sex in order to maintain an erection. Nick had gone to a doctor to determine why his penis no longer could "fill up with bone."[17] The doctor diagnosed stress impotence and prescribed Xanax. Nick sees the Xanax as a warrior in his battle to maintain his manhood:

> Xanax, the Sicilian champion come to fight for the Greeks, steps out from the ranks, and with a booming voice heard all around the countryside calls out the Trojan champion.

"Stressimpotence! Stressimpotence! Let's you and me settle this disputed with hand-to-hand combat. Winner take all!"[18]

He describes the encounter as a battle, a typical way for traditional men to gain honor. The battle recalls the mythic Trojan War and alludes to the way men fight over the possession of other humans, especially women. To Nick, a man is one who can conjure an erection and maintain it. In the next chapter, "Song of the Castrato," Nick tells of the non-man. Lefty has told him that he speaks the way Sinatra sings, but that "she doesn't hear me talk about her, doesn't hear my mellifluous baritone transform to a castrato, an impassioned castrato who, after he sings his aria of unrequited love, is so overwrought that all that remains to him are tears in his eyes, pain in his heart, utter exhaustion."[19] After telling this, Nick imagines that Johnny will want to meet Lefty, but then Nick realizes that Lefty would only complicate his relationship with Johnny because she won't be passive and will challenge Johnny's authority. He imagines that if he brought her to meet Johnny and she didn't like him, she would "sit demurely in her thigh-length, leopard-skin skirt and halter cut at the midriff, black-stockinged legs crossed, an attentive, intelligent, unreadable look on her face, which for an Italian male is worse than a show of hostility."[20] This would then cause friction, if not outright hostility, between the two friends. Nick imagines he will have to start fumbling around for excuses for why Lefty cannot make such a meeting—she is under pressure from promoting her new book, or she has a bad case of PMS. He decides it's better not to have the two get together after all.

The problem of attraction is addressed in a chapter entitled "Animal Magnetism." Here Nick claims that the Italian-American man has a natural way of attracting beautiful women. He refers to the attraction of Marilyn Monroe to Joe DiMaggio and Ava Gardner to Frank Sinatra, and explains that: "Especially, non-Italian women are drawn to the animal in us."[21] Then he refers to "Jake the Bull, Sly the Stallion. Each and every one of us is a fox. But the winds may be changing. Stallone has a script on his desk about the life of Giacomo Puccini."[22] Nick goes on to describe himself having the balls of an elephant, the wild fury of a rodeo bull, and the friskiness of a chimpanzee.

The discussion between Nick and Johnny does little but replay the same old problem for the stereotypical Italian-American man, that of being either the macho lover or the macho gangster. The next chapter, "Lesson on Paradise Island," introduces what could be read as a rough prototype for the future of Italian-American masculinity. Nick brings up another subject with Johnny that has been bothering him for a while—the Italian Kid Professor. Ted Nardack, originally Teodoro Nardacci, is a professor of literature " 'who's been mouthing off about his former life as a thief at literary functions and in the same breath puts down his wife like she's some bimbo or something.' "[23] He tells Johnny that the problem is that such acts seem ugly: " 'Para brutto, Johnny. It looks bad for you, me, all of us. Why, why do we put down our women in public? Do we feel we are not good enough for them?' "[24]

Nardack has received a grant from the Fiat Foundation of Italy to create an anthology of Italian writing. He gets invited to speak at colleges and has asked Nick for an autobiography that Nardack can include in his study. Nick is flattered but cautious, as he tells Johnny that the kid

> has this fascination with his father's line of work that could upset irrevocably the important work he's doing. The old man was a loan shark, independent, and was whacked in his apartment building, in the lobby. Expired in his son's arms. The kid naturally doesn't forget, but as he grows he's unable to separate his love for his father and his sorrow and the image of his father letting blood in his arms, from his father's line of work and his enemies. Everything gets mixed up, confused, which doesn't make for a genuine effort either in the life of a true criminal or in the life of a true cultural pioneer.[25]

What Nick doesn't know is that Nardack's position is typical of the culture hero, who in doing the wrong thing can actually save the very culture he is failing to be accepted into.

Nick goes on to explain that the Kid eventually became a thief who got caught and then was saved from the prison system by a connection. He started studying as a way of separating himself from that life. One of the books the Kid read was *The Godfather*: "Again he calls me: " 'That book and its ramifications were the turning point in my life' " ... as it enabled him to use the crime in his father's blood, his blood, and the blood in his culture as grist for the academic mill, and in his writing, too, as a tension, conflict. At the same time, in his real life, he begins to sort out images from their false, dangerous projections.' "[26] As Nardack starts making connections to the world outside his Little Italy, his progress is stymied by a professor who "berates him for being too emotional."[27] When the Kid calls Nick to complain, Nick offers the following advice: " 'Your sponsor's absolutely right. Hot on hot's no good, kid. When your subject is hot, you have to be cool.' "[28] Nardack follows Nick's advice and succeeds. In his work, he practices a cool detachment from the hot subject of his personal life. In essence, the Kid Professor has surrounded himself with the trappings of intellectual life. Reading, for him, becomes a way out of the streets and the academy becomes a refuge. Education is a viable path, Valerio suggests, by which the wiseguy can become the wise man.

Later Nick and Nardack are invited to read at a college in New Jersey. After the reading, in an Italian restaurant, the Kid Professor regales the diners with stories about crime and also "invokes an ugly picture of his wife, who is back home caring for their children. "One of those Midwestern types, dairy-fed, strong-backed, blonde. The Kid's actual words were 'a blonde with big tits.' "[29] Those at the table look to Nick "with startled, satisfied eyes, as if to say, 'You see, sooner or later the true Italian color comes out.' "[30] Nick, embarrassed by the events, asks Johnny if they could take this Kid down to Paradise Island and teach him a lesson, which would be spoken by Johnny:

> We understand about your father, that the image of his bullet-riddled body is all-powerful, that you feel profound pity and filial love and well-founded hatred and bitterness and shame— but all this can dwell inside side by side. Keep them the fuck that way. And your wife, it looks funny how you're talking about her … . Finally, remember, always remember, that you're a professor now and not a thief. For the time being, we have to tolerate our crime and our culture, but your job is to promote culture, not the crime." Here Johnny, I suggest you make a wide sweep of your free arm, taking in all of us and the trees and the ocean, and your face suddenly goes dead, and you say in your most ominous sweet tone: "Do this for me. Do this for Johnny, at least until the likes of us are gone. OK …? Good. Now let's all go to jai alai games

Nick, though keen on the problem that Nardack is having on his way to becoming a wise man, doesn't understand that in spite of a son's propensity to move beyond the father's way of being in the world, the father's way is the first model, and for Nardack, telling the stories of his family is a way for him to remain connected to his father's life. Nardack, in essence, is the messenger of the way to wise manhood. He is not the model. Through this character, Valerio has ingeniously signaled the end of the gangster as a way of being an Italian-American man.

Nick, obsessed with the way Ted characterizes his wife in public, tells Johnny that he'll take care of setting the Kid straight about love. He'll take him out for coffee and "in the guttural tone of a paesano," he'll say, " 'Ted, how exactly do you feel about your wife?' The truth will emerge, I'm certain, and then once we have it, we can prescribe the appropriate public posture."[32] As for their trip to the Bahamas, he wants Johnny to "plant the seed" of the subject, "in literature it's called simply a *plant*, an idea or character established and seemingly abandoned, the reader believes it's gone forever, but sometimes this idea or that character reappears and figures in a big way and the reader finds that it had etched itself in the memory and delights in the cohesiveness of it all."[33] The Kid Professor serves as Valerio's plant, and he returns at moments in the narrative that clarify the relationship of fear to love.

Nick believes that Nardack's feelings for his wife are "interrelated with his imaginary life of crime," and so he wants Johnny to put fear into Nardack by suggesting "that his wife's life will be in jeopardy if he doesn't shut up about the crime now."[34] Nick thinks the Kid will respond to this because "the sad truth is that, like love, only so much fear can be held at any given moment."[35] What happens in this exchange is the connection between the "gangster" and the "lover" becomes exposed. Fear and love are seen as key elements in the creation of the masculine identity, and how much of one feeling a man is able to show depends on his ability to hide the other feeling.

Nick goes on to admit that he's actually failed in love with Lefty after suggesting that they move to Key West, Florida, to live together, and she walks away. Later, when he tells her he'll love her until he dies, she tells him, " 'The word *love* is the biggest lie in the English language. But I'm crazy about you.' "[36] He is disappointed and invents his death scene in which his last words are " 'Please say you love me,' " and she doesn't respond. He smiles and turns his face to the wall and dies. She's intrigued by this scene and wants to use it in her new novel. When Nick says yes, if he too can use it, her response is no. Nick has revealed that he's actually addicted to love, and not to his lover. When he loses his own imaginative creation to the woman he loves, he begins to realize that his future as a lover is in as much doubt as is Ted's future as a gangster. His last conversation with Johnny focuses on how he wants to change from being a lover into being an ordinary man, in the way he treats women and in his general outlook on life. Johnny suggests that if Nick were more specific in his autobiography, perhaps he could " 'be convinced of the truth of the images and they'll stop haunting [you] and [you'll] be able to view life in all of its complexities, not just though a kaleidoscope of love.' "[37]

The future of the Italian-American gangster will not be how the figure is replicated in reality, but how it will be mythologized in story. Valerio presents Johnny the gangster and Nick the writer, hybridized through the Kid Professor, who is a little of both—a halfbreed who will become the culture hero. In fact, this is precisely what Nick himself becomes by the end of the novel; he takes his own and Johnny's advice (meant for Nardack) in the making of his own art, which results in the short story "The Last Godfather."

What Nick does is break the code of *omertà*: he talks to the world about what is going on inside himself, and that means inside his family as well. This happens in the chapter entitled "Autobiography," when the Kid Professor comments on Nick's autobiography. Nardack complains that what he has received from Nick isn't really autobiography because it is the story of Nick's parents meeting. Nick responds by telling Nardack that the world wants to know about Johnny, not Nick. Nardack says that while most of the world wants to know about Johnny, the rest, a sizable number, could be interested in Nick's life, especially because men like Johnny won't reveal what's going on inside themselves. Unlike the ideal gangster, the ideal writer will spill his guts. Nardack tells Nick, " 'You're one Sicilian who'll talk and write about anything and everything ... practically every word you've uttered and written breaks our sacred code of omertà.' "[38] The discussion continues and Nick ultimately asks the Kid to back off while he gives this autobiography writing further thought.

In the chapter entitled "Funny Writers," Nick is in the hospital after being hit by a car. Gay, a character Valerio uses to skewer Italian-American writers (meant to invoke Gay Talese), is visiting and walks into his room with a hatbox containing a black Stetson, which he gives to Nick, saying, " 'Now [you] could walk down the street and everybody would recognize [you].' "[39] Gay is "the top Italian banana," a dandy in the fashion of the film actor "Adolphe Menjou, dressing up morning, noon, as well as night in his bathroom, tennis court, in his bedroom."[40] The symbolism of the cowboy hat, a sign of traditional American masculinity, combines with the Italian notion of *figura*. Later Gay reads some of the autobiographical writing that Nick has produced and suggests that the book should start in the hospital and then move to the love story. Gay and another writer, Ralph Stiller, in unison, read aloud from a section of Nick's autobiography that recounts some of the images from Nick's earliest memories surrounding "the god, the creative touch [that] were the things he loved to do with his mother."[41] The words allude to the bond between mother and son that evolves into the son's penchant for creating images and worlds through words.

Nick proposes another problem to Johnny, one often encountered by artists and writers, especially those who do little more than make ends meet through their work. In "Casa Johnny," Johnny asks Nick what it is that he really needs, and Nick responds: " 'A home for aged Italian artists.' " When Johnny asks for clarification, Nick tells him he means Italian-American writers. Johnny tells Nick he can accomplish that with a six-room condo. After all, there couldn't be that many American writers of Italian descent. Johnny then calls for his lackey to " 'check out Fort Hamilton. They don't need the fort anymore. If that don't work, look into the Veteran's Hospital and Dyker Beach golf course. In the last resort we'll use Appalachia.' "[42] What we learn here is that the artist needs the gangster to help him struggle in the material world, and in exchange the artist can help the gangster deal with the spiritual world: the gangster is the body, the artist, the soul—and the prototype for the synthesis of the two lies in the Nardack figure.

As Nick takes leave of Johnny, he hands the gangster a copy of his latest book. Johnny asks Nick if he can read to him the selection he presented at the college reading. Nick takes a position, quite symbolically, behind a statue of Aphrodite and Apollo. Johnny has his worker hook up a public address system so that what Nick reads will be broadcast over the neighborhood. Nick chooses to read "The Last Godfather," a first-person narrative of Pippo Napoli-Sicilia, the last of the great dons. Don Pippo says:

> After me, after I join Dante in the empyrean, my family of thirty million will not need crime to get on because in their dark souls and untrustful minds I have placed love and beauty and imagination and understanding. Their olive faces will be raised to the Crystalline Heaven. They will be at the point of assimilation into the American race, prepared to ponder the

American Revolution and George Washington and Thomas Jefferson and Alexander Hamilton.[43]

Don Pippo becomes the "godfather" to end all gangster godfathers. Set in the year 2089, the story has the Don living in an apartment similar to Nick's in lower Manhattan. Each day the Don, ninety-four-years old at the writing of this tale, walks from his home to the river. He wears long underwear and a robe in a manner reminiscent of the real-life gangster Vincent Gigante. Each day, along the way, the Don stops to talk to neighborhood people. Charlie, the bread store owner, greets him and is told by the Don that he should pay more attention to his son: "It's not good for our sons to do as we do. My son, as you know, is an art historian,"[44] he says. Along the way he gathers a variety of people: Pretab Madar the jeweler from Bombay, Yang the Japanese shoemaker, Bella the female butcher, Juan the Spanish fish vendor, Jake the Jewish pizza maker. The Don leads the group to a parking lot where the Hudson River meets the Atlantic Ocean and wonders "exactly where the fresh water turns to salt."[45] He asks the question of his group, each one coming up with a possible answer, but nothing seems to be definitive. The Don is worried about the bass, but Juan tells him that if they died they would have been seen belly-up on the water's surface. The suggestion here is that there is a natural evolution that occurs when one species is introduced to the environment of another. Italian immigrants evolve differently in the United States. Over time, adaptation will occur or the species will die. This is what happens also to the Don's people, who by now are so intermingled that there is no possibility for the old, traditional version of the Italian gangster to exist and, anyway, there is no longer any need for the gangster.

The Don leads the group to a parking garage, where he explains to them that Jerry, the garage attendant, has no idea what went on in that place over the years. The Don uses Jerry to explain two types of ignorance:

intentional ignorance, from which I suffer—pray for me, Jerry!—and pure ignorance. Jerry will ascend to Dante with the goodness he showed me preserved in his heart, purely ignorant of the knowledge that through all the days he worked his lot, I owned it, and the men and women he guided in and out may have appeared like teachers of that college across the highway or like businessmen of Wall Street—but they were my soldiers.[46]

Nearby is where the Don used to dump the bodies of his enemies. He points to the river and says, "The water below us appears stagnant and foul, but I know the tides. I know them from observing the piers that used to jut into the river busted up. Ungathered wood lingers here for a while, then drifts out into the ocean."[47] The Don can see that just as the ocean takes care of itself, so does culture take care of itself.

"The Word" continues Don Pippo's monologue as he reveals to his nurse, Italia, that he wishes to die in "the old fashioned way, by assassination" and then be chopped into pieces and dropped into the river, so that

> My head rises to the surface and bobs, and the face is that of a young Don Pippo, handsome, sublime; his beautiful hazel eyes open to the immensity of the sky; and the brother and sisters on the embankment marvel at the curled lashes the way the old ladies under the el used to marvel at them. My black hat is on—nail it on if need be—and around my head like a nimbus, the fingers splayed, float my beautiful hands. So let out the word, sweet Italia, and seal my desire with a kiss.[48]

In death the Don becomes like the mythic Orpheus, whose head continued to sing as it floated down the river.

The last word in *Lefty* is given to the lover/writer, Nick, as he gives a reading to the Dante Society of Westchester, a social group of Americans of Italian descent. In this final chapter, Valerio presents Ruby, the character the narrator says was the model for Don Pippo's nurse, Italia. Nick tells Ruby:

> "The War of the Five Families is over, Ruby … . Johnny's trial and all that surrounded it was a charade, made for TV and the papers. Even Anthony Quinn and Mickey Rourke interviewed outside a courthouse was a stroke of genius on Johnny's part, actors playing out a supposed real scene."[49]

Here Nick makes the connection between his Johnny and the real gangster, John Gotti.

Nick loses touch with the real world of Gotti, though: "The last time I saw Johnny he had his Machiavelli with him, and he and Vinny were on their way to a plastic surgeon in Garden City who was going to transform them into blondes with big tits. Then Vinny was going to Vegas and Johnny to New Orleans."[50] Here Nick moves away from the real and into the symbolic. The "Machiavelli" in the quote could be an allusion to the author whose book *The Prince*—a key text in the production of noble notions of manhood—is popular in American prisons. "Blondes with big tits" could be a poke at how Gotti's name continues to live through his daughter, Victoria, and her writing and television show *Growing Up Gotti*.

Nick is contacted by Doris Carubba, the first woman elected into the Dante Society of Westchester, a friend of Ruby's who serves as the society's events coordinator. Doris asks Nick to come and lecture on Dante. At this lecture he speaks of great and wise Italian men—Dante, Mazzini, Garibaldi, and Silvio Pellico—and recites from Pellico's prison memoirs: "Woman is for me a creature so admirable, so sublime, the mere seeing, hearing and speaking to her enriches my mind with such."[51] This is where the novel ends, in midsentence, as though the narrator has been cut off before he can complete his thought. Through Nick, Valerio has transferred the power of the gangster into the power of the writer. Nick shows, as Scorsese's films and Ermelino's novels do, that it is through women that men can be redeemed and can turn from wiseguys into wise men.

DeLillo's Gangster Voice

Don DeLillo, a major contemporary American writer not known for portrayals of Italian-American characters, still uses the gangster figure in a number of his novels. The first instance of a DeLillo gangster is Arondella, a mysterious character in his first novel, *Americana* (1971). Arondella, who is not thoroughly described, could be a racketeer, similar to the one Richard Conte plays in the film *Cry of the City*. Arondella is the man with whom another character, Mary Valerio, runs away from home. Mary is the sister of Tommy Valerio, the best friend of the novel's protagonist, David Bell. Arondella, as Mary tells David, is a hit man she met in Boston. His "territory" is upstate New York and New England. She is running off with him because she knows he kills people, but " 'there are different kinds of death ... . And I prefer that kind, his kind, to the death I've been fighting all my life.' "[52] Mary is referring to the death of being trapped inside a traditional Italian family in a small American town. Arondella is later re-created as a character in David's autobiographical film through a monologue by another character named Mary:

> His sense of insult was overwhelming. If someone used an obscene word in my presence, he demanded an immediate apology. He always got it, of course, his reputation being what it was. He was prepared to kill, quite literally to kill, in order to avenge the honor of someone he loved. He was always swearing on his mother's grave. In his company of men, there was no greater promise or proof of honor than to swear on your mother's grave ... . He told me about a friend of his called Mother Cabrini. Cabrini got a lot of mileage out of his mother's grave until it was learned that his mother was not dead. Telling this, he managed to be both outraged and amused. They were all children, of course, but not in the same way the rest of us are children. We have learned not to be afraid of the dark but we've forgotten that darkness means death. They haven't forgotten this. They are still in the hills of Sicily or Corsica, wherever they came from. They obey their mothers. They don't go into a dark cellar without expecting to be strangled by a zombie. They bless themselves constantly. And us, what do we do? We watch television and play Scrabble. So there it is, children of light and darkness.[53]

What Mary and Arondella have in common, despite their different upbringings, is the "instinct that death is without meaning unless it is met violently."[54] Arondella represents a world that is dark and full of superstition, an in-your-face world that knows how to deal with death and, thus, with life.

Later in the monologue Mary refers to him as "very handsome, very much a leading man of the 1930s. He moved the way a proud, an almost overbearingly proud animal might move, an animal that is all sex and death."[55] This is another example of that animalistic quality of Italian-American masculinity that Anthony Valerio also writes about. Arondella is also a gentleman—he never swore in her presence, and he took her to the Copa; she says he was "everything to me, a man no more than a philosophy, and it's strange, isn't it, that someone like me, with my upbringing and education and presumably well-trained intellect, would have such a very significant thing in common with this man. It was his instinct that death is without meaning unless it is met violently."[56] DeLillo's first representation of the gangster is a minor character, but in Arondella's brief scenes DeLillo touches on some of the same themes that surface in other representations examined here.

The gangster figure reappears in DeLillo's *Running Dog* (1978) in the form of Vincent "The Eye" Talerico, a minor character who is in charge of acquiring first-run films for "one of the New York families." He's "the Hollywood one. The dresser. The fancy gangster type,"[57] and he suffers from facial nerve paralysis so that the right side of his face is collapsed and droops, hence his right eye stands out. "It was like an animal's eye, people said. A hawk, a snake, a shark."[58] Again, DeLillo's gangster character is associated with animal qualities.

Another DeLillo gangster appears in *Libra* (1988) and he comes right out of the pages of American history. The character, Carmine Latta, is a fictional representation of Carlo Marcello, a New Orleans mob chieftain supposedly connected to the John F. Kennedy assassination. There is not much in the way of a philosophical approach to the gangster figure in *Libra*. When the character David Ferrie comes to visit Latta, he sees:

> The white-haired man, bright-eyed, veined, ancient, was sitting on a sofa, drink in hand. He was frail and spotted, with the drawn and thievish look of a figure in a ducal portrait. There were times, entering his presence, when Ferrie experienced a deferential awe so complete that he found himself becoming part of the other man's consciousness, seeing the world, the room, the dynamics of power as Carmine Latta saw them.[59]

There is little more than this regarding Latta. There is a bit about the Chicago gangster Sam "Momo" Giancana, whose mistress was rumored to have had an affair with John Kennedy. In *Libra*, even though DeLillo plays with many facts in order to create his drama, he seems to have his hands tied by history regarding how much play he can give the gangster figure, especially when very little is told from the gangster's point of view. Yet the figure of the gangster serves as a critic of the WASP world in which the conspiracy of a president's assassination involves players from a variety of cultures. It is in his novel *Underworld* (1997)—the title echoes a famous 1927 gangster film—that DeLillo makes his most pronounced statements about the gangster, through his protagonist, Nick Shay.

As in *Libra*, DeLillo creates the action in this novel around a number of historical events that took place on 3 October 1951, the day Bobby Thomson hit his famous home run to win the National League pennant for the New York Giants, and the day the Russians test-exploded their first atom bomb. Within the frame of these events, DeLillo presents fifty years of American history through the persona of Nick Shay, son of an Italian-American bookie, Jimmie Costanza. A novel rich in many of the stories that have become American history and legend, *Underworld* takes the reader under the known world to a place where bookie-fathers disappear, where nuclear weapons are turned into hazardous waste eliminators, and where the dead get resurrected. Echoes of nearly all DeLillo's earlier novels can be heard throughout *Underworld*, but only faithful DeLillo fans who have read everything he has written will catch them all. Through the characters of Albert Bronzini and Nick Costanza Shay, DeLillo recreates life in a Bronx Little Italy.

Nick Shay tells his brother, Matt, that their father " 'did the unthinkable Italian crime. He walked out on his family. They don't even have a name for this.' "[60] This is why Nick's mother legally arranged for Nick to keep her last name. The ability to care for one's family is one of the key factors in determining one's masculinity in Italian-American culture. Matt believes his father was abducted by the mob, but Nick believes he simply ran away, abandoning his family responsibilities.

Even though his family had been affected negatively by gangster activity, Nick sometimes plays the gangster in his daily life. By doing so, he can connect to his past as he lives in a world that is far removed from the Bronx neighborhood:

> In my office in the bronze tower I made gangster threats that were comically effective. I said to a consultant who was late with a report, "I'm telling you once and for all that I, me, Mario Badalato, I'll sever your fucking family's head off." This in a scraped-raw voice faithful to the genre and evilly appreciated by others in the room.[61]

When his wife tells one of his coworkers that Nick is half Italian, the coworker says, " 'I hear it in that voice he does.' " She asks:

"What voice?

"The gangster making threats."

"What gangster?"

"It's a voice he does. Expert, stereotyped, pretty funny."[62]

Later, Nick reveals a secret from his past to his wife in the same mobster voice: " 'In udder words I took him off the calendar.' "[63] Nick's secret is that when he was a young boy, he accidentally killed a man. Nick's imitation of the gangster's voice shows that anyone can "become" a gangster figure. And he takes on the gangster persona as a way of distancing himself from the reality of his real life—of having killed someone.

However, beyond the idea of imitating the gangster, Nick relates to the gangster in terms of solitude: "I've always been a country of one. There's a certain distance in my makeup, a measured separation like my old man's."[64] He presents a Latin word that explains it, a word that interestingly connects the artist to the gangster; that word is *lontananza*:

> Distance or remoteness, sure. But as I used the word, as I interpret it, hard-edged and fine-grained, it's the perfected distance of the gangster, the syndicate mobster—the made man. Once you're a made man, you don't need the constant living influence of sources outside your self. You're all there. You're made. You're handmade. You're a sturdy Roman wall.[65]

DeLillo has actually taken the quality of the gangster and turned it into something to be emulated by those who want to achieve, if not independence, then certainly an ability to survive without much dependence on others. When the professional man takes on the gangster persona, he becomes a rebel public intellectual who can mock the very society in which he thrives.

This synthesis of the gangster and artist is revisited when Nick contemplates the creator of the Watts Towers in Los Angeles. The famous "Outsider art" monument was created by "an immigrant from somewhere near Naples, probably illiterate, who left his wife and family, or maybe they left him ... a man whose narrative is mostly blank spaces."[66] The more he looks at the towers, the more he thinks of his father: "I could imagine him rising this high, soaring out of himself to produce a rambling art that has no category."[67] While his father is the missing link between Nick and the gangster, the gangster also resides in the art of Sabato Rodia: "The work he did is a kind of swirling free-souled noise, a jazz cathedral, and the power of the thing, for me, the deep disturbance, was that my own ghost father was living in the walls."[68] When a boy loses his father, especially at a young age, he is likely to spend much time looking for him. That is why Nick glimpses his father in art, especially that of Italian-American artists.

Nick, though not a gangster himself, has grown up in an environment where he has seen and even spoken with actual gangsters. In a conversation with a fellow worker about mobsters, Nick mentions that he once spoke to Mario Badalato, a well-known gangster who was an acquaintance of his father. The coworker says that he once saw Badalato on TV getting into a police car: " 'He's always being photographed on the courthouse steps. He's the king of the steps.' " Those "steps" echo scenes in the films *Scarface* (where a young gangster is gunned down on the steps of a church) and *The Godfather* (where Don Barzini is shot on the steps of a courthouse). Later, Mario Badalato runs into Nick in a pool hall and explains that Nick's father was forced to leave the family and most likely did not meet with foul play, otherwise Mario would have heard about it sooner or later. This does little to relieve Nick's anxiety about his father's absence.

Another of the coworker's comments to Nick reveals the power that the gangster has to demand respect from total strangers:

> "In other words, I have to show respect. I have to be reverent when I mention his name. This guy who runs a criminal enterprise in narcotics, extortion, what else. Murder, attempted murder, what else."
>
> "Waste carting," I said." [69]

Nick, a white-collar worker in waste management, is well aware that he works in a business which, at least on the east coast, has been shadowed by the activities of organized crime. It would also become one of the businesses of that most contemporary of American gangsters, Tony Soprano.

DeLillo, in small strokes, and Valerio, with a much broader brush, both utilize the gangster figure to serve artistic purposes that help us see beyond the usual two-dimensional portrayal and into the possibilities of how the wiseguy might give way to the wise man.

8

FRESH GARBAGE: THE GANGSTER AS TODAY'S TRICKSTER—DAVID CHASE AND TONY ARDIZZONE

Look beneath your lid some morning
See those things you didn't quite consume.
The world's a can for your fresh garbage.[1]

—**Jay Ferguson**

 If you seek the monuments of the bourgeoisie, go to the suburbs and look around.[2]

—**Robert Fishman**

In my neighborhood when I was growing up, there was a character we used to call the "Ragsaline Man." He got his nickname because he would call out "Ragsaline, ragsaline," as he drove an ancient truck slowly through the neighborhood looking for rags, old iron, and other

149

junk. Since I had grandparents who were Italian immigrants, I was not surprised that this man could treasure other people's garbage. We were all taught that it was a sin to waste, and to avoid that sin we had to develop new ways of seeing. In our house we were admonished for anything that might potentially be wasted. If an adult saw a child had not consumed all of the food on his or her plate, the adult would first chide the child, and then, quite often, take what was left on the plate and eat it. Many of our meals consisted of animal parts that butchers threw away or sold very cheaply. When it came to meals, we simply did not leave food on our plates. Anything not eaten in one meal would find its way into subsequent meals. Clothes that no longer fit were passed on to those who could wear them, or they were shipped to Italy. When clothes became unwearable, they were torn neatly into cleaning rags. Nothing was wasted. Our immigrant grandparents, trained to behave this way out of poverty, passed on their frugal habits.

Recycling as a way of sustaining one's resources was not lost when immigrants moved into the art world. The work of Sabato Rodia is a good example of what happens when this immigrant recycling mentality is applied to the creation of art. His "Watts Towers" in South Los Angeles were made from junk he found: seashells, shards of glass, ceramic tile. Nick Costanza Shay, the protagonist of Don DeLillo's novel *Underworld*, refers to these famous towers as "a kind of swirling free-souled noise, a jazz cathedral," where Nick finds that his "own ghost father was living in the walls."[3] This tradition of seeing garbage in a fresh light, of not wasting anything, of making something out of nothing and seeing one's ancestors in the result, provides a good frame for understanding the new version of the American gangster presented in David Chase's HBO television series *The Sopranos* and in Tony Ardizzone's novel *In the Garden of Papa Santuzzu*.

THE SUBURBAN TRICKSTER: DAVID CHASE AND *THE SOPRANOS*

David Chase, the creator and executive producer of the hit series *The Sopranos*, conceived the program in the tradition and spirit of the traditional U.S. gangster film, but he executed it as a commentary on both the genre and contemporary life in the United States. As a crafty ragpicker, he cast an eye over the garbage heap of film characters, picked up the discarded gangster, dusted him off, and gave him new life by setting him back down in the suburbs, where today over 60 percent of

U.S. Americans live. But Chase has done more than simply reuse the gangster figure, he has fashioned it into what I call "fresh garbage."

A character not mentioned in my earlier discussion of Don DeLillo's novel *Underworld* is a "garbage archaeologist" who presents the keynote address at a waste management industry convention. Nick Costanza Shay explains the professor's theory that civilization is the result of garbage: "We had to find ways to discard our waste, to use what we couldn't discard, to reprocess what we couldn't use. Garbage pushed back. It mounted and spread. And it forced us to develop the logic and rigor that would lead to systematic investigations of reality, to science, art, music, mathematics."[4] This is an interesting notion, especially when applied to the development of American bourgeois culture.

Thorstein Veblen's classic notions of "conspicuous consumption" and "conspicuous waste" can help us overcome the knee-jerk responses to *The Sopranos* that tend to dismiss the show as trash.[5] *The Sopranos* matters because it reflects U.S. capitalism at the height of its impact on the world. "In order to be reputable, it [consumption] must be wasteful," wrote Veblen.[6] *The Sopranos* fulfills this mandate better than any other television program. It is creative and critical. It is historical and hysterical. Tony Soprano (played by James Gandolfini) is a partner in a waste management company (among other legal and illegal businesses); he is not only a purveyor of garbage, but also a dramatic embodiment of the waste produced by postmodern U.S. consumer culture.

Michael Kimmel has observed that contemporary masculinity has been defined by the consumption of manhood ever since men lost control over their labor, the classic way of "producing" masculinity. Avi Santo makes the same point about *The Sopranos*: "*The Sopranos* depicts a world run rampant with consumption, where middle-class masculinity has come to define itself not by what it produces but by what it consumes, and where even the attempt to reassert control over production outside of the body cannot be achieved."[7] Santo sees Tony's overweight body, and those of many of the other gangster characters, as indicative of this hyper-consumer, making him and his type targets for social ridicule, if not persecution, in an age when men are expected to be fit and not fat: "Tony's body is the self-destructive body, not because fatness is unhealthy or aesthetically devalued, but because it represents the barbarous failures of self-made manhood to sustain itself without resort to cannibalistic consumption and, hence, destruction, of the very ideals of inner-directed masculinity it adheres to."[8] The gangster as Tony

Soprano represents a last gasp of old-fashioned manhood dying in the stranglehold of an economically different American man.

What makes *The Sopranos* worth watching and worth talking about is the fact that Tony Soprano's actions speak to contemporary life in the United States. As Wallace Katz writes, "Even though Tony Soprano is a criminal, he is a mirror image of ourselves. Which is why his existence opens up a window on the dilemmas of American society at the dawn of the twenty-first century."[9] Katz sees Tony Soprano as "a kind of contemporary Babbitt, who embodies the culture wars—between virtue and happiness, between disciplined 'character' and the protean self, between dying traditions and a vacuous modernity—that currently tear apart the American soul and keep us from creating the new moral perspective, cultural identity, and, above all, new politics that we need."[10]

Tony Soprano's movement from urban ethnic to assimilated suburban American is mirrored in the show's signature opening montage, which Katz says "tells a story about generational change and social mobility, the American Dream."[11] The sequence begins with a shot of the ceiling of the Lincoln Tunnel, which connects Manhattan to New Jersey. A vehicle drives west, away from the city. Most of the images are presented through the driver's point of view, and all one sees of the driver is his eyes in the rear-view mirror. The car clock reads 10:22 a.m., so Tony Soprano is coming home either from an all-nighter in the city or from an early morning meeting. In any case, he is returning home. He sees a plane coming in, he lights a cigar, and he's on the New Jersey Turnpike, bypassing the city of Newark. This is followed by a series of images of working-class sites: oil tanks, factories, a blue-collar neighborhood, a church, a cemetery, Satriale's Pork Store, Pizzaland. Soon the working-class neighborhoods give way to wider, tree-lined streets that lead up into upper-middle-class suburban developments. The sequence ends with the car stopping at the top of the Sopranos' driveway. The viewer has just completed a journey from the old city to the new suburb, through tunnels once forged by people like Tony's ancestors, through a working-class neighborhood where Tony might have been born, ending up in the gangster's plush suburban "estate." This is the stereotypical journey taken by those who chase the American dream.

These opening images are accompanied by the series theme song, "Woke Up This Morning" by the group A3, which sets up a commentary on the internal life of the protagonist. The song recounts a philosophical bout with mortality that happens when a middle-aged man returns home after a three-day drinking binge and plays music that reminds him of blues and jazz greats such as Charles Mingus, Eric Dolphy, Billie Holiday, Ella Fitzgerald, Muddy Waters, and Howlin' Wolf. The lyrics contain the lines, "You woke up this morning, got yourself a gun, / Mama always said you'd be the Chosen One."

As the oldest child, and only son in an Italian American family, Tony is the one expected to take over his father's way of life, the gangster's way. His father never explained that life to Tony; Tony simply imitated his father's actions, dropped out of school, and entered organized crime. In fact, Tony is a rarity among real Italian Americans. Most sons of gangsters never did follow in their father's footsteps, as each generation, through money and education, found more socially acceptable ways of acquiring the trappings of middle- and upper-class American life.

Chase's success with this series depends not on his ability to represent Italian-American culture—his version has irked quite a few Americans of Italian descent, some of whom have tried to stop the projection if not the production of the program—but on his ability to make us see the "garbage" produced by contemporary American life. His genius lies in the fact that he chose to tell this story through the gangster figure, a proven audience attractor as well as a model for the American Everyman. Through Tony Soprano, the Italian American has become American. Examining the way Chase uses the gangster figure and its migration into postmodern U.S. suburban culture offers great insight into the alienation caused by U.S. capitalist culture of the twenty-first century. Chase, an American of Italian descent himself, returns artistic attention to the primal mother–son relationship that is and always has been so important in Italian art and so unimportant in American art.

Hardly an episode of *The Sopranos* passes without some nod to or comment on an earlier classic depiction of the gangster. In the first episode, there are cutaways to Al Capone and head shots of famous actors playing gangsters (Humphrey Bogart, Dean Martin, and Edward G. Robinson) as the character of Christopher Moltisanti shoots a rival. Over time, the gangster has become a marker of ethnicity and manliness in contemporary American life, and David Chase is no stranger to the power of the gangster figure as a vehicle for his own commentaries on both ethnicity and manliness.

To Tony Soprano, the history of organized crime is poetry, an art that comforts him as it gives him a sense of being connected with a past. He has mythologized the actions of past gangsters, as though his father belonged to some type of gangsterhood golden age. Tony becomes philosophical whenever he contemplates these myths, but the more he thinks about them, the more he sees that they are only constructions that shatter easily. The values of the immigrant generation are lost, transformed from using waste to making waste.

Ultimately the audience, if not Tony himself, can see that he has never matured. Tony has not become a wise man, but he has the possibility of becoming one if only he would listen to the women in his life. When he does, though, as in an early episode when he hears his daughter refer to sex at the kitchen table, he exclaims that such talk is inappropriate and that "in this house it's still 1954." Tony's immaturity keeps him from adapting to a changing world in which women and even children might speak frankly about sex at the dinner table. However, when it comes to himself, Tony has no problem enjoying all the extramarital sex he can get his hands on. His problem comes when women start talking to him, and especially when they start talking back to him. Tony is a twenty-first-century American example of Old-World Italian patriarchy.

Tony Soprano believes in the type of life he leads and feels that he is constantly being besieged by outside forces bent on making him conform to various expectations—the FBI sees him as a capo of organized crime; his neighbors see him as a colorful mob kingpin; his mistress sees him as a generous lover; to his children he's the father who takes care of them, and to his wife he is the provider of material goods. Without a solid sense of self, he constantly wavers from the various attacks on his ego. As he begins to explore just who he is, he opens up the possibility that being a gangster might not be such a good choice after all.

Tony, unlike most of the sons of America's real gangsters, stays in the business of organized crime after inheriting the role from his father, and, therefore, can never become the wise man. He is constantly under surveillance by the FBI. This forces him to constrain his speech and, when he can, his behavior in public. Thus, the performance of his masculinity must take place inside the private spaces of his home or work, and as a suburbanite he brings a new look to the traditional notion of the gangster.

A look around the suburbs today shows that they are no longer the utopian havens that once promised wealthy urbanites refuge from the ills of city life. Some—literally built atop lands filled with the waste of cities bursting beyond their original boundaries—are quickly succumbing to the same overcrowding and pollution that led to their creation. The suburbs became a refuge where a man who worked in the city could get away from the overcrowding and increasing industrialized environment that the city had become. The cities had alienated man from nature and the suburbs became a good place to renew that connection.

The television representation of suburban life in *The Sopranos* invites viewers to recall many earlier American television shows that portrayed suburban family life, such as *Father Knows Best* (1954–1960) and *Leave It to Beaver* (1957–1963). In those shows, the father had a steady white-collar job, spent plenty of time with the kids, and was always there when the kids needed him. This time, the father's job is being a boss in New Jersey organized crime. Suburbia not only restructured man's relationship to his work and his family, says Fishman, it also expressed "a complex and compelling vision of the modern family, freed from the corruption of the city, restored to harmony with nature, endowed with wealth and independence yet protected by a close-knit, stable community."[12]

Flashbacks throughout the series explain that Tony Soprano is the only son of Johnny and Livia Soprano. He was raised with two sisters, one older and one younger, in Newark's Little Italy. At some point after the death of his father, he and his nuclear family—his wife, Carmela, and their children, Meadow and Anthony Jr.—take up residence at the symbolically loaded address of 633 Stag Trail Road, North Caldwell, New Jersey 07006, in Essex County, one of the wealthiest counties in the United States. "Stag" is an appropriate name for the street address of this gangster, who maintains the promiscuous life of a stag in spite of being married to Carmela for nearly twenty years.

The Sopranos' move from the city to the suburbs mirrors the migration of ethnic groups who, after spending a generation or two in the city, move away searching for their promised land. As the immigrants leave their old neighborhoods, they also leave their old ways of being. City life requires identity with one's neighborhood and one's culture. Movement to the suburbs requires assimilation that often demands that one lose the trappings of the original culture, including one's original language. Tony Soprano learns to think of himself as a white, assimilated American, but he also sees himself as different from those Anglos he calls "mayonnaise," or in the case of assimilated Italians like his neighbor and personal physician, Dr. Bruce Cusumano, "Wonder Bread Wops."

During the course of the series, there are only the briefest references to the immigrant generation. One of these occurs when Tony walks his daughter into a church and tells her that his grandfather helped to build the church, not as an architect but as a bricklayer. He is proud that his grandfather contributed to one of society's fundamental structures, even though he has long stopped attending church. The history of immigration is filled with people who made incredible sacrifices, and while Tony comes to know the past, he cannot foresee his future. Like the people in Marshall McLuhan's metaphor, Tony is driving forward while looking in his rear-view mirror. His sense of the future is not developed because of his obsession with the past.

Much of what Tony and his suburban family do throughout the series is to consume, and much of all the characters' identities depends not on what they produce but on what they consume. Like the rest of the United States, they are being assimilated. As a card-carrying suburbanite, Tony surrounds himself and his family with all the appropriate accessories that enable them to consume conspicuously. He drives a Chevrolet Suburban, and his wife has a Mercedes-Benz. His children attend a prestigious Catholic preparatory school, interestingly named Verbum Dei (Word of God). He has an in-ground pool in his backyard and gym equipment in his basement. The suburban home, surrounded by greenery, enables privacy and invisibility from neighbors, essentially insulating what happens in the Soprano family from outside influences and from the attention of outsiders.

Another middle-class accoutrement is Tony's boat, appropriately named the *Stugots*. If it isn't already apparent that Chase, as a writer, is playing with Italian-American culture, then this detail ought to do it. The likelihood of this Italian American naming a power boat after his penis (*stugots* is a dialect form of '*sto cazzo* or *questo cazzo*, "this penis") is very low, as it reflects a self-conscious play more likely to be enacted by an artist than by a gangster. These powerboats are commonly referred by critics to as "penis boats," and the *Stugots* serves as a site for male homosocial behavior—Tony's bonding with his son, disposing of problems, and regular rendezvous with his mistress. The naming of boats becomes significant again in episode 13, when Tony kills one of Junior's hit men in a boat appropriately named *Villain II*. Chase creatively uses these props obliquely to condemn the actions of his characters, and to poke fun at the gangster figure.

Tony's entrée into the middle class does not come without its downside. In episode 10, Tony presents his doctor with real Cuban cigars, the illegality of which tantalizes Dr. Cusumano and tempts him to offer Tony a golf outing at the country club. Tony joins the doctor and two businessmen, who are obsessed with Tony's reputation and try to get him to reinforce the stereotypes and myths about the Mafia that they hold. These men, who discuss their business ventures in the same secretive tones that Tony and his wiseguys use to plan their crimes, reveal that they are really not morally superior to the gangsters. Outwardly there is no difference between them, but on the inside, Chase makes us identify with the honesty of Tony Soprano and not with the two-faced behavior of the suburbanites. Dr. Cusumano and his buddies represent the traditional, accepted way up the economic ladder into upper-middle-class suburbia—through education. Tony Soprano made it into their neighborhood with no more than a year and a half of college. His presence shatters the illusion that the suburbs belong to those who work hard and follow the moral high road; in fact, it is the accumulation of money that matters.

Although Tony has made it to the world of the wealthy, he struggles to remain loyal to what he perceives as his ancestral heritage. Just what this heritage consists of is never defined by Chase, and it is so rarely articulated in dramatic productions generally that one feels that no director out there has a good sense of just what Italian-American culture is. This is another reason why critics should not become obsessed apparently negative portrayals of Italian Americans in the series. As a storyteller, Chase uses what every major storyteller has depended on since the beginning of time to tell a story—easily identified types that represent not realities, but possibilities. It's not Chase's job to represent reality. After all, he's not shooting a documentary. Chase provides many signals to remind viewers that he is telling a story from the titles of episodes to the continuous dialogue with entertainment history that goes on in each episode. If there is any group of Italian Americans who might have a right to protest representation in the series, it is the tiny number of contemporary Italian-American gangsters.

If life in the suburbs conditions Tony Soprano to act as if he is not a criminal, it also exposes him to greater female influence than experienced by the gangsters who came before him. This is Chase's greatest contribution to the reinvention of the gangster figure as a means of connecting the wiseguy to wise manhood. With the move to the suburbs, work and home, formerly integrated in urban life, became separated, and the home became the sphere of female power. Men's sphere of influence remained outside the home in the city. If Tony finds it necessary to conduct business in his home, he takes it to the basement and talks in code, a gangster jargon that conceals his meaning. Within the home, Carmela has the power and the opportunity to lead the family down a morally correct path. This, as Fishman suggests, was inherent in the creation of the earliest suburbs:

> The city was not just crowded, dirty, and unhealthy; it was immoral. Salvation itself depended on separating the woman's sacred world of family and children from the profane metropolis. Yet this separation could not jeopardize a man's constant attendance to his business … . This was the problem, and suburbia was to be the ultimate solution.[13]

As mentioned in chapter 2, this idea was advanced early on in American history by Catharine Beecher, who wrote that "the 'cult of true womanhood' is linked to the home with piety and purity."[14] Modern-day women struggle with the earlier tropes of womanhood created by men and sustained and disseminated by writers such as Beecher. The gains made by the women's movement are reflected in the independence represented by many of Chase's female characters. Chase makes this important point by placing Tony frequently in situations where he must depend on women. Tony's relationship with his female psychiatrist, Dr. Jennifer Melfi, has already been written about to such an extent that I will restrict my discussion of Tony's female relationships to that with his wife and especially with his mother.[15]

Carmela Soprano's power inside the house is usually manifested in her kitchen, where she feeds her family and friends, and where she often disciplines and counsels her children. Seduced by the materiality of middle-class life that provides her with safety and comfort, she compromises her morality in order to build a sense of security through the accumulation of wealth. Carmela's power dynamics are often played out at the kitchen table, where she, as the provider of good food, can seduce her guests into giving her sympathy, providing favors, and listening to her instructions. Carmela uses food the way her husband uses threats of violence. For example, in episode 21, Carmela's power of suggestion, expressed through the gift of a homemade ricotta pie, exacts an important letter of recommendation for her daughter's college application from an influential and initially reluctant sister of Jeannie Cusumano, a successful alumna of the school.

Although the Soprano household shares much with those of other contemporary Italian Americans, it is often very different. For many years, Italian-American culture has been preserved in the homes and, more likely than not, in the basement (which Italian Americans have come to call the *basciument*, an Italianized version of the word), where grandpa made wine, where grandma had a second kitchen, and now where many Italian Americans store material legacies and memories. Outside celebrations such as religious *feste* (feasts) became the most important public presentation of Italian-American culture, but these annual events were never frequent enough to protect that culture from the mass-media bombardment of negative stereotypes. Italian American identity, for the most part, has been practiced in the home, where Italian-American culture is safe inside family celebrations. Tony and Carmela Soprano's basement is void of such legacies. Instead they have some workout equipment, a washer and dryer, and not much else. Chase understands that he cannot make a gangster film like the old ones, and this understanding extends to Tony, who realizes that he cannot be a gangster in the old-fashioned sense of the word, and that in order to survive in this new postmodern world, he has to find a language that he can use to communicate with himself and to manipulate the world around him. A great example of this occurs when Tony moves his aging mother out of her home. In the process of relocation, which threatens to destroy her power, his mother turns on him and suggests to her brother-in-law that Tony might be better off dead, a statement that her brother-in-law construes as her permission to have Tony killed.

The absurdity of any mother, especially an Italian-American mother, ordering her own son's murder should alert anyone that connecting what happens in this series to real Italian-American culture is an exercise in futility. What is worth exploring is the symbolism involved in the dramatic presentation of a mother who is able and willing to issue her son's death warrant, for it is in this representation that Chase holds the key to transforming, once and for all, a wiseguy into a wise man. *The Sopranos* has reintroduced the mother–son paradigm. Doing so results in the opportunity to explore alternatives to the development of male identity in relation to the way Western men usually separate themselves from their mothers.

Returning to Christina Wieland's analysis in *The Undead Mother: Psychoanalytic Explorations of Masculinity, Femininity and Matricide,* Wieland believes that the symbolic matricide that separates a man from his mother can also be responsible for much of the violent tendencies that often mark the onslaught of male adolescence, the point of male development that she sees as crucial to the evolution of the notion of woman as an object that needs to be possessed:

> The stronger the attraction toward the female body, the stronger the banding together of young males because of the way this attraction unleashes the terror of being possessed by a woman, of being merged with a woman and becoming feminine. Thus the paradox: the ultimate expression of maleness—the sexual act—entails fears of loss of masculinity. The solution traditionally sought for this basic, masculine anxiety entails that the woman/mother becomes a possession, a part of the narcissistic self, under male control.[16]

The search for this control over women leads to men's objectification of women, something very much a part of the gangster's persona. Women who resist this objectification, argues Wieland, enact what men perceive as the return of the "revengeful mother." The reactions of Tony Soprano and his band of gangsters should be read with this in mind. Wieland attributes this development of male attitudes toward women as revengeful mothers to Western society's preoccupation with the Oedipus conflict and its virtual ignorance of the symbolism at work in another profound work of myth, the *Oresteia*, especially in the matricide carried out by Orestes. Aeschylus's *Oresteia* trilogy (*Agamemnon, Libation Bearers,* and *Eumenides*) is a central text that considers the relationship between power and violence, tribalism and democracy, and struggles between males and females. These are all themes addressed in *The Sopranos*. Wieland states that the *Oresteia* has usually been interpreted as marking the move from matriarchy to patriarchy. On the contrary, she writes: "The *Oresteia* portrays the transition only from one type of patriarchy to another, but that this represents a cultural advance."[17] In this advance the father becomes the invisible protector of "the matricidal psyche" (the idea that the mother must be eliminated for the boy to become a man), something Tony Soprano experiences.

He always speaks of his father as a good man, without faults; his mother does also, but her children say she never did so while her husband was alive. *The Sopranos* invites us to watch this mother–son drama play itself out, not only through the first two seasons in which Livia actually appeared, but also throughout the other seasons as Tony's therapy sessions bring him close to understanding how his mother has affected his psychosocial development.

In a particularly illuminating reading of the behavior of Raskolnikov, the protagonist of Dostoyevsky's *Crime and Punishment*, Wieland presents some insights that work for reading Tony Soprano. Like Raskolnikov, Tony is fatherless, a state that Wieland suggests "signifies his lack of protection by a paternal super-ego, and its replacement by a grandiosity which is matched only by his contempt for all weakness and need."[18] This contempt for weakness, says Wieland, creates a " 'false father', an omnipotent part of the self which offers protection in the manner of … a 'gang' or 'mafia' … (or of the Devil in Christian mythology)."[19] That Tony literally has this other "family" is telling support to Wieland's interpretation. Interestingly, Tony faints and feels weak whenever he experiences things that remind him of his father's violent acts. Tony, who has characterized his father as a saint, is unable to process his father's violence and instead directs his anger toward his mother, but not until after he has begun to understand her role in contributing to his mental state.

Livia, who feels spurned by her son when he sells her house to put her into a retirement home, attempts to enlist Junior, her brother-in-law, to help get revenge on her son. She suggests to Junior that Tony is snubbing the older Junior's natural authority by having meetings inside the retirement home with Junior's capos, without including Junior. It turns out that a couple of Junior's capos have placed their mothers in the same home. "I don't like to be put in the middle of these things," Livia says, suggesting Tony's impropriety to Junior. Junior does his thinking out loud and suggests that he must act, "blood or no blood." Livia responds, "I suppose I should have kept my mouth shut. Like a mute. Then everyone would have been happy." What Chase has created is exactly what Wieland depicts as "the return of the revengeful mother." Livia, unchecked, is as capable of killing her son as she was of controlling her husband, or as Tony says, "She rubbed him down to a nub."

162 • From Wiseguys to Wise Men

Wieland suggests that the only way to move beyond this under-developed sense of masculinity is to employ a slow working-through of the Oedipus complex, not simply its dissolution. Since motherhood has been one of the few power centers for women, it has been used to challenge the father's power, and its site "has become a place from which the father is excluded."[20] In order to move beyond this, men have employed symbolic matricide, something Wieland believes led to the creation of "the myth of the Virgin Mother, the infinitely loving and non-threatening mother who can control neither her fertility nor her (Divine) Son—a very reassuring version of the mother."[21] This is the typical presentation of the Italian-American mother, one replayed over and over, from Pietro Di Donato's Annunziata in *Christ in Concrete* (1939) to Puzo's Mama Corleone in *The Godfather* (more than in his *The Fortunate Pilgrim*). Livia is not like these mothers and, thus, her figure helps fracture the notion of the powerful/powerless woman. In the process, she represents an all-powerful woman who knows "how to speak to people" and how to manipulate them to serve her purposes. What keeps most men from understanding this dynamic, argues Wieland, is the act of repression which is so important a part of Freud's theory of the unconscious. As long as Tony's unconscious remains hidden, he can continue to be the unchecked gangster. As he gets more and more in touch with his unconscious, he begins to question his actions as a wiseguy and even, at times, to check his violent behavior.

It is doubtful that Tony will ever achieve what Wieland calls the "alternative space," which would enable a proper mourning of the separation of son from mother and would break "this cycle of destructiveness" that Western civilization has created.[22] Tony Soprano is the last of the wiseguys and a pivotal figure in the development of wise men. The end of the wiseguys and the beginning of wise men, therefore, is in developing the skills to gain knowledge and to use knowledge instead of violence to solve problems. It is by using one's knowledge, not physical force, that boys become men and wiseguys become wise men.

Chase's *The Sopranos* joins the fiction of Italian Americans such as Giose Rimanelli's *Benedetta in Guysterland*, Anthony Valerio's *Lefty and the Button Men*, Frank Lentricchia's *The Music of the Inferno*, Louisa Ermelino's *Joey Dee Gets Wise*, and Don DeLillo's *Underworld* in creating a different future for the gangster figure in American culture one that completes the maturation cycle of Italian-American figures as they move from wiseguys to wise men. Yet only if Tony Soprano is also considered as a trickster figure can America's fascination with *The Sopranos* be explained fully.

In *Trickster Makes This World: Mischief, Myth and Art*, the noted mythologist and poet Lewis Hyde says that the trickster, unlike the Devil, "embodies and enacts a large portion of our experience where good and evil are hopelessly intertwined."[23] Hyde sees the figure of the American "confidence man" as "one likely candidate for the protagonist of a reborn trickster myth."[24] The gangster figure embodies aspects of the confidence man, especially in the way he attempts to swindle people out of their money through various schemes, but the gangster takes the notion of the trickster a bit farther by creating the possibility of unchecked appetite in a consumer-driven capitalist economy. He redefines the notion of survival of the fittest in a postindustrial capitalist society by returning a sense of the hunter and hunted to the human dynamic. Hyde points out, "Trickster intelligence arises from the tension between predators and prey. Behind trickster's tricks lies the desire to eat and not be eaten, to satisfy appetite without being its object."[25] What the gangster does is cross the line between what is proper and improper, between right and wrong: "What tricksters in general like to do is erase or violate that line between the dirty and the clean."[26] All along, the gangster has served as a trickster figure who goes to places outside the boundaries of traditional and normal society, who proves that culture is human-made and who shows us that those who reach for too much will eventually lose everything. Society needs a figure that can represent fringe behavior against which the center of society can formulate its values and identity. The Mafia myth, thus, has served an important function in American society in defining, by contrast, what is American and what is acceptable behavior in American society.

David Chase's recovery of this dramatic gangster figure in *The Sopranos* gives new insight into contemporary U.S. society's position high atop the junk heap of a postmodern consumer society. It is also a reminder that people need to pay more attention to the legacy left for future generations. And while Chase's gangster, Tony, never quite makes it to wise manhood, he does show the way. If Tony cannot become the wise man, then who can? Chase shows that the wise man is the artist, the one who uses his gangster qualities to demonstrate what he has learned about life. One of the things that Chase has learned about American life is that the movement from urban to suburban life has accompanied a change in traditional notions of American masculinity. Chase has moved the gangster into American suburbs that have changed significantly since they were first developed as extra-urban refuges.

There is no doubt that Tony Soprano is a much wiser man than most of his gangster predecessors. The question is whether he can complete that transformation. That Chase does not accomplish the transition from wiseguy to wise man through Tony Soprano is one of the shortcomings of this artistic effort. Then again, I am writing this at least one year before the series's final season, so I cannot make a definitive pronouncement on that. It remains to be seen how Chase will end the story of Tony Soprano, but whatever happens, Tony's actions will always be informed by an awareness of the effect his mother had on his life. By utilizing the strong mother–son dynamics of Italian culture, Chase moves the gangster figure toward a higher level of maturity, if not to the actual level of the wise man. This is something the next artist to be discussed, Tony Ardizzone, accomplishes wonderfully in a single chapter of a novel which takes a look at the gangster through the lens of magic realism.

Tony Ardizzone's "Mafioso Wolf Man"

Tony Ardizzone, an Italian-American author whose work has earned such prestigious recognition as the Flannery O'Connor Award for Short Fiction, the Pushcart Prize, and the Milkweed National Fiction Prize, has been dipping into his Sicilian-American background sporadically throughout his career. In his most recent novel, he embraces Sicilian culture from different points of view. *In the Garden of Papa Santuzzu* (1999) tells the story of a man who knows that *La Merica* (America) holds a fortune for his family. Reluctant, if not afraid, to leave the land where he was born, he sends child after child, until he is left alone with his visions and his memories. Twelve stories, each presented in the voice of a different child or relative of Santuzzu, tell of the trials of traveling across the ocean, of how the Mafia came to be, of work in Sicily as a fisherman and in the United States as a baker, and how to survive selling newspapers in Chicago. Ardizzone's clever imagination rises above reality to create a sense of a super-reality, a magical experience with words. The influence of the greats of magic realism, such as Gabriel García Marquez, Ben Okri, and Toni Morrison, is apparent as Ardizzone creates a different sense of reality to show how the mafioso-gangster is created by society and how that figure evolves cyclically. Ardizzone retells ancient origin myths and creates original myths of his own. It is hard to tell where one begins and the other ends. What will be discussed here is the tale of Luigi Girgenti, "The Wolf of Girgenti."

Luigi Girgenti is one of Santuzzu's sons and his chapter in this novel is a story of right and wrong, and of how Luigi is transformed into a mafioso one restless night when he was listening to the wolves up in the hills, thinking that they were calling to him. Luigi sneaks out of his Sicilian village home and sings out: "Hey wolves, why don't you come out and play / Or else shut up so I can sleep! / I'm a village boy who's roamed this way / To romp and frolic, gambol and leap."[27] In his midnight rambles he comes upon a wolves' campsite and steals food and eats until his stomach is full for the first time in his life. He then notices a bag of gold, and after he places a few of the coins in his pocket, he gets hit by lightning "right through the crack of my culu [ass]."[28] In no time, he is transformed into a wolf and begins to run with the wolf pack.

Luigi's adventures as a wolf teach him that he can achieve justice in a world where the power is held by the *baruni* (often absentee landlords) and administered by their henchmen, the *gabbilloti*. Ardizzone here is presenting the social structure of much of Sicily during the nineteenth and early twentieth centuries, out of which it is believed the Mafia evolved. Ardizzone's wolves are Robin Hood-like bands out to balance the scales of justice for the *campagnoli*, the country folk. The wolves have transformed from men because when a man witnesses others starving, "How can he remain a man? Thus, wolf packs formed in the Sicilian forests and hills and commenced to rob the robbers, taking back a small portion of what was rightfully ours."[29] The wolves take care of one another and when a woman is widowed through the death of "a man of honor," she is taken care of by the others.[30]

Wolves are often used to symbolize characteristics associated with the gangster: loyalty, success, perseverance, intuition, independence, thought, intelligence, and the shadow. Ardizzone utilizes these in creating his *banditi* (bandits). These are local men who fight for the honor of their existence. Ardizzone flips the historical association of the Mafia with the barons by having his mafiosi or *banditi* become the wolves who fight those in power. The typical weapon of the Sicilian Mafioso is the *lupara*, a short-barreled shotgun good for spraying the shot out to drive away packs of wolves. Years later, when Luigi leaves the life of the wolves and comes to the United States, he goes to the movies and sees cowboy films that remind him of his days of running with the mafiosi. While this seems a simplistic comparison, it works to show the acclimation of the immigrant to American society and helps him see himself as part of this new country. Luigi Grigenti presents a story within his own story that tells of the creation of good and evil and supports his belief that if one wants to learn about life, "Talk not to the saint but to the sinner! The outlaw is always wiser than the sheriff."[31] Luigi's story tells that when God created the world, he created lightness and darkness, and in between the two worlds there is the world of shadows. "To be whole, a complete woman or man, one learns to move through both of these worlds. You teach your feet to walk the path in between light and darkness."[32]

As punishment for creating trouble in the heaven, Satan was banished to the world of darkness, but eventually he was able to work his way out through a crack he created by scratching endlessly against the barrier God placed between the two worlds. This is why Luigi warns his listeners that it is through the cracks that Satan can enter humans. After recounting this story of how evil enters through cracks, he supposes his listeners can "understand what happened to me that night when I heard the wolves howling in the woods, when I smelled their campfire, saw their stolen lambs, gnawed their discarded bones, fingered their gold coins, drank their water. These things opened in my mind cracks through which the desire for riches beyond my imagination spread."[33] And when he goes to a priest to confess his sins, the priest tells him he is beyond forgiveness. Luigi, the wolf, strikes the priest and realizes that the priest is nothing but a slave for the *gabbilloti*. It is after this confrontation that he returns to his human shape. His fellow wolves claim he's been bewitched and say he's cursed. When Luigi returns to his parents' house, his mother "beat all of my sins right out of me."[34]

Although this is a minor appearance of the gangster figure, it represents an advancement of the figure in that Ardizzone returns to the origins of the Sicilian mafioso to show that there are two sides to the figure—the repressive, represented by the *gabbilotti*, and the revolutionary, represented by the wolves. Significantly, it is the boy's mother who administers the punishment for his absence from home. Luigi transforms from a boy into a gangster, and while he does little more than serve as a cook to the other wolves, he still identifies strongly with their gangsterlike ways. He successfully transforms from wiseguy into wise man through being beaten by his mother, as his story about the origins of good and evil reveals. The wolf also represents the instructor or guide, and it is in this spirit that Luigi ends his tale: "Listen to me and learn these lessons well / So you don't burn for all eternity in Hell."[35] The key to understanding Ardizzone's use of the gangster figure is to see that it is a state that can be transcended. Just as Luigi is transformed as young boy into the gangster-wolf, he also is able to transform from gangster-wolf into wise man.

Both Ardizzone and Chase have renewed the figure of the gangster and employed it in the service of reviewing the role of good and evil in today's society and how that affects the rethinking of American masculinity. Chase uses the gangster figure as the emblem of a modern man who will not settle for the socially accepted "normal" life. Ardizzone uses it in the form of a Sicilian mafioso, a soldier in the class war of early twentieth century Italy who uses his experiences to teach the next generation about good and evil. The effect of both these uses of the gangster is to achieve what Jung attributes to the trickster figure: they place "the earlier low intellectual and moral level before the eyes of the more highly developed individual, so that he shall not forget how things looked yesterday."[36] In fact, both writers begin their works with figures whose masculinity is nostalgic, harkening back to a prefeminist time when manhood was predominantly male, defined by the display of one's physical powers. In both these examples, the gangster figure serves an important function in American storytelling by providing a model for what is and is not acceptable masculine behavior in American society. The next chapter examines two dramatists who have utilized the gangster figure to show new possibilities for the creation of wise men.

IV

Looking for a Few New Men

9

NEW DIRECTIONS IN
ITALIAN-AMERICAN MANHOOD

The works examined in this chapter, in one way or another, offer new models for Italian-American manhood and suggest that it is possible for a wiseguy to become a wise man. They all start from the premise that there is a gangster figure out there that nearly everyone who sees plays or movies or reads books can recognize immediately, and that to repeat the same story of that gangster figure is to embrace stagnation. These writers create new images which, though shaped by history, extend beyond history; they take the gangster figure to a place outside history where new ideas of manhood can be proposed, explored, and realized.

THE GANGSTER IN POETRY

Since his first book of poetry, *River Full of Craft* (1956), Felix Stefanile has labored steadily, quietly, and independently in the field of American letters. In 1954, with his wife Selma, he founded *Sparrow*, a journal of poetry. A veteran of World War II and in 2005 Professor Emeritus at Purdue University, Stefanile has received such prestigious awards as the Balch Prize of the *Virginia Quarterly Review* and the Pushcart Prize. His poetry has appeared in many of the most prominent U.S. journals, but he has always maintained a low profile, focusing his time and effort on his art. His major collections include *A Fig Tree in America* (1970), *East River Nocturne* (1976), *The Dance at St. Gabriel's* (1995), and *The Country of Absence* (1999). In the introductory essay to his latest volume, he argues that the Italian mindset in the United States is in disrepair, and that the antidote to a culture in disrepair is what he calls "the culture of one."[1] Stefanile, a staunch advocate of artistic integrity through independence, sees the "culture of one" as "that congeries of rules, yearnings, memories, groping, even glimmerings of transcendence most individuals carry in their breasts."[2] At its worst, the culture of one is seen "in the fragmentation of our times."[3] At its best, it gives us "the good teacher in the bad school, or the Elder—a rare but valuable resource in these times, who tells the tales of the tribe to the children."[4] When Stefanile turns his pen to the issue of the gangster, he is acting as the Elder to tell the tale of this misunderstood figure:

A Review of the Film *Godfather VII*

Italian gangsters,
all my life, Italian gangsters:
there's the one with the scar;
there's the good-looking one with the curls
who is a coward;
there's the little murderer who loves his mother;
there's the ratty one in the white car
blowing on his nails;
there's the dignified old Don who turns good,
and dies;
there's the big, oily one being gunned down
in the restaurant—his head sinks
into his bowl of spaghetti;
the man with the machine-gun is Italian too,
and grinning.
Italian gangsters,
all my life Italian gangsters;
you too, Leonardo, and Galileo,
and you too Pop.[5]

Stefanile's poem, written before *The Godfather Part III* appeared, presents a series of expected images, all quite stereotypical, of the gangster. These images pile up until the surprise ending, "Leonardo, and Galileo, / and you too Pop." Eventually the stereotype comes to represent all Italian-American men, even those most remote from the image. The Italian-American gangster has eclipsed all the "good" history of Italians. Stefanile voices in this poem his frustration with the fact that years of powerful media-driven imagery can and eventually will distort even the historical and personal images one may construct of Italian men, so that simply putting together the two words "Italian" and "man" is likely somehow to evoke the gangster. Italian-American organizations claim that the majority of people identify Italian Americans with organized crime. One of the more recent protests involved the title of a Public Broadcasting System documentary on the Medicis which had the subtitle "Godfathers of the Renaissance." Stefanile's poem, written more than two decades ago, remains relevant today. The gangster has come to represent every Italian-American man.

Sandra Mortola Gilbert, a leading feminist literary scholar and poet, has a long history of acknowledging her Italian-American ethnicity in her work. Her important contributions to American culture, often written in collaboration with the critic Susan Gubar, include *The Madwoman in the Attic* (1979) and its three-volume sequel, *No Man's Land* (1988–1994). Gilbert often dramatizes in her poetry some of the theory that she has developed and applied in her critical studies. Although she has not produced a critical study of Italian-American masculinity, her poem "Mafioso" poses a question about its portrayal. Her twist is a play on another stereotype once used to denigrate early Italian immigrant men.

Mafioso

Frank Costello eating spaghetti in a cell at San Quentin,
Lucky Luciano mixing up a mess of bullets and
calling for parmesan cheese,
Al Capone baking a sawed-off shotgun into a
huge lasagna—
Are you my uncles, my
only uncles?
Mafiosi,
bad uncles of the barren

cliffs of Sicily—was it only you
that they transported in barrels
like pure olive oil
across the Atlantic?
Was it only you
who got out at Ellis Island with
black scarves on your heads and cheap cigars
and no English and a dozen children?
No cars were waiting, gallant with paint,
no little donkeys plumed like the dreams of peacocks.
Only the evil eyes of a thousand buildings
stared across at the echoing debarkation center,
making it seem so much smaller than a piazza,
only a half dozen Puritan millionaires stood on the wharf,
in the wind colder than the impossible snows of the
    Abruzzi,
ready with country clubs and dynamos
to grind the organs out of you.[6]

Though getting some facts wrong—Luciano was the only Sicilian among those mentioned, and Costello never did time in San Quentin—Gilbert exercises her poetic license to ask the question, "Where are the alternative images of Italian-American men?" The Puritan millionaires who watch the Italian men debark, ready to "grind the organs out of you," reminds us of how the Italian immigrant man was used by the great U.S. industrial machine to create profits for the rich, often to the physical detriment of many of the real Italian men who never became gangsters. This image also invokes another earlier stereotype of the Italian immigrant man, the organ grinder. Gilbert seizes the opportunity to show the reader that the gangster story has overshadowed many other immigrant stories, and what has been lost is the tragic tale of the honest worker who literally sacrificed his life for his family. Like Stefanile's poem, Gilbert's asks just where one can find an Italian-American wise man.

Robert Viscusi provides a glimpse of the answer in his poem "Goons and Lagoons." Viscusi, one of the foremost critics of Italian-American literature and culture, has published essays and poetry on Italian-American subjects. His award-winning novel *Astoria* is examined in the next chapter. Here I look at one of his poems that references gangsters in a much more obscure way than Stefanile's or Gilbert's poetry:

Goons and Lagoons

Gangsters in gondolas glide down the streets of Las Vegas.
What does it matter that this is a desert?
The water is a form of liquidity.
The gangsters are my leaders insofar as I am an Italian in
    America.
Desert lakes glitter with pumped cash.
Don't tell me I'm not special, because I have been to Italy.
In the Biblioteca San Marco I have read manuscript
    codices.
The water climbs the marble stairs in the entrance halls.
Seaweed hangs from every stone you can see of the
    library's foundation.
Albert Anastasia was murdered in a barber's chair at the
    Sheraton.
He had a brother who was a priest at Saint Lucy's in the
    Bronx.
Father Anastasia didn't speak English too well.
We used to go to the Bronx just to make our confessions.
The Cadillacs would silently turn the corner of Allerton
    Avenue.
Gangsters in cherrywood coffins would slide into the
    church.
The Island of San Michele in the lagoon is the cemetery.
The water eats everything.
After a few decades the graves are empty.
Venetians one after another have lain in the same graves.
In America it is the cities we bury.
The money eats them the way water eats corpses.[7]

Viscusi's reference to gangsters being the leaders of Italian America is ironic, but it also reflects the more literal interpretation of the gangster phenomenon that many Americans see as the *only* style of Italian-American masculinity. By the end of this poem, Viscusi achieves the presentation of an alternative to the gangster—the intellectual. Paired with the gangster, both contemporary (as evoked by the Las Vegas images) and historical (through the presence of the infamous Albert Anastasia[8]) is the Italian-American intellectual who reads in a Venetian library. Viscusi also juxtaposes the idea of gondolas in the Las

Vegas desert with their original Italian site of Venice, an image that brings to mind the placement of Italian culture in American culture. The gangsters in this poem form a point by which we can reference the wisdom of the poet. The light cast on the important archival literary work of the scholar and poet throws the superficiality of the gangster's material world into the shadows. Viscusi's alternative to the wiseguy who has captured America's imagination for so long is the wise man whose work can actually save Italian-American culture from drowning in a sea of gangster images.

CHAZZ PALMINTERI'S ONE-MAN SHOW

The movie *A Bronx Tale* (1993), Robert DeNiro's directorial debut, was adapted from a one-man show written and performed by Chazz Palminteri. On the surface the film might seem stereotypical in its portrayals, but Palminteri's gangster, based on a real man he knew in his youth, is a more rounded character than almost any examined so far in this book. The film, thus, is more a father–son story than the portrait of a gangster. The story involves two periods of young Calogero Anello's life, at the ages of nine and seventeen. Calogero is growing up in the Bronx under the influence of his father and a local gangster, who both try to shape his sense of masculinity.

The film opens with a camera shot that drops down from the sky into the Bronx neighborhood where the story takes place, creating a mythic perspective. Calogero, as a young boy, witnesses a local gangster's murder of another thug. When he is questioned by the police, he does not reveal what he knows. For that show of support, the gangster, Sonny, takes a liking to the boy and keeps an eye on him as he grows up. Much of the film covers ground familiar from films such as Scorsese's *GoodFellas*. There is the same use of the protagonist's voice over the action, creating a documentary effect; there are a number of shots that seem right out of Scorsese's film, emphasizing the perfect shine on the gangsters' shoes, the men with big stomachs, and the men gathering on the street. In spite of these stylistic similarities, however, there is a major difference in the story line. Through the character of Calogero's father, Lorenzo, Palminteri provides a moral compass that is conspicuously absent from almost every other gangster film. Calogero is attracted to Sonny's power, but from time to time during the course of the film his actions are checked by Lorenzo, who knows very well the dangers of attraction to the world of the local gangsters.

The beauty of this story is seeing young Calogero making the choice between living the life of Sonny and that of his father, a bus driver. He actually has a choice.

Chez Bippy is the club where Sonny hangs out and from which he unofficially governs the neighborhood. Sonny is first seen from Calogero's perspective, from a low angle looking up, and as Sonny is framed, Calogero's voiceover calls him "The Man." The shot is the culmination of that first sweep of the neighborhood, including scenes of what the narrator calls "young Italian men romancing their women"—a man driving his car down the street and yelling out at a woman walking on the sidewalk, "Get in the fucking car!" There are also shots of young boys in action—playing around an opened fire hydrant, standing outside a candy store listening to music, teasing and stealing from a horse-cart peddler, and hopping on the back of Lorenzo's bus for a free ride. These scenes are juxtaposed with shots of what the neighborhood men are doing—talking on the street corner, hanging around the bar at Chez Bippy, and playing craps in the building's basement. At the beginning of the film, Calogero is nine years old and dying to be an adult. He imitates the adult men he sees; he makes the sign of the cross just after his father does when they pass a church and when his father lets him off the bus at his stop, Calogero sneaks into Chez Bippy to watch the men gamble. The voiceover repeats a roll call of the men's nicknames — Tony Toupee, Eddie Mush, Jo Jo Whale, Frankie Coffee Cake, Jimmy Whispers, and Bobby Bars. Calogero's mother finds him in Chez Bippy and pulls him out to their building's stoop, scolding him for going near the bar and warning him not to do it again. But the attraction is too strong. Calogero and his friends imitate Sonny's speech and gestures and the men's racism, chasing the black kids who ride buses through the neighborhood.

When Calogero witnesses Sonny shooting another thug, Lorenzo grabs him and takes him home. The police investigate, but father and son both say nothing, in traditional *omertà* fashion. When the police let them go, Calogero turns proudly to his father and says, "We fooled 'em. I didn't rat," and his father nods, but says, "You did a good thing for a bad man." Calogero's face shows his confusion and Lorenzo launches into a lecture about doing the right thing. "You can be anything," he tells his son. "There's nothing worse than wasted talent. When you do right, good things happen." The lesson has been heard, but it will not be learned for a while.

Soon after, Calogero goes to confession to repent his sins, and when he confesses having witnessed the murder, the priest asks him if he knows what "the Fifth" is, meaning the fifth commandment. Calogero answers by giving a definition of the self-incrimination response connected to the Fifth Amendment, made famous by U.S. gangsters in the courtroom. This scene shows clearly that the gangster's hold on the boy is stronger than his religious upbringing. When the priest chastises Calogero for this, the boy replies: "Your guy's bigger than my guy up there, but my guy's bigger down here." He is acknowledging the power that Sonny has over his world of the neighborhood and the priest agrees. This is a power that Calogero finds deeply attractive and one that he tries to obtain.

Sonny summons Calogero and asks the boy if he's afraid of him. Calogero responds with a crisp and simple "No," endearing him to the gangster even more. He tells the boy that his name, Calogero, is tough, and renames him "C." Sonny takes C under his wing, and the boy starts serving drinks in Chez Bippy to the gamblers. Sonny gives the dice to C, who has a streak of winning throws, and afterwards, when Sonny hands him money, he also gives C what he thinks is sound advice: "The working man's a sucker. You get two educations—in the street and in school." Sonny adopts him as the son he never had and starts to take him everywhere, introducing C as "his boy."

It's not long before C's new life is discovered by his mother. She finds the money he has hidden in his room and turns it over to Lorenzo. She begs Lorenzo to keep the money for the family's use. Lorenzo demonstrates stronger values than his wife when he returns the money to Sonny. In the confrontation that follows, Sonny defends his actions by saying, "I treat him like he's my kid," to which Lorenzo responds, "You don't fool with a man's family." Sonny takes Lorenzo's action as an insult, and one of his soldiers asks if he should "take care" of Lorenzo. Sonny shakes his head and watches as Lorenzo walks off holding Calogero, explaining to his son that he can't keep the money because it's bad. Then Lorenzo gives him the following advice about good money and good people: "You try getting up every morning and going to work. The working man is a tough guy. They don't love him [Sonny], they fear him."

The time frame of the film then shifts eight years later, to the year 1968. Now the boys have their own storefront club called Deuces Wild. As C gets older, he strays from his father and is reluctant to join Lorenzo on the bus route as he used to. C and the boys are more interested in girls and the continuing antics of the older gangsters they have come to emulate. At this point the influence of Sonny and Lorenzo on C's developing sense of masculinity is apparent. C moves away from Lorenzo's influence as he moves closer to Sonny.

Sonny teaches C life lessons from a gangster's point of view. Sonny's lesson in how a leader should behave in public is one he got from reading Machiavelli's *The Prince*: "Availability: they [meaning the people in the neighborhood] feel safe when they know I'm close." When he's close, a leader can see trouble developing and, as Sonny says, "Trouble's like a cancer; if gets too big, it gets you." A final lesson, "Nobody cares," basically means that a man must look out for himself. Sonny then launches into another lesson he picked up from reading Machiavelli: leaders can rule by fear and or love. Sonny says, "I'd rather be feared than loved. Fear keeps you loyal, but don't be hated."

C witnesses Sonny's leadership in action as Sonny's boys beat the hell out of a motorcycle gang that starts trouble in Chez Bippy. Later, when Sonny notices that C is trying to emulate him by hanging around with the troublemakers at Deuces Wild, he warns C, "Don't do what I do. I do what I have to do; this is not for you."

A major conflict between Lorenzo and Sonny occurs when C tells both of them about his interest in a black girl from school. C has no problem telling Sonny that he's interested in the girl. He presents it to his father as though it is a friend who is attracted to the girl. Sonny tells him that her skin color is not important. What is important is "how you feel about each other." Sonny then goes on to tell C that there are three great women who come along in a man's life, "every ten years, like in the fights," referring to great boxers. He's proud of C and lends him his car for the date. Unlike Sonny, Lorenzo tells his son that he should "Marry within our own. I'm not prejudice, but you would never do that." Here, the advice from the gangster is more helpful. When C tells his father he's going to be using Sonny's car, Lorenzo tells his son that he doesn't want him to. Then Lorenzo tells C: "That man [Sonny] can't be trusted. They don't respect him, they fear him. Be somebody, go to work and take care of your family." When C asks his father to call him by his new name, "C," Lorenzo tells him that changing his grandfather's name shows great disrespect to the family.

C finally begins to see through Sonny's bravado when Sonny, after finding an unexploded bomb in his car, accuses C of planting it there. C yells back at him, "You're like a father to me. Don't you trust anyone?"

When Sonny tells him he doesn't, and that "It's the only way," C tells him, "Not for me." C joins his friends in his buddy's car as they head toward the black kids' hangout with a back seat full of Molotov cocktails. When Sonny sees C get into the car, he comes over and forces C out. He tells the boys to stay away from C. Later the car explodes when one of the gang's bombs is tossed back into it. When C sees his friends' bodies, he runs back to thank Sonny for saving his life.

As he gets to Chez Bippy, C sees Sonny get shot by the son of the man whom Sonny had shot years before. A vendetta has been enacted, and another boy has become a man by avenging his own father's murder. At Sonny's wake we hear "Ave Maria," a song normally reserved for weddings. The use of it here suggests the suffering mother who must see her dead son, a nod to the *mater dolorosa* role of the Italian woman.

The last scene finds the new head gangster, Carmine, paying his respects at Sonny's wake. When he leaves, Lorenzo comes in to tell C, "Everything's going to be OK." Then he turns to Sonny's corpse and thanks him for keeping an eye out for his son. C has the last word to Sonny and tells his body, "Nobody cares, you were wrong about that one." Then he says, "Wasted talent." This signals that Calogero has learned from both his father and the gangster. As the father and son walk away, the voiceover returns and C says, "I did understand. Give and get love unconditionally, accept who they are. The choices you make shape your life forever." There can be no doubt that Palminteri's protagonist is on his way to becoming a wise man.

BEYOND THE INVETERATE WISEGUY WITH RICHARD VETERE

Richard Vetere is a poet, playwright, novelist, and film and television writer and actor. Once nominated for a Pulitzer Prize for his play *One Shot, One Kill* (2002), he is the author of more than forty plays, including *Gangster Apparel* (1996), *The Engagement* (1998), *First Love* (1998), *The Marriage Fool* (1998), *Hale the Hero!* (1996), and *How To Go Out on a Date in Queens* (2000).[9] His first novel, *The Third Miracle* (1998), was made into a film starring Ed Harris and Ann Heche. Although most of his work does not deal directly with Italian-American culture, most of the plays that do have a gangster figure. More often than not, Vetere's gangster is presented in a humorous light and reveals the absurdity of gangster behavior as a model for contemporary masculine behavior.

Gangster Apparel is Vetere's first and only play dealing directly and exclusively with the gangster figure. The two-act comedy features two characters, Louie Falco and Joey Pugg, small-time hoods who get a chance to kill somebody for the mob. Louie is a slick, fancy dresser who, as the writer's note says, "believes that style is more important than substance." Joey, his partner, is a slob who thinks nothing of how he dresses. The play deals with how the two of them confront the surfaces and depths of the gangster life.

The first act focuses on Louie's obsession with looking good at any cost. He tries to teach his partner how to dress as well. Louie is a city boy who is quite uncomfortable in nature: "I hate sand, I hate rocks in my toes, and I hate that smell that comes up from Jersey. And no matter what beach you are on, I don't care where you are, you are going to get hit with that smell that comes up from Jersey! Plus, you walk on a beach and you step on dead things."[10] Louie's discomfort with nature, echoing Charlie Cappa's reaction to nature in *Mean Streets*, sets him up as an urban boy who is at home in the horizonless city. Louie believes in a good shoeshine: "I noticed the other day with the boss … . And I was sittin' out in the car like always and I watched him get into the limo and saw how his shoes were shining all the way over there! I mean, I was across the street and saw them shine!"[11] Through Louie, Vetere establishes the wiseguy's obsession with how he looks. For Louie, it's important to be dressed well, even when you're being arrested: "The cops bust in on you and see you dressed in a nice robe with silk lining, a silk pair of pjs and good slippers and they will treat you like SOMEBODY!"[12] The key to being important is to look important.

In an attempt to help his friend Joey look better, Louie gives him a new $1,200 tailor-made suit to put on. As they rehearse the hit, Louie stresses to Joey that they must look good doing it: "Come on, pal, you don't have to go to college to know how to look good when you are shootin' somebody! Don't you watch TV?"[13] Joey puts on the suit and loves the way it makes him look. He thanks Louie "for making me see myself as I was, so I can change myself to be better."[14] Louie concludes that "one day when we are famous the papers will say 'Louie Falco and Joey Pugg are the two best-dressed hoods in town.'"[15] In this first scene, Vetere establishes the connection between the wiseguy's wardrobe and the wiseguy's mind.

Scene Two finds the boys in a jail cell. They were caught because one of the witnesses to the hit identified Louie by the distinguished handkerchief in his jacket pocket. Joey has been in jail before, feels comfortable there, and now becomes Louie's teacher. Louie feels quite vulnerable. Now that he's dressed like everyone else, there's nothing to distinguish him from others so that people will know who he is. He cannot separate himself from the slick gangster image he had created out on the streets. As the two recount the actions leading up to and through the hit, Louie comments on how good their newspaper photographs looked and laments the fact that they didn't make the front page. Even Joey admits that the photos "gave me some pride."[16] In the course of their discussion Louie realizes that he cannot survive in jail, while Joey feels right at home and even sees a number of his friends and family inside. Joey teaches Louie that the key to doing time is to accept things as they are: "What you see in front of you, that's what it is. There ain't nothin' else. A thumb is a thumb. A wall is a wall. A guy is who he is and that's it."[17] In jail there are no distractions like fancy clothes to disguise the fact that everyone there is equal. Louie suggests that they should take the district attorney up on the offer of immunity in exchange for testifying against the boss. Joey is appalled at this suggestion that they violate the gangster code of doing time with dignity and says he could never be disloyal, especially by giving the boss up to the Feds. In the end, Louie convinces him that "there are no rules anymore, Joey. There's no justice. So I say, we have to change with the times."[18] Louie continues his argument by emphasizing the discomfort they will have to endure and the possible emasculation that will happen to them if they don't take the deal: "If we stay here we gotta face fifteen years with no women? No real food? No cars to drive? No women? Do you know what happens to guys who don't have women for fifteen years? They get distorted upstairs. They start to think that young boys are girls! … . I ain't pretendin' some guy is a girl for no boss."[19] Joey reminds him that once they enter the witness protection program they can no longer be who they were. But Louie thinks he can "be one of those people"—a Louis Smith if he has to be.[20]

Act Two is set in a trailer camp in Yuma, Arizona. Joey and Louie are dressed as cowboys and the scene is laden with Western paraphernalia and, oddly, a Confederate flag. Vetere is trying to connect the gangster figure with what he sees as its cultural ancestor, the cowboy. Joey has adapted well to the move and his new identity as "Jesse." He's become engaged to Holly May Butane (Willow Jane, in a later version of the play), who belongs to a family "that has been in these parts since

Geronimo."[21] Louie can't take his new life as "Roy": "I'm no Roy Rogers."[22] He can't stand the desert, hates western food, and longs for "some scungeli [*sic*] and calamari and some clams casino."[23] Joey, on the other hand, is beginning to find his way to becoming a wise man:

> JOEY: Louie, when you first suggested this Witness Protection program, I was skeptical, I'll admit. But now, I do see the wisdom of your vision. You really knew what you were talking about. Thanks to you convincing me, I am now going to mix my blood with the blood of a blue-blooded woman. Joey Pugg will have kids who will have blood in their veins that goes back to the Civil War.[24]

Since entering the program, Joey has started reading and growing plants. He tells Louie, "Thanks to the Witness Protection Program my blood line will advance and my children will become PEOPLE."[25] The program has enabled Joey to see beyond the restrictions of his earlier upbringing.

In a revision of the original 1993 production, Vetere strengthened his earlier renunciation of the gangster and used the figure in a sincere attempt to make sense of the influence of Italian culture on American culture. Vetere understands that Italian-American culture is a culture of indirection in which people can hide what they really feel behind actions and clothes. He makes the point that to leave Little Italy is to move into the world, and to use a language that is not ambiguous, and therefore seemingly less deceiving. This becomes evident in an exchange toward the end of the play in a section added since its 1996 publication. Joey tells Louie about how life with his new girlfriend is different from what they've experienced thus far:

> JOEY: The words she uses, Louie. Willow Jane wouldn't even think about using that kind of language [swear words]. She reminds me of my mother that way. Let me tell you something, I am learning out here that out here you are what you say, you are what you think, you are what you do.
>
> LOUIE: And where is "out here," my friend?
>
> JOEY: It's America, Louie. The America I never knew was real. When I was growin' up, I thought we had only

three choices. Be a cop, a priest or a wise guy. Now
I know there are other ways to go.[26]

Through this exchange Vetere suggests that renunciation of
the gangster mindset requires learning things one never knew
before, and learning how to use language to express what one
wants and not to hide it. Joey shows Louie the books that he's
been reading about the contributions Italians like Galileo have
made to the world. He then rattles off a litany of Italian-American inventors, scientists, and other *prominenti* who contributed
to Western civilization:

JOEY: How come I don't know this, Louie? How come
        nobody told me? All they told me was about *The
        Godfather*. There's more important things to read
        about than war. There are more important people
        than generals. Nobody told me about other things
        I could have been … other things I could have seen
        myself as …

(then)

        Don't you get it? We could have been these guys.[27]

"These guys" to Joey means anything but the gangsters that they've
become. Like Louisa Ermelino's Joey Dee, Vetere's gangsters find a
way out of their past by traveling west. Vetere's Joey learns new ways
of behaving from his new girlfriend. But for Louie, it's a different story.
It's not long before Louie reveals that he's not going to be able to handle
his new life as well as he had hoped, and it's not long before their past
comes to visit them.

Louie confesses to Joey that he's reverted to some of his old habits,
one of which is playing cards, and Joey yells at him:

JOEY: Look, we came out here to start new lives. We were
        bad and now we're good. We were from the neigh-
        borhood and now we're cowboys. We were killers
        and now we are upstanding citizens. And upstand-
        ing citizens do not play poker in whorehouses! [28]

Louie lets him know that the mayor's brother was there too, but Joey shakes it off and says he wants to go straight this time: "At least you can try and change your spots."[29]

> LOUIE: You're talkin' like Joey Pugg was some saint before he met me. Who did time for robbin' a bar? Who used to hijack trucks for a living? You [Joey] used to run numbers! You used to dress like some low-life on the street! [30]

For Joey change is possible; for Louie, it's impossible. Louie reveals that he played cards with a couple of guys from the old neighborhood who were sent out to kill him and Joey. The guys offered Louie the opportunity to make good by killing Joey. When Joey asks Louie why they wouldn't kill him as well, Louie reveals to Joey that when they were still in jail he told the other guys it was Joey's idea to go into the program, and that this is the word that got back to the boss.

The Witness Protection Program has become, for Joey at least, a kind of school in which he can make the transition from wiseguy to wise man. Louie, stuck on superficialities, cannot make that transition. He can't reach deeper than the surface of things. Perhaps that's how he was able to take care of the thugs who came out to kill him and Joey. For a while, Joey thinks that he and Louie will have to kill each other, but ultimately he realizes that he needs to keep moving, and that means he must stay far away from being the old Joey Pugg:

> JOEY: A man should be from someplace, he should have thoughts about things, he should be proud of what he is. But the minute he ain't any of those things, then it's time for him to become somebody else. (*A beat*) It's time I turn my back on Joey Pugg forever.[30]

Louie realizes that he can't be anyone else but Louie. The answer is for them to split up. And so this comedy turns dramatic and presents a resolution of the wiseguy versus wise man dilemma.

If Joey and Louie should be seen not as separate characters, but as two voices inside the same man, the challenge the young Italian-American boy faces as he travels down the road to manhood becomes apparent. Vetere parodies the many gangster characters who have come before his, but unlike more obvious gangster parodies and comedies—*The Freshman* (1990), *My Blue Heaven* (1990), *Jane Austen's Mafia* (1998), *Analyze This* (1999), and *Analyze That* (2002), none of which were created by Italian Americans—his play attempts to say something serious about the gangster and, therefore, it offers a fresh way of looking at the plight of the gangster figure. At the end of the play, while Louie is admirable for his prowess and his ability to see trouble coming and deal with it, it is Joey who proves that a wiseguy becomes a wise man when he begins to use his intellect to move beyond the limitations of a life lived only on the surface. For Vetere, a wise man is one who can change when he needs to.

Vetere continued to use the gangster figure in a number of other plays, most obviously in *The Classic* (1998) and the book he wrote for the musical *A Hundred Years into the Heart* (2004). In *The Classic*, the gangster never makes it onto the stage, but by hovering in the background throughout much of the play, he functions as a reminder that the gangster figure lies at the lower end of the evolutionary scale for the Italian-American male.

In this play, the Italian-American man becomes a writer and an intellectual as the gangster figure recedes into the background. When the gangster surfaces in the play, it is to serve a humorous purpose and then disappear. Vetere achieves a depiction of the wiseguy's struggle to become the wise man by becoming an artist. For Michael Forte, the main character in *The Classic*, nothing is more important than being a writer, and his life has been totally devoted to his writing. Michael creates art, not children, because "When you have a child, something of yourself is diminished, lost, and when you create a work of art, something of yourself is heightened: you create but you remain intact."[31] His main girlfriend, Carmela, is from the neighborhood and her grandfather is the reigning local don.

During the two-act play, Michael is confronted by his car mechanic, an aspiring writer who has come to him for advice, a crazed lawyer who believes that Michael has plagiarized his work, a publisher who wants Michael as a lover, a lover who wants Michael as a husband, and a young tenant who he believes is the key to finding true love. As he works his way through these conflicts, he comes to realize that he is not happy with his life. He is trying to figure out what it means to be a man:

CARMELA: Oh, be a man, for God's sake.
MICHAEL: What is that supposed to mean?

CARMELA: You know what it's supposed to mean.

MICHAEL: No, I don't know. And I hate it when people use that expression: "Be a Man." No, I don't want to be a man. YOU be a man. Try it and see how you like it!

CARMELA: My grandfather is a real man, and he never complains.

MICHAEL: Oh great, I knew he was going to come into the conversation. The great Capo De Vico. He kills people for a living, Carmela! That's not the kind of man I have in mind when I say the word MAN!

CARMELA: He provides for his family! He keeps the neighborhood safe! He is a general doing battle against the federal government and the other families who sell drugs and prostitutes.

MICHAEL: You're making him sound like the Lone Ranger.

CARMELA: He's my hero!

MICHAEL: Of course he is! And if you had two balls and a dick, you'd be out there killing along with him! [32]

Michael is smart enough to realize that the traditional way of being a man, especially when it's connected to the gangster life, is not always the answer.

When Michael's agent arrives, she brings him news of the rejection of his latest manuscript by most of the publishers she's shown it to. That manuscript is an autobiographical book entitled *Bread and Veal*. One of the rejection letters says, "Mr. Forte writes like a young Anne Tyler."[33] Another says, "'Mr. Forte is a fifties throwback. He's a macho dinosaur. If we publish this book, we'll be seen as archeologists."[34] The one publisher who is willing to take it is Vivian Smit, who sees in the book "What it means to be male today. What it means to live the perfect male life with all its vulnerability and imperfection. To redefine and make new the male perception." She goes on, "The masculine mind is under siege .... The realization that his testicles produced 100 million sperm a day—Michael, what a moment. And then he goes on and discovers that sperm can be deformed and still impregnate."[35] Michael's book might be a throwback to the old notions of masculinity, but it is something that excites Vivian to no end.

Michael is on the phone when another call comes in. It's Carmela's grandfather:

> MICHAEL: Oh, Mr. DeVicio! (*MICHAEL turns white*.) You just saw Carmela run down the street naked and run into my house. Your granddaughter is not naked, sir. Capo, o great-godfather... (*MICHAEL bows*.) Don't come over sir. There's no need. [36]

The phone goes dead and Michael panics. He asks his car mechanic to keep an eye out for Carmela's grandfather. When asked what the guy looks like, Michael replies, "He's about four-foot-four with a fedora. Without the fedora he's two inches shorter."[37] Later on the fedora appears in the window. The hat is the only visible presence of the gangster in this play and works as a humorous threat that is never realized.

The final scene features Michael alone on stage as the voices of the other characters speak out to him. Carmela asks if he's received the sauce she made for him, and she tells him that her grandfather was called a "mobster kingpin" in the local newspaper. "They said he was extorting money from the unions! I told him he should get a lawyer and sue the reporter. He said he'd thought he'd just blow up the guy's house instead."[38] The humor here signals the end of the road for the gangster figure, and the play ends with Michael, obviously inspired by all these voices, furiously writing, creating something new. He does not succumb to the wishes of the others in the play, especially not to his girlfriend's plan for him to become a "man" like her grandfather. Michael has become the "classic" writer, and he is on his way to being a wise man.

Vetere's most recent use of the gangster figure is in the musical *A Hundred Years into the Heart* (2004). The story revolves around two men whose lives came together when they were children. A boy, Vincent, happens to catch baby Sal, who has been thrown out of an apartment window. The two meet again later in life and fall in love with the same woman, Stephanie. The gangster figure appears as Carmine, the lover of Stephanie's mother, Regina, and secretly Stephanie's father. He is a former gangster turned legitimate businessman who resorts to his old ways to protect his daughter.

From the beginning of the play, it is obvious that its creators wanted to use the gangster figure for dramatic purposes to tell a story about love and not to tell the gangster's story itself. The character Carmine serves as the action's narrator and as catalyst to the plot. Carmine is described as "handsome, sensual, in his 50s. With all of his streetwise cunning, Carmine also manages to be straight-forward and sympathetic. Wise, he is uneducated. Not wealthy, he likes to spend and dress well."[39] For all intents and purposes, Carmine is a gangster. He also speaks with the urban New York accent that has come to represent the gangster's voice.

Carmine is well aware of his image, as is evident in his first song: "It's the kind of macho posturing you'd class as asinine."[40] Carmine knows himself well: "All I'm saying is I didn't make the world. But I ain't afraid of it either."[41] He embraces his tough, macho behavior as a necessary way of being a man in his world—as the women note in a line from their duet: "But yank his chain? / The man turns into Mister Bah-Da-Bing!"[42] Carmine becomes the guide both to the setting and action of the play.

A Hundred Years into the Heart begins with Stephanie, who is engaged to Vincent but later falls in love with Sal, a cement worker who has come to work at her mother's house. Sal is described as "A wannabe. A wiseguy in the making."[43] Vincent and Sal are examples of two types of men that Stephanie's mother has experienced so far in her life. Regina was in love with Carmine, the gangster, but settled down with Phillip, a professor, because she thought he'd take better care of her. After Phillip died, Regina and Carmine started seeing each other again. Regina sees the wiseguy element in Sal and looks to Carmine to do something to help her stop him from seeing her daughter. Carmine thinks about calling the local don, Frankie Nomo, "Somebody who can make sure this Sal goes away. Like gone."[44]

In Scene Nine of Act One, Sal sings a song which characterizes his philosophy and which strongly echoes some of Louie's speeches in Vetere's *Gangster Apparel*.

> Point is … to look your best
> Bally shoes? They'll be impressed.
> Comb the hair … back and slick
> Lay the oil on … nice and thick
> Silk shirt … Armani threads
> Guaranteed to faze the Feds
> Diamond stud … for a thrill.

Brand new "piece"? You're dressed to kill!

Care in what you'll wear'll
Send the message you're Okay.
Sharpen your apparel
'Til they notice you, and hey …
It wouldn't hurt to pray.

Decked out—a fashion plate
You're gonna make the grade, man
Drinking deep and sleeping late …
You're gonna have it made.
No longer second-rate;
Straight ain't they way it's played man,
You're gonna be a made-man
You're gonna … you're gonna have it made! [45]

Like Louie, Sal believes that the way one is treated by others depends on how one is perceived, and that dressing well is one of the best ways of ensuring that one will get attention and, subsequently, respect. Vetere uses the gangster figure not to document the life of an exotic but to serve as a foil to a better form of manhood. This technique comes through clearly in the scene where Carmine tries to talk some sense into Sal. After they come close to blows, Carmine warns Sal about the gangster life.

You'll run a couple numbers …
Go collecting some guys "Vig" [loan interest]
Why? So you can thumb yer
Nose like mister "Frigging" Big,
'Til they stick you like a pig?!

Shallow graves, tossed with lime …
Keeping the capos [crime bosses] paid, kid.
Getting screwed and doing time?
You're gonna have it made!

Sweet stuff this life of crime
And everyone needs a trade, kid
When you're a man who's made kid,
Oooh, you're gonna have it made! [46]

Carmine warns Sal to stay away from Stephanie and Sal defies him. Carmine returns to Regina and she pleads for him to do something. He agrees to phone Frankie Nomo, who's been interested in becoming a partner in Carmine's restaurant. Carmine thinks it over during the shift to a scene in which Stephanie decides to move in with Sal. She does, and a little while later the news comes that Sal has been killed trying to hold up a bank, but not before getting Stephanie pregnant. Vincent returns to Stephanie and decides to marry her and adopt the baby. Carmine counsels Vincent, saying that there was nothing he could have done to save Sal: "What could you have done? Make him see that his life was worth something? He thought it was. He just wanted respect. And he thought being a wiseguy was going to bring him that."[47] The purpose of the gangster figure in this play and in much of Vetere's work is to serve as a springboard for the creation of the wise man.

The characters of Calogero from *A Bronx Tale*, Joey Pugg from *Gangster Apparel*, and Michael and Carmine from *A Hundred Years into the Heart* are all examples of what happens to young Italian-American boys exposed to the gangster lifestyle. And yet all of them are also examples of men who have learned from their gangster experience and have found better ways of moving through life. The work of Palminteri and Vetere is especially important for showcasing the process by which a wiseguy can become a wise man. Their work also uses an evolved, creative gangster figure to portray more about Italian-American life and culture than were seen in the works discussed earlier.

10

FROM MACHO TO ZERO: REDESIGNING ITALIAN-AMERICAN MASCULINITIES

The American artists of Italian descent whose work has been discussed through the course of this book have used the gangster figure to reflect various notions of what it means to be a man in American society. Those notions have shifted from the very narrow, tough, macho version of masculinity seen in Puzo's novel and Coppola's film *The Godfather*, to the more varied and fluid versions presented by Frank Lentricchia, Louisa Ermelino, and many contemporary dramatists, poets, and novelists. From the poet Robert Bly's *Iron John* (1990) to Gabriel Costans's *The Penis Dialogues* (2003), a spate of publications have appeared dealing with changing notions of masculinity. My study of the gangster figure joins this conversation by unpacking what Italian culture has brought to American ideas in the creation and performance of masculine identities through the gangster figure. This figure, in the hands of Italian-American storytellers, offers a better understanding of how masculinity has been forged and transformed over the years. In his essay " 'I'm the King': The Macho Image," Rodolfo Anaya suggests a redefinition of the word "macho"—that includes consideration of the more feminine side of humanity:

> We are not all male at any given time, nor are we all female. We need to find balance and give harmony to the deep currents of our nature. Macho need not be all male, "puro hombre." Nothing is pure one thing or the other, especially when we speak of human nature. The old dictates of the fathers have to be transformed to create a new macho, and of that we need to listen to the feminine sensibility. To listen within.[1]

Anaya is not alone in his view of how we might redefine masculinity. Feminist author bell hooks, in her book-length essay *We Real Cool* (2004), posits the notion that in order for African-American men to move away from violent versions of patriarchal manhood, they must look to the females of their culture. What I have tried to show in the previous chapters is that the gangster figure, as portrayed by Italian-American writers and artists, has shifted from modeling of masculinity from wiseguy characters to wise men. In this final chapter, I examine how we might further this progression, and I present a number of interesting recent works that point to this redirection and redefinition of Italian-American masculinities.

We are trained to believe that scholars are objective, that they write from a perspective that does not betray their upbringing, their prejudices, or their personal lives. When I first started researching masculinity, I thought there was no one more objective than I. I had read many of the major studies of masculinity and its expression in cultures American and Italian. I had read all the works in Italian-American culture that mattered, and so when it came to putting the two together, there was no one better for the task than I. I had given a few public presentations on the subject and I sold this book to a publisher before I had written it. I was on a roll. I wrote two chapters in two months. But something happened while I was writing this book that made me begin to rethink the way I was made and the way I behave, and only now, a couple of years later, am I ready to talk about it.

I use the word "design" in the title of this chapter because I see notions of masculinity and femininity as conceptions and inventions that are fashioned by humans and that can and should change over time. What follows comes from the research I have done on how "macho" got here, what it is doing here, and where it is going. In my personal fall from traditional macho masculinity, I went into a limbo state where fear and self-doubt ruled, until I learned how to work my way into maturity by leaving the macho behind. I see this as my own personal transition from being a wiseguy to becoming a wise man.

At one recent talk, I asked the audience to name a wise man, a man who models the behavior we expect from mature, wise males in our society. A long silence followed and the first name to come up was Gandalf, a character in J. R. R. Tolkien's *The Lord of the Rings*. Someone else mentioned Jimmy Carter, and that was it. One reason why people have trouble naming models is that according to what we see reflected in mass media, our society doesn't expect or even want men to mature. The models of men presented in the media continue to encourage the behavior of the explorer or the conquering playboy, even among men long and happily married. The characteristics of the men most often presented as powerful are among those that are called "macho." The song "Macho Man," recorded by the Village People, is a good example of the characteristics of macho, including male physicality and the use of that physicality to attract and conquer.

> Body ... wanna feel my body?
> Body ... such a thrill my body
> Body ... wanna touch my body?
> Body ... it's too much my body
> Check it out my body, body.
> Don't you doubt my body, body.
> talkin' bout my body, body,
> check it out my body.
>
> Every man wants to be a macho man
> to have the kind of body, always in demand
> Jogging in the mornings, go man go
> Works out in the health spa, muscles glow
> You can best believe that, he's a macho man
> ready to get down with, anyone he can. [2]

This song has become an anthem of the macho myth and its place in marking out masculinity.

"Macho" is about the way a man presents his self, his body, in public. Recently, a "new macho" has been noted in relation to U.S. President George W. Bush. From Barbara Ehrenreich's coverage of the 2004 Democratic National Convention in *The New York Times* to David

Ford's take on hypermasculinity in the Bush administration published in the *San Francisco Chronicle*, there is concern that this new macho can be quite destructive.[3] Paraphrasing the work of Stephen Ducat from his book, *The Wimp Factor: Gender Gaps, Holy Wars and the Politics of Anxious Masculinity* (2004), Ford writes: "Ducat said that men with the extreme type of masculinity afraid of characteristics traditionally considered feminine—self-reflection, attunement to others, appreciation for human interrelatedness—may become sociopaths—those possessed of a guilt-free capacity to hurt others for personal gain."[4]

The answer that both these writers and many others suggest is a deeper embracing of feminism, and this is also hinted at by the authors discussed in this book who have reinvented the gangster figure. That figure, as presented in romantic and realist fiction, has done a good job of preserving old-fashioned, tough-guy macho that keeps men connected to physical power and its expression in violence. Only if we begin to see macho posturing as performance can we ask the questions that will help us redesign what we see as "American male." Somewhere between the Italian and the American man, a balance can be achieved in a new way of being a man which Italian-American writers are discovering. This point is the state of being I call "zero."

Anaya, a Latino writer, suggests that we must know the history of masculinity in order to move beyond it: "The essence of maleness doesn't have to die, it merely has to be understood and created anew. To re-create is evolution's role. We can take an active role in it, but to do so we have to know the history of false behavioral conditioning."[5] This "false behavioral conditioning" can be seen in the way the gangster figure has functioned in American storytelling.

Mario Puzo's version in *The Godfather* humanized the gangster figure. However, Vito and Michael Corleone remained staunchly macho, even in the face of increasing rights for women. Scorsese's gangsters reinforced this notion and firmly established the Italian-American gangster as the prototype for a postfeminist masculinity that remained untouched by social and political developments stemming from the women's movement of the 1970s. Both the romanticization and the realization of the gangster in American popular culture set up the Italian-American male as one of the last survivors of old-fashioned macho masculinity. However, the strong, silent type of man who settled scores with his fists instead of diplomacy became politically incorrect. When Tony Soprano asks his psychiatrist, "What ever happened to the

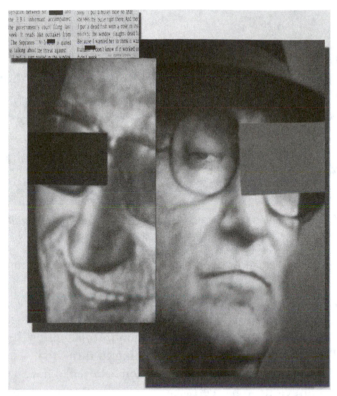

Figure 10.1   Antonio Petracca, *Sopra Nono,* 2004, oil. (Courtesy of the Kim Foster Gallery, New York City.)

strong silent type played by Gary Cooper?" in the first episode of *The Sopranos*, he is asking a question that his very presence in the media answers. It is through the reinvention of the gangsters created by David Chase, Giose Rimanelli, Frank Lentricchia, Louisa Ermelino, Anthony Valerio, Richard Vetere, Chazz Palminteri, and many others that new possibilities are available for the old stock characters. Ultimately, the power of the gangster figure shifts from reinforcing macho masculinity to freeing the power of the writer, the creator, the artist to question the status quo.

This shift of power is also seen in the art of Antonio Petracca. In "These are not my Shoes (Queste non sono mie scarpe)," an exhibition of Petracca's recent work at the Kim Foster Gallery in New York City, the gangster figure appears in a number of pieces, performing versions of masculinity.[6] What is unique about Petracca's gangster is that when visible in the paintings, he is never a completed or whole image. He

Figure 10.2 Antonio Petracca, *Natura Morta/Un Tavolo Stereotipico per Due, Grazie,* 2004, oil. (Courtesy of the Kim Foster Gallery, New York City.)

often appears as a shadow or is distorted, as in a piece titled *Sopra Nono* (Figure 10.1). In this work, the artist has placed red and black blocks over a portrait of Junior Soprano, Tony's uncle. One of the blocks covers an eye, as if to keep the audience from being seduced by the gangster's gaze, or to show that there is limited vision in this figure. This distortion led some viewers at the show's opening to think that the portrait was of Paul Castellano, a real-life Mafia don believed to have been murdered by John Gotti. What Petracca attempts in this work, and in others, is the erasure of the gangster. By revealing the incompleteness of the gangster figure, he drains the figure of the power it has to represent Italian-American culture.

In *Natura Morta/Un Tavolo Stereotipico per Due, Grazie* (Figure 10.2), or "Dead Nature" (the Italian phrase for what in English is called "still life"), the display of a gangster's shadow in the painting's background turns the real-life gangster into a silhouette; though still shadowing other aspects of Italian-American culture, he is on his way out of the picture. Through Petracca's revisioning of the gangster figure and his use of it in his art, he shows the damage the stereotype has done by narrowing the perspective on Italian-American masculinity.

Maria Manhattan, a New York artist, has painted a portrait of John Gotti (Figure 10.3) that makes a statement about family connections; she has told me that she recognized similarities between Gotti and the males in her own family.[7] She suggests that to see an Italian-American man is to see John Gotti all over again, since the dominant image of the Italian-American male is the gangster. Art like these works emphasizes

Figure 10.3 Maria Manhattan, *The Death of Macho*. (Reprinted by permission of the artist.)

the importance of moving Italian-American masculinity away from macho toward zero.

Zero is the absence of macho. However, more important for my argument is that zero means less an absolute degree than a point of balance. For many years the gangster has been the dominant way Italian-American masculinity has been portrayed in American popular culture, even by Italian-American writers. However, during this same time many other Italian-American writers have been involved in redefining Italian-American masculinity, even if their work has been more obscure. What interests me is what *these* Italian-American artists are saying and how they themselves are redesigning notions of Italian-American masculinity. There are many doing the brave work of dismantling the armor of macho and with a new sense of vulnerability trying to connect to and express their feelings.

One last theme being tackled again is the centrality of the mother–son bond in the Italian-American experience. Early Italian-American writers knew the power of the mother, and novelists like Puzo celebrated this in works like *The Fortunate Pilgrim* before they felt the pressure to create a patriarchal version of masculinity that was more expected and accepted in the United States, as Puzo did in *The Godfather*. What follows is a discussion of a number of works in which women in general, and mothers in particular, form the center of a young boy's experience of becoming a man. These works restore the image of the mother to its place of power in Italian-American culture and offer alternatives to the traditional versions of patriarchal manhood. I am not saying that by simply writing about the mother these writers humanize notions of masculinity and, thus, eliminate socially destructive macho ways. Rather, these portrayals are unique to U.S. literature and offer new ways of seeing men and being a man in the United States.

NEW WAYS TO WISE MEN

Robert Viscusi's Astoria (1995)

A key work that turns away from macho and toward a more balanced human masculinity is Robert Viscusi's novel *Astoria*. To understand Viscusi's novel, which won the American Book Award, it helps to know a little about how the Baroque and Rococo styles of art are manifested in literature, painting, and music, for in this innovative work Viscusi paints the past and composes music with words in these styles. Like the later Romantic movement, the Baroque suggests emotion through sensory perceptions and the Rococo elaborates that excess. It also helps to know how fundamental the mother–son relationship is in Italian culture, and the powerful way that relationship has been depicted in Italian art, especially in images of the Madonna and Child. Viscusi, one of the foremost critics of Italian-American literature and culture, a president of the Italian-American Writers Association and director of the Wolfe Humanities Institute at Brooklyn College, has captured what it means to be an Italian-American man in a way no one has attempted before. In direct defiance of the simple masculine portrayals in *The Godfather*, Viscusi's version of masculinity goes a long way toward realizing what a wise man could be; and he shows that to be wise is not to be glamorous or hip and that wisdom comes with great effort and through much difficulty.

Opening with a Prologue subtitled "The Stendhal Syndrome," Viscusi sets up an unreliable narrator who presents his story of traveling from America to Paris during the 1980s. The narrator explains that what we are reading could be real history, but also could be pure story. It is in fact both. "Astoria," the name of an area in New York City (so called after John Jacob Astor), is also a play on Italian *la storia*, "history." But in Italian, prefixing a word with *a-* can change the root word into its antonym, much as the prefix *un-* works in English. And so "Astoria" cannot be read as pure history. It is a place between history and story, and there lies the magic and metaphor for Italian America.

"The Stendhal Syndrome" is something that happens to tourists and others who travel to historic, beautiful places and are so overwhelmed by the art they view that they swoon, or they go slightly mad and even hallucinate. Macho men, of course, don't swoon. Viscusi uses this syndrome as a way of describing the social mobility of post-immigrant generations: "You feel guilty seeing what your parents couldn't and you want to go home," he writes.[8] Great art makes great demands on the viewer and sometimes the effects can be physical.

The Prologue then introduces a travel storyline about a professor who goes to Paris and then meets his family in Italy, and it also chronicles the travel of his immigrant predecessors. Much of the writing works as a form of meditation—an extended meditation on the meaning of cultures European and American, on travel and migration, on mother and Madonna and father and *padrino* (godfather), and on one's love of the lost and the lost loves of one's past. In the opening, "A Note from the Author," Viscusi admits the dominance of the mother in the artistic life of a son: "This is a woman's book written by a man. The writer is totally dominated by his mother's imagination. He struggles to escape, but keeps falling back. Think of an ambitious dolphin trying to climb onto dry land."[9]

The novel's importance, in terms of rethinking Italian-American masculinity, resides in the poignant, poetic phrases which evoke haunting images, like this one of his mother on her deathbed:

now lying still in the bright cheerful room as the priest went through the motions and my son kept imagining that either it wasn't really his grandmother in the bed with her face sagging on the side or else she was suddenly going to get up and be bet-

ter, a belief I myself never got rid of even after all these emer-
gencies, sudden pulmonary edema, sudden pneumonias, sudden un-nameable infections, oceans of mucus drawn through
a tube in her from her lungs with a machine.[10]

In "Part I, The Invalids," the narrator is a tourist walking through the
streets of Paris looking for the dead. In Paris, the ghosts of European
history meet the ghosts of the narrator's history at Napoleon's tomb in
Les Invalides, originally an old soldiers' home founded by Louis XIV in
1670, and now the site of many of Paris's museums. This is a fitting loca-
tion for the narrator's meditation and retrospection. It is here, two years
after his mother's death, that the narrator, burdened by grief and history, begins to write the weight off his shoulders by composing a travel
book that could be a novel. He confronts the ghosts of both Napoleon
and his family as he wanders through the monument-rich precinct of
Les Invalides, a metaphor of those in his past whose lives have yet to
be validated through history and through literature. In one masterful
stroke, Viscusi validates Italian Americans through a meditation on
a mother's death. This narrator's meditation contains the essence of a
new way of viewing Italian American masculinity. His meditations on
the meaning of migration, sensitized by the feminine perspective he
has gained through his mother, comprise some of the wisest and witti-
est observations on Italian-American culture ever to find their way to
the printed page:

> How do you love your mother? You do not love her in the con-
> templation of her beauty, her swift fingers and her grace at con-
> versation, admiring these excellences of course even as you tot
> up the things that, over the years, their sustenance might have
> cost you or drawn from you as a sign of your own always amaz-
> ing "virtù," as you know, because loving her in the contempla-
> tion of these things is only too likely to lose itself in their own
> goodness and estimability, but you love your mother differently,
> from all these perfections she has surrounded you with and left
> ready to hand like so many ripe pears and plums set down for
> you on the table (as in the poem) when you come home from
> school even though she is out for the moment, love her with
> something very terrible to name, some desire to stand at her
> door and hold up a mace or a club against all possible entrants,
> tell someone else, not me, that you don't, or never knew, even a

moment that you did, which was, under everything else, under the spirals of fear and delight and resentment and tenderness, what I had discovered, a plain black animal inside that would not let her die and would fight her death for her when she could not, no reasoning able to reach him, so that he only howled at his failure when she died, only later quite enough to hear the "all's for the best" and the rest of it, him loving his mother as an involuntary act, as a form of breathing and turning under water in his sleep as he dreamed of it.[11]

This sentence goes on for another page or so in the very heart of this novel. Viscusi uncovers the center of the mother–son relationship which makes a man want to protect his mother from all harm and believe that he can even protect her from death—and if he doesn't, then he's a failure. Viscusi reveals here a dynamic central to understanding a weakness inherent in the mother–son relationship. That weakness is the unacknowledged pact between mother and son in which a mother acquires the son's protection by bartering her ability to deflect and absorb much of the feelings that assault the young boy. In exchange for this care, the mother expects nothing less than total loyalty from her son. Viscusi sees the narrator's mother as a version of Napoleon, or rather he turns Napoleon, an immigrant from Italy, into the narrator's mother. This mother has real power over her son and, in fact, when the narrator shifts to a meditation about her grave in Gate of Heaven Cemetery in Valhalla, New York, it is apparent that in her death, he considers her to have become a saint.

In "Part II, The Terror," Viscusi once again uses a word associated with French history, "terror," in a meditation on his Italian-American upbringing and a recollection of his childhood. the philosopher Giambattista Vico wrote that it is terror that creates "fantasia," and Viscusi supports this idea as his narrator unearths "terrible" childhood memories of life in Astoria to examine their significance in the creation of his self and sense of manhood.

"Part III, The Revolution" finds the narrator in Italy, now reunited with his family. The use of revolution is ironic, because Italy never experienced the violent revolution against monarchy that happened in France. Italy's revolution was more psychological than physical and took place in individual Italians, many of whom revolted by leaving Italy for new lands. This section is a literal re-turning, a second wishing, a spinning of the narrator's mind around the significance of Italian immigration to America and its effects on the identities of those who call themselves Italian Americans. Sentences such as: "For make no mistake, my grandparents told me to be Italian only because they knew I was already indelibly an American,"[12] signal a long-awaited intellectual exploration into the way cultural revolution affects individual identities, and it is this intellectual pursuit that marks the work it takes to become a wise man.

Joseph Bathanti's East Liberty (2001)

Like Viscusi's novel, Joseph Bathanti's first novel builds its core narrative around a mother–son relationship. *East Liberty* is set in a Pittsburgh neighborhood during the 1960s, when the Pirates were baseball's world champions, when everyone was singing the songs from *West Side Story*, when nuns were the queens of corporal punishment, and when single-parent families were rare. Bathanti, a poet, playwright, and Pushcart Prize nominee for short fiction and the essay, teaches creative writing at Appalachian State University. In the novel, he employs a style that is a unique synthesis of impressionism and realism, distorting reality and portraying the kaleidoscopic nature of memory as it reconstructs a past needed in the present. The terror that creates fantasy and the history that creates memory are deeply entwined, so that the reader is never really sure just what is real. The narrator, Robert "Bobby" Renzo, describes himself as "a boy who has always said [he] will marry [his] mother, even past the age when [he's] realized [he] would not."[13] He lives with the fear that his mother, whom he always refers to as "Francene," will abandon him permanently as she does temporarily from time to time—sometimes with her parents, Italian immigrants from Naples, sometimes with friends he calls "uncle" and "aunt." His father is a vague memory who reappears in times when Bobby needs a hero. To be fatherless is shameful, as he notes when his mother gives him a bicycle that once belong to Hugo, "a tall, ascetic boy, always it seemed in his dead father's oversized white shirts and ties. An egghead, a sissy, a mama's boy, someone to be made fun of because of his unfortunate name, his fatherlessness (though I have no father), his physical clumsiness, and the fact that he dared stretch the limits of what was necessary to learn."[14]

Bobby learns a lot from his grandparents, with whom he is sometimes forced to live. His Nonna, her head wrapped in a black kerchief, speaks no English and warns him not to go near her steamer trunk filled with the bones of her ancestors, who will drag him into the trunk. She also tells him about Spacaluccio, a monster that grabs kids who wander alone too far from home. His mother, Francene, explains that Spacaluccio, who takes on the identity of the latest immigrant tragedy (a construction worker buried in concrete or a cuckolded soldier) is "just a story made up by crazy Italians to scare their children. They are in love with misery. It is their genius, and out of it they conjure a monster. They really are the monsters. East Liberty is a monster. Its enemy is happiness; it eats children."[15] Bobby witnesses the struggle between Francene and her parents for control over her life as a single mother and her ability to love as an independent woman.

Bobby's passion is for baseball, something his mother comments on: "She [Francene] feels I substitute baseball for religion—for God—and attributes my obsession to the fact that I do not have a father. But she is wrong. Baseball and God are the same to me."[16] Francene's preferred escape from life's troubles is watching classic films, and she and Bobby watch them together on television. These films feed the young boy's imagination and help him form an early sense of what it means to be a man. To Bobby, they are "good stories" and serve as "morality tales, like the Old Testament and Jesus' parables." But these celluloid romances are a crashing contrast to life on the streets of East Liberty, a black and Italian neighborhood, where if the school nuns don't get you, then the street gangs will. The street parables Bobby hears center on misfits "like Mooch or Montmorrissey Hilliard, or any of the neighborhood freaks that parents point out to their children as warnings."[17] Another lesson he learns from his experiences in the neighborhood is that: "Memory is a pimp. It sells off for its own comfort what is most precious. I don't trust it and never will."[18] Bobby soon learns that his job is to protect his mother, whom he sees as a movie star, a heroine in his imaginary life. Through the focus on Bobby's relationship with his mother, Bathanti, like Viscusi, sheds light on how a boy raised by a single mother comes to understand that life is much more than what happens in competitive sports or exploited love relationships, and through Bobby's story, he shows a different way of viewing Italian-American masculinity.

Frank Ingrasciotta's **Blood Type: Ragu** (1999)

In *Blood Type: Ragu*, a one-man show written and performed by Frank Giano Ingrasciotta, a young man, Frank, tells the story of his family by taking on all of their personalities and behaviors. The key to this story is the relationship between Frank and his mother. Mom, as she is referred to in the script, is the opening voice. As she puts on an apron, she says, *"Ah Frengine, quando naciste tu la madre, mi spakste in mezzo.* When you were born you ripped me in half. It took 3 doctors to sew me shut, the stitches got infected. Ah, a mother suffers for her chulli [children]. But it's nothing, because you my son, my life … my husband."[19] This reference to her son as her husband is quite revealing and is essential for insight into the complexity of the mother–son relationship in Italian culture. Placing a child into an adult's position in one's emotional life is a form of abuse that is common, yet its impact is often overlooked.

The voices in the opening of the show alternate among the Narrator, Frank, and Mom. The storyline is Frank's coming of age as his parents' marriage falls apart. He often finds himself caught in the middle of his parents' fighting and once actually has to restrain his father after he has slapped his wife. This event leads Frank to realize that while he doesn't want to be like his father, he doesn't know what else to be: "So I fine tuned myself into my mother's every thought and feeling."[20] Frank returns to Sicily with his mother after she attempts suicide. There he learns first hand what Sicilian life is like, and it becomes obvious that his relationship with his mother will be the source of many problems later in his life.

Most of the characters in the play are women and through them Ingrasciotta reveals a side of Italian-American culture that is rarely seen in public. One of the key phrases that Mom uses whenever she wants Frank to understand that she can't give him something is to tell him it's "alla casa della Madonna" (in the Madonna's house). She tells him this when he asks her for a new, expensive bicycle. And when he comes of age sexually, he imagines his father saying, "Frengie, you want you manhood, ah, it waits for you alla casa della Madonna."[21] Frank realizes that he must escape home in order to become sexual. When he sees the Broadway play *The Best Little Whorehouse in Texas*, he decides to travel to where no one knows him to gain some sexual experience and soon finds himself in a brothel, Cherie's Cherry Patch, in Pahrump, Nevada, where prostitution is legal. He feels better after losing his virginity. For Frank, it takes the physical act of sex to make him feel: "The years of cling wrap around my heart melted just enough to allow me … a feeling. I sobbed in her arms for a boy who wasn't allowed to feel."[22] When he returns home, his parents split up and he stays with his mother. It's not long before his father dies, and one day, as Frank is taking his mother to get her Social Security survivor's benefit, he is asked by the clerk what his relationship is to her. He responds: "My wife, I mean my mother, my wife, my mother, my wife, my mother,"[23] in a frenzy that reveals his subconscious confusion, and echoes as it fulfills the mother's opening statement that he is her husband. Frank eventually explodes when his mother doesn't want to deal with a Social Security clerk in a wheelchair. He screams: "No, we're not going to do this anymore! They're my balls, not yours. Dad, where the fuck were you? It's not my rope to tug, it was yours *(Frank eventually releases the chair as a symbol that he's the one who needs to let go and not pull anymore)*."[24]

It is interesting that Frank's awareness that his mother is holding him back comes only after he has traveled west. Like Gay Talese's Bill Bonanno, Louisa Ermelino's Joey Dee, and Richard Vetere's Joey Pugg, Frank's road to becoming a wise man runs westward. This is the same thing Michael Corleone was trying to achieve when he thought he could make the family legitimate by moving to Las Vegas. Once a young man has his horizons widened, he can begin to imagine ways of being a man that are not always obvious while he is smothered inside an Italian family and trapped inside a Little Italy. Once Frank realizes this fact about his mother, he is able to develop a serious relationship with a Sicilian-American woman and, by the play's end, Frank is telling the audience about his marriage to her and their honeymoon in Sicily. Ingrasciotta, thus, has acknowledged the impact the mother figure has on the development of Italian-American masculinity—it is not always a positive impact, but understanding the mother–son relationship is vital to the maturity of any Italian-American boy.

Jim Provenzano's Pins *(1999) and Anthony Giardina's* Recent History: A Novel *(2001)*

Another way in which Italian-American authors are challenging traditional notions of masculinity is by exploring alternatives to the heterosexual model of manhood. Jim Provenzano's *Pins*, well received by reviewers in the gay press, has attracted little attention by mainstream book reviewers. The novel presents fifteen-year-old Joey Nicci, a wrestler whose Italian-American family has chased the American dream from Newark, New Jersey, to the suburbs. Joey is a good student and a rising star on the high school wrestling team. He has known all along that he is gay; he is beginning to experiment with his sexuality and wants to express his feelings, but only to someone he considers to be the right guy. What Joey must go through to defend not only his body but also his soul is the material Provenzano approaches well in this novel. Whether in the gym during practice or in the showers afterward, young men constantly test each other's sexual loyalties. In the gym there is a good look at how young boys perform their masculinities for each other: "How they appreciated or accused each other of loving each other's bodies was the source of tension, constantly broken by small faked punches, blurted words ... popped open by induced giggles."[25] These scenes, part of every male's experience, are rarely shown in the work of straight writers. Provenzano's depiction of the mistakes all men make with macho show the shortcomings of traditional representations of Italian-American masculinity. It also defies mistaken notions of homosexual versions of masculinity.

Another novel that explores the confusion involved with identifying and asserting one's sexuality on the road to becoming a man is *Recent History* by Anthony Giardina, author of two previous novels, *Men with Debts* (1984) and *A Boy's Pretensions* (1988), and a story collection, *The Country of Marriage* (1997). In *Recent History*, Giardina takes on the controversial topic of a young boy growing up in the 1960s who fears that his father's homosexuality means that he, too, must be homosexual. Like Provenzano's Joey, Giardina's protagonist, Luca Carcera (whose last name means "prisoner"), is surrounded by his nuclear and extended family. They become the spectators of Luca's remarkable life, in which he feels trapped. The novel is divided into two major sections, "Inca Boy" and "History Teacher." The first part deals with the shattering of Luca's innocence and his realization of how sexuality marks not just a man but everything that man touches. Giardina explores this well, and he adds a twist because Luca's sense of sexuality starts in relation to his father and then becomes complicated by his own physical interaction with his best friend.

Recent History opens with a traditional father–son scene in which Luca's father takes his son for a ride to see the lots on which he and Luca's uncle will build their families' dream homes. But the dream soon vaporizes when Luca's father unexpectedly abandons his family. What the family keeps secret from Luca is that his father has left his mother for another man. This happens at the same time that a schoolmate is banned from gym class after he displays an erection in the showers, and Luca begins to understand the division of the world into men who like women and men who like other men. This first section ends with an experimental homosexual encounter between Luca and his friend Eric that has Luca wondering about his own sexuality and worrying about his family.

Later in life Luca realizes that there is an emptiness that comes in the form of his family's history:

> Recent history has moved us all on. I inhabit a house that other families have inhabited before me; mine is more a tenancy than a creation. And even if this weren't a house I'd bought jointly with my more well-paid wife, even if I'd lifted it, literally, out of the earth, I doubt I'd allow myself the sense of completion that Meolo and Semenza and my Uncle John once indulged. We have passed that simple male moment, I'm afraid; it is unrecoverable. The necessary goal of a man's life is no longer dominion, the settled claim; it is now something else, it is intimacy.[26]

In this passage Giardina hits on the very essence of what I have been suggesting is the key for the transformation of wiseguys into wise men—the achievement of intimacy in relationships. This intimacy is achieved only after a man, once conditioned not to acknowledge his feelings so that eventually he has none, becomes aware of his feelings, gains the ability to process them, and then takes the risk of expressing them to others.

Writers like Lentricchia, Provenzano, and Giardina, who move beyond typical, expected portraits of masculinity, pierce the darkness that often surrounds the way Italian-American men look at themselves and at each other. These novels go a long way toward envisioning new ways of being men in a postmodern world. They strive to replace yelling with listening, threat-filled body postures with invitations to intimacy—new ways of marking out a balanced masculinity that take us from macho to zero.

THE FUTURE OF THE GANGSTER FIGURE

Shifting from the behavior of wiseguys to that of wise men is based on education. Until recently, Italian-Americans have not associated formal education with strong masculinity. To be facile with words often signals femininity. An old proverb goes, "Parole femmine, fatti maschi" ("Words are feminine, actions masculine").[27] The cultural critic Phillip

Brian Harper addresses this in relation to African-American culture in the first chapter of *Are We Not Men?* (1996):

> If verbal facility is considered an identifying mark of mascu-
> linity in certain African-American contexts, however, this is
> so only when it is demonstrated specifically through use of the
> vernacular. Indeed, a too-evident facility in the standard white
> idiom can quickly identify one not as a strong black man, but
> rather as a white-identified Uncle Tom who must also, there-
> fore, be weak, effeminate, and probably a "fag."[28]

Although nothing, to my knowledge, has yet been written about the role that intellect plays in signifying Italian-American masculinity, I can tell from personal experience that the more a man's intelligence is perceived to be academic and not practical (i.e., useful, as in medicine, law, or business), the more suspect a man's masculinity is. Again, this is something that Harper identifies in the African-American experience:

> In some black families where reading is encouraged in girl chil-
> dren, a boy who likes to read is perceived as suspect, as on the
> road to being a "sissy." Certainly as long as black people buy
> into the notion of patriarchal manhood, which says that real
> men are all body and no mind, black boys who are cerebral,
> who want to read, and who love books will risk being ridiculed
> as not manly.[29]

I am not arguing that the solution to the problems of perpetuating traditional notions of macho can be solved if we simply turn all our young boys into intellectuals and encourage them to write heady books. What I want to suggest is that more exposure to public versions of mas-culinity that value intellectual development and sensitive expression of thoughts will go a long way toward enlarging the scope of possible mas-culinities presented as models for young boys. In the works discussed in this chapter, the protagonists all develop notions of masculinity that move beyond traditional concepts because they have incorporated what has traditionally been called feminine into their ways of being and behaving. The way beyond the wiseguy begins with a better sense of the impact a mother has on the development of a young man.

One thing not dealt with in this study is the plethora of stories about how "I am, was, or shoulda been a gangster." Typically, these are told by gangsters to professional writers. Among the best is Bill Bonanno's *Bound by Honor* (1999), but besides feeding "the facts" to the large number of gangster junkies in the population who thrive on trivial details that never make the press, such books do not come near the cultural impact that the filmed or televised fictional gangster has on models of U.S. manhood. Harper's notion of "'simulacral realism'—whereby television programming is conceived as propounding scenarios that might subsequently (and consequently) be realized through the larger social field, regardless of whether they actually preexist there"[30]—also explains the role that representing the gangster in the media plays in forming desirable ways of being a man in the United States. How many young boys have imitated the gangsters from dramatic films and music videos? A shift from macho to zero demands more dynamic and diverse portrayals of Italian-American masculinity which will move away from immature gangster-based models and toward a more complex and rewarding sense of how young boys become wise men.

This portrayal of a preferred masculinity through the gangster figure is not something peculiar to Italian-American culture. According to bell hooks, a similar dynamic has long been present in African-American culture:

> Black power militants, having learned from Dr. King and Malcolm X how to call out the truth of capitalist-based materialism, identified it as gangsta culture. Patriarchal manhood was the theory and gangsta culture was its ultimate practice. No wonder then that black males of all ages living the protestant work ethic, submitting in the racist white world, envy the low-down hustlers in the black communities who are not slaves to white power. As one young gang member put it, "working was considered weak."[31]

This is an echo of Chazz Palminteri's "the working man's a sucker," a line used by Sonny and then Calogero in *A Bronx Tale*. Another passage from hooks rightly connects this gangster behavior to the way men are conditioned to create identities around the potential for creating violence:

> If black males are socialized from birth to embrace the notion that their manhood will be determined by whether or not they can dominate and control others and yet the political system

they live within (imperialist white-supremacist capitalist patri-archy) prevents most of them from having access to socially acceptable positions of power and dominance, then they will claim their patriarchal manhood, through socially unaccept-able channels. They will enact rituals of blood, of patriarchal manhood by using violence to dominate and control.[32]

Thus, hooks suggests that the way out is to "choose a partnership model that posits interbeing as the principle around which to organize fam-ily and community."[33] This partnership model relies on shifting the emphasis of interaction away from competition and toward collabora-tion. Without such a shift, the culture of death that produces ideas such as "the mother of all bombs" will continue to dominate the way humans interact on a national, and ultimately, on a personal level. According to hooks, "The black power movement with its faulty embrace of gangsta culture and violence colluded with the dominant culture in producing a cult of death that is the current ethos of black male life."[34] This is an ethos that is not restricted to black males. The solution offered by hooks is similar to Christina Wieland's notion of an "alternative space" that can be achieved only by "the working-through of the Oedipus com-plex"[35] such that it stops "the slaying of the maternal monster" from being seen as a "triumph of phallic narcissism"[36] that expresses itself as "a turning away from intimate relationships, or else—at times—as an orgy of destruction."[37] The working through of what she sees as "the depressive position" requires seeing "the parental couple as the source of life"[38] and reconnecting the earlier split between father and mother that has been "expressed as a breach between mind and body, or mind and matter."[39] This reconnection of the male and female, of the mind and body, is precisely what the writers and artists profiled in this chap-ter—those I have called reinventors of the gangster figure—accomplish in their work. It remains to be seen if any of this work will transfer significantly to electronic media and, thus, have a greater impact on the imaginations of tomorrow's young boys.

What does all this mean for the future of the gangster figure? Is it played out? What could possibly follow David Chase's six years of gang-ster portrayals in *The Sopranos*? Will the gangster figure morph from Italian to Russian, Korean, or any other newer immigrant culture in the United States? There is no doubt that the Italian-American gangster will always have a role in storytelling, especially if he is perceived as a sure way of attracting consumers. One of the latest attempts at this is

Bill Bonanno and Joe Pistone's novel based on their "real experiences." *The Good Guys* (2004) is the collaboration between an ex-gangster and an ex-undercover cop.[40] Written as alternating chapters from the point of view of an Italian-American gangster and an Italian-American FBI agent, the novel dramatizes the arrival of the Russian mob in U.S. organized crime. The writing of this novel signals the mainstream's failure to do anything new with a stock figure.

Traditional notions of what it means to be a man have always been changing as the work of such scholars as Michael Kimmel and David Gillmore has demonstrated especially well.[41] What has been called "the first empirical study of Italian masculinity" has been conducted by David Tager and Glenn E. Good of the University of Missouri–Columbia. Entitled "Italian and American Masculinities: A Comparison of Masculine Gender Role Norms in University Students," their study "supports the notion that there are cross-cultural differences in masculine gender role norms. Italian male students report less conformity to traditional masculine norms as conceived of by American psychologists."[42] Although the study is small in scope, its results support much of what I have found in this look at the representations of gangsters in the work of Italian-American writers, and it points the way for more work in the social sciences and humanities.

As a trickster figure, the gangster continues to portray behavior that is deemed unacceptable in "proper" society. As a symbol of traditional patriarchal manhood, in which men use their physicality to gain power and maintain social control, the traditional gangster character has outlived his utility as a mode for modern masculinity. Unlike some Italian Americans, I do not see the elimination of the gangster figure as a way of avoiding the infliction of a stereotype on a people. The way around this is to be sure that alternative images of Italian-American men compete with gangster images. We must try not to censor art, but to enhance society's abilities to interpret it. As a model for masculinity, I believe the gangster is exhausted for all but those who are unable to move beyond the traditional notion of patriarchal manhood. When the connection between young men and their mothers is brought out in the creative works of men, I believe the notion of what it means to be a man, in Italian-American or any other ethnic American culture, will change from the violent type of the traditional wiseguy into the more mature figure of the wise man, and, therefore, show that to survive in this world, men must abandon the cult of death and cultivate alternative ways of living.

NOTES

INTRODUCTION

1. Felix Stefanile, "A Review of the Film *Godfather VII*," *The Black Bough* (Spring 1985), 13.
2. Quoted in Jonathan Munby, *Public Enemies, Public Heroes* (Chicago: University of Chicago Press, 1999), 105.
3. William DalCerro, journalist and media officer for the Italic Institute of America, conducted a study based on his observations of 1,233 films identified as "Italian related." He found that nearly two-thirds of them presented Italians in a negative light. Results of the study can be found at http://italic.org/imageb1.htm.
4. David A. J. Richards, *Italian American: The Racializing of an Ethnic Identity* (New York: New York University Press, 1999).
5. Many Italian-American organizations in the United States have taken a stand in protest of the HBO television series *The Sopranos*. On April 5, 2001, legal action was begun by the American Italian Defense Association (AIDA) in an attempt to have the series banned from broadcast on the grounds that it violated the Illinois Constitution's guarantee of "individual dignity." Although AIDA lost the lawsuit, organizations such as the Italian American One Voice Committee (led by Dr. Manny Alfano), the National Italian American Foundation, the Order of Sons of Italy in America, and UNICO (just to name the larger ones) continued to protest and recommend boycotting HBO. A visit

to these organizations' websites will provide a sense of what the protests encompassed.

6. Interaction on the Internet among Italian-American scholars and activists regarding *The Sopranos* can be found in the archives of the Humanities Italian American discussion group (H-ITAM), located at http://www.h-net.org/~itam/.

7. Fredric Jameson, "Reification and Utopia in Mass Culture," in his *Signatures of the Visible* (New York: Routledge, 1992), 22.

8. Ibid., 32.

9. I use the word "parasite" in the Michel Serresian sense as he developed it in Michel Serres, *The Parasite*, trans. Lawrence Schehr (Baltimore: Johns Hopkins University Press, 1982).

10. Michael Klein, "Beyond the American Dream: Film and the Experience of a Defeat," in Michael Klein, ed., *An American Half-century: Postwar Culture and Politics in the USA*, (London and Boulder, CO: Pluto Press, 1994), 221.

11. Robert Warshow, "The Gangster as Tragic Hero," in his *The Immediate Experience: Movies, Comics, Theatre and Other Aspects of Popular Culture* (Cambridge, MA: Harvard University Press, 2001), 101.

CHAPTER ONE

1. Remo Franceschini, A *Matter of Honor: One Cop's Lifelong Pursuit of John Gotti and the Mob* (New York: Simon & Schuster, 1992).

2. David Ruth. *Inventing the Public Enemy: The Gangster in American Culture, 1918–1934*, (Chicago: University of Chicago Press, 1996).

3. Norman O. Brown, *Hermes the Thief: The Evolution of a Myth* ([1947] repr. Great Barrington, MA: Lindisfarne Press, 1990), 3.

4. Ibid., 76.

5. Ibid., 13.

6. Ibid., 47.

7. Ibid., 48.

8. Ibid., 50.

9. Ibid., 52.

10. Ibid., 81.

11. Ibid., 85.

12. Ibid., 101.

13. Ibid., 123.

14. Stanley Diamond, "Introductory Essay: Job and the Trickster," in Paul Radin, ed., *The Trickster: A Study in American Indian Mythology* (New York: Schocken, 1956), xiii.

15. Ibid., xxi.

16. Paul Radin, "Prefatory Note," in Paul Radin, ed., *The Trickster: A Study in American Indian Mythology* (New York: Schocken, 1956), xxiv.

17. Ibid.

18. Karl Kerényi, "The Trickster in Relation to Greek Mythology," in *The Trickster*, 185.

19. Carl Jung, "On the Psychology of the Trickster Figure," in *The Trickster*, 201.

20. Ibid., 207.

21. Ibid., 207.

22. Giambattista Vico, *The New Science*, trans. Thomas Goddard Bergin and Max Harold Fisch (New York: Columbia University Press, 1968).

23. David Bidney, "Vico's New Science of Myth," in Giorgio Tagliacozzo, ed., *Giambattista Vico, An International Symposium* (Baltimore: Johns Hopkins University Press, 1969), 274.

24. Richard Gambino, *Blood of My Blood* (New York: Anchor, 1975), 277.

25. Robert Warshow, "The Gangster as Tragic Hero," in his *The Immediate Experience* (New York: Atheneum, 1975), 100.

26. Ibid., 100.

27. David E. Ruth, *Inventing the Public Enemy: The Gangster in American Culture, 1918–1934* (Chicago: University of Chicago Press, 1996), 3.

28. Ibid., 120.

29. Jonathan Munby, *Public Enemies, Public Heroes* (Chicago: University of Chicago Press, 1999), 2.

30. Ibid., 4.

31. Eric Lott, *Love and Theft: Blackface Minstrelsy and the American Working Class* (New York: Oxford University Press, 1993), 25.

32. Ibid., 25–26.

33. Ibid., 52.

34. *Ibid.*, 149.

35. Jack Shadoian, *Dreams and Dead Ends: The American Gang-ster/Crime Film* (Cambridge, MA: MIT Press, 1977), 4.

36. *Ibid.*, 5.

37. Henry James, *The American Scene* (Bloomington: Indiana University Press, 1968), 231.

38. A good example of the patrolling of the neighborhoods is the murder of Yusef Hawkins. Yusef Hawkins was a sixteen-year-old black youth who was killed on 23 August 1989 by young residents of Bensonhurst, New York, a predominately Italian neighborhood. He was looking for a used car near where local youths had gathered to confront a black youth who had been invited to a local girl's birthday party. They mistook Hawkins for that youth and killed him.

CHAPTER TWO

1. Mario Puzo, Preface, in his *The Fortunate Pilgrim* (New York: Random House, 1997), xii.

2. Robert Viscusi brought my attention to this during a presentation he made on Italian-American film in Rome in 2002.

3. Warshow, "The Gangster as Tragic Hero," 102 (see Introduction, note 11).

4. Mario Puzo, *The Godfather* (New York: Fawcett, 1969), 386.

5. The National Italian Foundation held a public forum on the question "Do the stereotypes found in *The Sopranos* hurt real-life Italian Americans?" Participants included writers Camille Paglia, James Wolcott, and Bill Tonelli; Ted Grippo of the American Italian Defense Association; psychologist Elizabeth Messina; and Joseph Scelsa of the John D. Calandra Italian American Institute. For more information see the NIAF website, http://www.niaf.org/image_identity/stereotyping_activities. asp.

6. Robert Viscusi, "Professions and Faiths: Critical Choices in the Italian American Novel," in Remigio U. Pane, ed., *Italian Americans in the Professions, Proceedings of the XII Annual Conference of the American Italian Historical Association* (Staten Island, NY: American Italian Historical Association, 1983), 41.

7. Robert Viscusi, "A Literature Considering Itself: The Allegory of Italian America," in Anthony J. Tamburri, Paolo Giordano, and Fred L. Gardaphé, eds., *From the Margin: Writings in Italian Americana* (West Lafayette, IN: Purdue University Press, 1991), 272.
8. Ibid., 274–75.
9. Puzo, *The Fortunate Pilgrim*, 3.
10. Ibid., 4.
11. David Gilmore, *Manhood in the Making: Cultural Concepts of Masculinity* (New Haven, CT: Yale University Press, 1990), 48.
12. Puzo, *The Fortunate Pilgrim*, 9.
13. Ibid., 27.
14. Ibid., 29.
15. Ibid., 31.
16. Judith Halberstam, *Female Masculinity* (Durham, NC: Duke University Press, 1998), 1.
17. Ibid., 9.
18. Ibid., 28–29.
19. Puzo, *The Fortunate Pilgrim*, 41.
20. Ibid., 42.
21. Ibid., 45.
22. Ibid., 65.
23. Ibid., 65–66.
24. Ibid., 66.
25. Ibid., 76.
26. Ibid., 81.
27. Ibid., 107.
28. Ibid., 140.
29. Ibid., 144–145.
30. Ibid., 189.
31. Ibid., 192.
32. Ibid., 203.
33. Ibid., 204.
34. Ibid., 248.
35. Ibid., 275.
36. Ibid., 276.
37. Robert Fishman, *Bourgeois Utopias: The Rise and Fall of Suburbia* (New York: Basic Books, 1987), 206.
38. Ibid., 190.

39. Ibid., 6.
40. Ibid., x.
41. Kenneth T. Jackson, *Crabgrass Frontier: The Suburbanization of the United States* (New York: Oxford University Press, 1985), 62.
42 Robert Fishman, *Bourgeois Utopia*, 38.
43. Christian Messenger, *The Godfather and American Culture: How the Corleones Became "Our Gang"* (Albany: State University of New York Press, 2002), 132.
44. Puzo, *The Godfather*, 287.
45. Ibid., 36–37.
46. Ibid., 37.
47. Ibid., 37–38.
48. Ibid., 203.
49. Ibid., 192.
50. Ibid., 16.
51. Ibid., 16.
52. Ibid., 16.
53. Christina Wieland, *The Undead Mother: Psychoanalytic Explorations of Masculinity, Femininity, and Matricide* (London: Rebus Press, 2000), 222.
54. Ibid., 210.
55. Puzo, *The Godfather*, 281.
56. Ibid., 123.
57. Ibid., 112.
58. Ibid., 324.
59. Ibid., 329.
60. Ibid., 338.
61. Ibid., 343.
62. Ibid., 294.
63. Ibid., 192.
64. Ibid., 192.
65. Ibid., 192.
66. Ibid., 213.
67. Ibid., 214.
68. Ibid., 443.

CHAPTER THREE

1. Ruth, *Inventing the Public Enemy*, 1 (see chapter one, note 27).

2. Gay Talese, *Contemporary Authors,* New Revision Series 9 (Farmington, MI: Gale Research, 1982), 485.

3. Gloria Nardini, *Che Bella Figura! The Power of Performance in an Italian Ladies' Club in Chicago* (Albany: State University of New York Press, 1999), 7.

4. Tom Ventsias, "FUHGETABOUTIT: America's Love Affair with the Mob," http://www.inform.umd.edu/cpmag/fall02/mob.html, accessed 14 April 2005.

5. Ibid.

6. Gay Talese, *Honor Thy Father* (New York: Fawcett Crest, 1971), 6.

7. Ibid., 447.

8. Ibid., 450.

9. Ibid., iii

10. Ibid., xv.

11. Gay Talese, "Filmmaker Michael Corrente and Author Gay Talese Tear at the Image of the Italian-American Male," *Interview* (December 1994), 46. Also available at http://www.dynomind.com/p/articles/mi_m1285/is_n12_v24/ai_16501850, accessed 17 July 2005.

12. Talese, *Honor Thy Father,* 9.

13. Ibid., 26.

14. Ibid., 37.

15. Ibid., 52.

16. Ibid., 37–38.

17. Ibid., 43.

18. Ibid., 44.

19. Ibid., 162.

20. Ibid., 164.

21. Ibid., 163.

22. Ibid., 71.

23. Ibid., 77.

24. Ibid., 127.

25. Ibid., 310.

26. Ibid., 270.

27. Vito Genovese was a Mafioso who made an overt effort to seize overall mob leadership to become the "Boss of Bosses." He ultimately failed and was arrested by the FBI. Thomas Lucchese was a more peaceful Don, thought to be very fair. He was a

good hit man and also had many political connections. He died of brain cancer at 67.

28. Talese, *Honor Thy Father*, 271.

29. Ibid., 310.

30. Remo Franceschini, *A Matter of Honor: One Cop's Lifelong Pursuit of John Gotti and the Mob* (New York: Simon & Schuster, 1992), 241.

31. Gay Talese, *Honor Thy Father*, 312.

32. Ibid., 313.

33. Ibid., 442.

34. Ibid., 442.

35. Richard Capozzola, *Finalmente! The Truth about Organized Crime* (Altamonte Springs, FL: Five Centuries Books, 2001).

36. Gay Talese, *Honor Thy Father*, 447.

37. Ibid., 449.

38. Ibid., 451.

39. Gay Talese, *Unto the Sons* (New York: Knopf, 1992), 51.

40. Ibid., 4.

41. Ibid., 15.

42. Ibid., 24.

43. Ibid., 25.

44. Ibid., 26.

45. Ben Morreale, *A Few Virtuous Men (Li cornuti)* (Plattsburgh, NY: Tundra Books, 1973), 11.

46. Bill Bonanno, *Bound by Honor: A Mafioso's Story* (New York: St. Martin's, 1999), xv.

47. Morreale, *A Few Virtuous Men*, 14.

48. Ibid., 17.

49. Ibid., 31.

50. Ibid.

51. Ibid., 56.

52. Ibid., 70.

53. Ibid., 80.

54. Ibid., 81.

55. Ibid.

56. Ibid., 159.

57. Ibid., 160.

58. Ibid., 162. *Trimalchio* was an early title of F. Scott Fitzgerald's *The Great Gatsby*.

59. Ben Morreale, *Monday, Tuesday ... never come Sunday* (Platts-burgh, NY: Tundra Books, 1977), 23.

60. Ibid., 68.

61. Ibid., 68–69.

62. Ibid., 121.

63. Ibid., 132–133.

CHAPTER FOUR

1. Pellegrino D'Acierno, "Cinema Paradiso: The Italian American Presence in American Cinema," in his *The Italian American Heritage: A Companion to Literature and Arts* (New York: Garland, 1999), 613.

2. Nicholas Pileggi, *Wiseguy: Life in a Mafia Family* (New York: Simon & Schuster, 1985) and *Casino: Love and Honor in Las Vegas* (New York: Simon & Schuster, 1995).

3. Franco La Cecla, *Modi Brusci: Anthropologia del maschio* (Milan: Bruno Mondadori, 2000), 39. *Modi Brusci* has yet to be translated, but there is an article by La Cecla, "Rough Manners: How Men Are Made," in Giannino Malossi, ed., *Material Man: Masculinity, Sexuality, Style* (New York: Harry N. Abrams, 2000), which contains the essence of the book.

4. La Cecla, *Modi Brusci*, 44.

5. Ibid., 39.

6. Ana Castillo. *Massacre of the Dreamers* (New York: Penguin, 1995), 66.

7. Ibid., 82.

8. Ibid.

9. Ibid., 71.

10. Ibid., 75.

11. Ibid., 68.

12. D'Acierno, "Cinema Paradiso," 638.

13. La Cecla, *Modi Brusci*, 41.

14. D'Acierno, "Cinema Paradiso," 636.

15. LaCecla, *Modi Brusci*, 39.

16. Ibid., 43.

17. Ibid.

18. Pileggi, *Wiseguy*, 17.

19. Ibid., 21.

20. Ibid., 29.

21. Ibid., 25.
22. La Cecla, *Modi Brusci*, 41.
23. D'Acierno, "Cinema Paradiso," 648–649.
24. Ibid., 640.
25. Mario Puzo, *The Sicilian* (New York: Simon & Schuster, 1984), 25.
26. Ibid., 29.
27. Billy Jaynes Chandler, *King of the Mountain: The Life and Death of Giuliano the Bandit* (DeKalb, IL: Northern Illinois University Press, 1988), 6.
28. Ibid., 53.
29. Ibid., 67.
30. Ibid., 169.
31. Gaetano Cipolla, *What Makes A Sicilian?* (Brooklyn, NY: Legas, 1996), 16.
32. Ben Lawton, "America through Italian/American Eyes: Dream or Nightmare?" in Anthony Julian Tamburri, Paolo Giordano, and Fred Gardaphé, eds., *From the Margin: Writings in Italian Americana* (West Lafayette, IN: Purdue University Press, 1991), 417.
33. Ibid., 421.
34. Puzo, *The Sicilian*, 241.

CHAPTER FIVE

1. Giose Rimanelli's novels, such as *Tiro al piccione* (1953) have been rediscovered and republished. Long before moving to America, Rimanelli was beginning to examine the American influence on life in Italy in his *Peccato originale* (1954), also translated by Johnson and published by Random House in 1957.
2. Anthony Burgess, "Introduction," in *Alien: Poems (1964–1970)*, *Misure critiche: Su/Per Rimanelli: Studi e Testimonianze 17–18.65-67* (1987–1988): 244–245.
3. Giose Rimanelli, *Benedetta in Guysterland: A Liquid Novel* (Montreal and New York: Guernica, 1993), 44.
4. Ibid., 44.
5. Ibid., 65.
6. Ibid., 45.
7. Ibid.

8. Ibid., 65.
9. Ibid., 58.
10. Ibid., 60.
11. Ibid., 64.
12. Ibid., 77.
13. Ibid., 79.
14. Ibid., 92.
15. Ibid., 113.
16. Ibid., 183.
17. Ibid.
18. Ibid., 81.
19. See Mary Dockray-Miller, "Tears of Fatherhood," in her *Motherhood and Mothering in Anglo-Saxon England* (New York: St. Martin's, 2000).
20. Christina Wieland, T*he Undead Mother: Psychoanalytic Explorations of Masculinity, Femininity, and Matricide* (London: Rebus Press, 2000), 14.
21. Ibid., 10.
22. Ibid., 29.
23. The review by James C. Mancuso can be found at http://www.amazon.com/exec/obidos/ASIN/0791443477/omega23/104-1368011-7015914, accessed 17 July 2005.
24. Frank Lentricchia, *Music of the Inferno* (Albany: State University of New York Press, 1999), 72.
25. Ibid., 18.
26. Ibid., 27.
27. Ibid., 72.
28. Ibid., 47.
29. Ibid., 51.
30. Ibid., 93.
31. Ibid., 94.
32. Ibid.
33. Ibid., 95.
34. Ibid., 51.
35. Ibid., 138.
36. Ibid., 140.
37. Ibid.
38. Ibid., 143.
39. Ibid., 164.

40. Ibid.
41. Ibid.
42. Ibid., 179.
43. Frank Lentricchia, *Lucchesi and the Whale* (Durham, NC: Duke University Press, 2001), 25.
44. Ibid., 26.
45. Ibid., 25–26.
46. Ibid., 27.
47. Ibid., 28.
48. Ibid.
49. Ibid., 29.
50. Ibid.
51. Ibid., 33.
52. Ibid., 39.
53. Ibid., 40.
54. Ibid., 31.

CHAPTER SIX

1. Ana Castillo, *Massacre of the Dreamers* (New York: Penguin, 1995), 13.
2. Louisa Ermelino. *Joey Dee Gets Wise* (New York: St. Martin's, 1991), 1.
3. Ibid., 1.
4. Giovanni Dall'Orto, http://digilander.libero.it/giovannidal-lorto/cultura/checcabolario/checcabolario.html, accessed 17 July 2005.
5. Ermelino, *Joey Dee Gets Wise*, 2.
6. Ibid., 3.
7. Ibid.
8. Ibid., 25.
9. Ibid., 9.
10. Ibid., 11.
11. Ibid., 10.
12. Ibid., 13.
13. Ibid., 14.
14. Ibid., 16.
15. Ibid., 20.
16. Ibid., 33.
17. Ibid.

18. Ibid., 39.
19. Ibid., 40.
20. Ibid., 41.
21. Ibid., 42.
22. Ibid., 43.
23. Ibid., 22.
24. Ibid.
25. Ibid., 26.
26. Ibid., 30.
27. Ibid., 54.
28. Ibid., 55.
29. Ibid., 74.
30. Ibid.
31. Ibid., 82.
32. Ibid., 77.
33. Ibid., 80.
34. Ibid., 82.
35. Ibid., 89.
36. Ibid., 90.
37. Ibid., 92.
38. Ibid., 100.
39. Ibid., 103.
40. Ibid., 98.
41. Ibid., 125.
42. Ibid., 110.
43. Ibid., 107.
44. Ibid., 70.
45. Ibid., 128.
46. Ibid., 143.
47. Ibid.
48. Ibid., 139–140.
49. Ibid., 142.
50. Ibid., 96.
51. Ibid., 148.
52. Ibid., 150.
53. Ibid., 151.
54. Ibid., 153.
55. Ibid., 169.

56. Lucia Chiavola Birnbaum, *Black Madonnas: Feminism, Religion and Politics in Italy* (Boston: Northeastern University Press, 1993), 3.

57. Louisa Ermelino, *The Sisters Mallone* (New York: Simon and Schuster, 2002), 12.

58. Information about Saint Rita was gathered at http://www.catholicforum.com/saints/saintr01.htm, a site operated by the Catholic Community Forum of Ballwin, MO, accessed 17 July 2005.

59. Ermelino, *The Sisters Mallone*, 53.

60. Ibid., 45.

61. A "blackjack" is batonlike, hand-held weapon, often made of leather or rubber-wrapped lead, which is used to knock out people, usually by hitting them on the back of the neck near the skull.

62. Ermelino, *The Sisters Mallone*, 62.

63. Ibid., 64.

64. Ibid., 110.

65. Ibid., 55.

66. Ibid., 248.

67. Ibid., 258.

68. Josephine Gattuso Hendin, *Heartbreakers: Women and Violence in Contemporary Culture and Literature* (New York: Palgrave Macmillan, 2004), 25.

69. Ibid., 9.

70. Ibid.

71. Ermelino, *The Sisters Mallone*, 55.

72. Hendin, *Heartbreakers*, 244.

73. Ibid., 262.

CHAPTER SEVEN

1. George Guida, "Novel *Paesans*: The Reconstruction of Italian American Male Identity, in Anthony Valerio's *Conversation with Johnny* and Robert Viscusi's *Astoria*," *MELUS* 26.2 (Summer 2001), 104.

2. Anthony Valerio, *Lefty and the Button Men* (Xlibris Corporation, 2000), 14.

3. Ibid., 45.

4. Ibid., 14.

5. Ibid., 15.
6. Ibid.
7. Ibid., 16.
8. Ibid.
9. Ibid.
10. Ibid., 21.
11. Ibid.
12. Ibid., 22.
13. Ibid.
14. Ibid., 21.
15. Ibid., 22.
16. Ibid., 27.
17. Ibid., 36.
18. Ibid., 37.
19. Ibid., 40.
20. Ibid., 41.
21. Ibid., 55.
22. Ibid.
23. Ibid., 43.
24. Ibid., 42.
25. Ibid., 43.
26. Ibid., 43–44.
27. Ibid., 44.
28. Ibid.
29. Ibid.
30. Ibid., 44–45.
31. Ibid., 45.
32. Ibid., 94.
33. Ibid., 94–95.
34. Ibid., 95.
35. Ibid.
36. Ibid., 99.
37. Ibid., 106.
38. Ibid., 69.
39. Ibid. 76.
40. Ibid., 75.
41. Ibid., 79.
42. Ibid., 87.
43. Ibid., 90.

44. Ibid., 91.

45. Ibid., 92.

46. Ibid., 93.

47. Ibid.

48. Ibid., 98.

49. Ibid., 112.

50. Ibid.

51. Ibid., 119.

52. Don DeLillo, *Americana* (New York: Penguin, 1971), 163.

53. Ibid., 278.

54. Ibid., 280.

55. Ibid.

56. Ibid.

57. Don DeLillo, *Running Dog* (New York: Vintage, 1989), 125.

58. Ibid., 175.

59. Don DeLillo, *Libra* (New York: Viking, 1988), 170.

60. Don DeLillo, *Underworld* (New York: Scribner, 1997), 204.

61. Ibid., 104.

62. Ibid., 165.

63. Ibid., 300.

64. Ibid., 275.

65. Ibid.

66. Ibid., 276.

67. Ibid.

68. Ibid., 277.

69. Ibid., 332.

Chapter Eight

1. "Fresh Garbage," lyrics and music by Jay Ferguson of the group Spirit.

2. Robert Fishman, *Bourgeois Utopias*, 4 (see chapter two, note 42).

3. DeLillo, *Underworld*, 277 (see chapter seven, note 60).

4. *Ibid.*, 287.

5. The show has created a great deal of controversy in the Italian-American community. See the Commission for Social Justice of the Order Sons of Italy in America's website http://www.nyscsj-osia or the National Italian American Foundation's site

http://www.niaf.org/ for information on the evolution of various campaigns to stop the series from being aired.

6. Thorstein Veblen, *The Theory of the Leisure Class* [1912] (New York: Viking/Mentor, 1967), 77.

7. Avi Santo, "'Fat Fuck! Why don't you take a look in the mirror?' Weight, Body Image, and Masculinity in *The Sopranos*," in his *This Thing of Ours: Investigating* The Sopranos (New York: Columbia University Press, 2002), 73.

8. Ibid., 94.

9. Wallace Katz, "Sticking Together, Falling Apart: *The Sopranos* and the American Moral Order," *New Labor Forum* (Fall/Winter 2001), 95.

10. Ibid., 93.

11. Ibid., 95.

12. Fishman, *Bourgeois Utopias*, x.

13. Ibid., 38.

14. Kenneth T. Jackson, *Crabgrass Frontier: The Suburbanization of the United States* (New York: Oxford University Press, 1985) 62.

15. For other works that deal with women in *The Sopranos* see Regina Barreca, "Why I Like the Women in *The Sopranos* Even Though I'm Not Supposed To," and Sandra M. Gilbert, "Life with (God)Father," both in *A Sitdown with* The Sopranos: *Watching Italian American Culture on TV's Most Talked-about Series* (New York: Palgrave Macmillan, 2002); Kim Akass and Janet McCabe, "Beyond the Bada Bing!: Negotiating Female Narrative Authority in *The Sopranos*," Cindy Donagelli and Sharon Alward, "'I dread you'?: Married to the Mob in *The Godfather*, *GoodFellas*, and *The Sopranos*," and Joseph S. Walker, "'Cunnilingus and Psychiatry Have Brought Us to This': Livia and the Logic of False Hoods in the First Season of *The Sopranos*," all in *This Thing of Ours: Investigating* The Sopranos, David Lavery, ed., (New York: Columbia University Press, 2002).

16. Wieland. *The Undead Mother*, 62 (see chapter two, note 53).

17. Ibid., 43.

18. Ibid., 208.

19. Ibid., 209.

20. Ibid., 216.

21. Ibid., 217–218.

22. Ibid., 229.
23. Lewis Hyde, *Trickster Makes This World: Mischief, Myth and Art*, (New York: Farrar, Straus and Giroux, 1998), 10.
24. Ibid., 11.
25. Ibid., 37.
26. Ibid., 177.
27. Tony Ardizzone, *In the Garden of Papa Santuzzu* (New York: Picador USA, 1999), 75.
28. Ibid., 76.
29. Ibid., 79.
30. Ibid.
31. Ibid., 84.
32. Ibid., 85.
33. Ibid., 91.
34. Ibid.
35. Ibid., 94.
36. Carl Jung, "On the Psychology of the Trickster Figure," in Paul Radin, ed., *The Trickster: A Study in American Indian Mythology* (New York: Schocken, 1956), 207.

CHAPTER NINE

1. Felix Stefanile, "The Culture of Descendants: Archeology and Ontology." *Romance Languages Annual, 1992.* Eds. Jeanette Beer, Charles Ganelin and Anthony Julian Tamburri. (West Lafayette, IN: Purdue Research Foundation, 1993), 353.
2. Ibid., 355.
3. Ibid.
4. Ibid.
5. Felix Stefanile, "A Review of the Film *Godfather VII*," in *The Black Bough* (Spring 1985), 13. Reprinted by permission of the author.
6. Sandra Mortola Gilbert, "Mafioso," in Helen Barolini, ed., *The Dream Book: An Anthology of Writings by Italian American Women* (New York: Schocken, 1985), 348–349. Reprinted by permission of the author.
7. Robert Viscusi, "Goons and Lagoons," in *A New Geography of Time* (Toronto: Guernica, 2004), 53. Reprinted by permission of the author.

8. The poet connects himself to the legendary gangster Albert Anastasia by letting the reader know that his brother was a priest to whom kids would go make their confessions to because his English was poor and he probably didn't understand everything they were saying.

9. *Gangster Apparel* was first produced in London in 1993, in the United States in 1994, and in New York City in 1995. *First Love* was first produced in the United States in 1996. *How to Go Out on a Date in Queens* was first produced in New York City in 1993. *Hale the Hero!* was first produced as a teleplay on the A&E network in 1992. *The Engagement* was first produced at the George Street Playhouse in New Brunswick, New Jersey in 1992. *The Marriage Fool* was first produced in the United States in 1994. *One Shot, One Kill* was first produced at Primary Stages in New York City in 2002.

10. Richard Vetere, *Gangster Apparel* (Woodstock, IL: Dramatic Publishing Company, 1996), 8.

11. Ibid., 10.

12. Ibid., 13.

13. Ibid., 16.

14. Ibid., 17.

15. Ibid., 18.

16. Ibid., 32.

17. Ibid.

18. Ibid., 35.

19. Ibid., 37.

20. Ibid.

21. Ibid., 43.

22. Ibid., 42.

23. Ibid., 43.

24. Ibid., 44.

25. Ibid.

26. This section, not in the original publication, was written for a later production and comes from a manuscript the playwright shared with me. The Vetere Papers are housed in the Special Collections of Stony Brook University's Melville Library. A finding aid for the Vetere collection appears on the website of Special Collections, http://www.sunysb.edu/libspecial/collections/manuscripts/ vetere.html.

27. Vetere, *Gangster Apparel,* 44.
28. Ibid., 47.
29. Ibid.
30. Ibid.
31. Richard Vetere. *The Classic* (Woodstock, IL: Dramatic Publishing Company, 1998), 15.
32. Ibid., 26.
33. Ibid., 30.
34. Ibid., 31.
35. Ibid., 45.
36. Ibid., 63.
37. Ibid., 64.
38. Ibid., 82.
39. Richard Vetere, *A Hundred Years into the Heart: A Musical Play* (unpublished ms., 2004), 1.
40. Ibid., 3.
41. Ibid., 7.
42. Ibid., 5.
43. Ibid., 42.
44. Ibid., 43.
45. Ibid., 45.
46. Ibid., 47.
47. Ibid., 79.

CHAPTER TEN

1. Rodolfo Anaya, " 'I'm the King': The Macho Image," in *Muy Macho: Latino Men Confront Their Manhood* (New York: Anchor/Doubleday, 1996), 73.
2. Barbara Ehrenreich, "The New Macho: Feminism," *The New York Times* (29 July 2004), reprinted at http://www.christusrex.org/www1/news/nyt-7-29-04e.html; David Ford, "Shrinking Bush", *San Francisco Chronicle* (17 September 2004), reprinted at http://www.sfgate.com/cgi-bin/article.cgi?f=/c/a/2004/09/17/WBGDT8LS5A1.DTL. (Accessed November 16, 2005)
3. Ford, "Shrinking Bush."
4. Anaya, " 'I'm the King': The Macho Image," 73.
5. Antonio Petracca's recent exhibition "These are not my shoes: (queste non sono mie scarpe)," included the works reproduced here. The exhibition took place at Kim Foster Gallery, 529 West

20th Street, New York, New York 10011, February 12–March 19, 2005. Work reprinted by permission of the artist.

7. I first met Maria Manhattan through Jeanette Vuocolo at her Manhattan home and studio. At that time she had just finished work on the painting reproduced here, which she calls "The Death of Macho." Maria is a painter, illustrator, and computer graphic artist who has also worked as a ceramic sculptor, video and conceptual artist, performer, and teacher. For more information, see her website, http://www.mariamanhattan.com/. Work reprinted by permission of the artist.

8. Robert Viscusi, *Astoria* (Toronto: Guernica, 1995), 16.

9. Ibid., 7.

10. Ibid. 91.

11. Ibid., 94–95.

12. Ibid., 293.

13. Joseph Bathanti, *East Liberty* (Simpsonville, SC: Banks Channel Books, 2001), 31.

14. Ibid., 25.

15. Ibid., 126.

16. Ibid., 31.

17. Ibid., 107.

18. Ibid., 32.

19. Frank Giano Ingrasciotta, "Blood Type: RAGU" (unpublished ms., 1999), 1.

20. Ibid., 11.

21. Ibid., 29.

22. Ibid., 34.

23. Ibid., 44.

24. Ibid., 45.

25. Jim Provenzano, *Pins* (San Francisco: Myrmidude Press, 1999), 8.

26. Anthony Giardina, *Recent History* (New York: Random House, 2001), 145.

27. "Fatti maschi parole femine" [*sic*] happens to be the motto of the state of Maryland, something that was pointed out to me by Frank Pesci, co-coordinator of the American Italian Historical Association's annual conference held there in 2004. The motto is translated as "manly deeds, womanly words," or "strong deeds, gentle words."

28. Phillip Brian Harper, *Are We Not Men?: Masculine Anxiety and the Problem of African-American Identity* (New York: Oxford University Press, 1996), 11.
29. Ibid., 40.
30. Ibid., 160.
31. bell hooks, *We Real Cool: Black Men and Masculinity* (New York: Routledge, 2004), 25.
32. Ibid., 58.
33. Ibid., 66.
34. Ibid., 153.
35. Wieland, *The Undead Mother*, 225.
36. Ibid., 228.
37. Ibid., 228–229.
38. Ibid., 228.
39. Ibid. Here Wieland uses Melanie Klein's phrase, "depressive position."
40. Bill Bonnano and Joe Pistone with David Fisher, *The Good Guys* (New York: Warner, 2005).
41. Michael Kimmel, a professor of sociology at Stony Brook University, is one of the leading contemporary thinkers and writers on U.S. American masculinity. His major books on the subject include *Manhood in America: A Cultural History* (New York: Free Press, 1996); *The History of Men: Essays in the History of American and British Masculinities* (Albany: State University of New York Press, 2005); *The Gender of Desire: Essays on Male Sexuality* (Albany: State University of New York Press, 2005); and *Handbook of Studies on Men and Masculinities*, edited by Michael S. Kimmel, Jeff Hearn, and Robert W. Connell, (New York: Sage, 2005).
42. David Tager and Glenn E. Good, "Italian and American Masculinities: A Comparison of Masculine Gender Role Norms in University Students," in *Psychology of Men and Masculinities*, 6(4) (Oct. 2005), 264–274.

INDEX

238 • Index